BANKING ON THE STATE

STANFORD STUDIES IN MIDDLE EASTERN AND ISLAMIC
SOCIETIES AND CULTURES

BANKING
ON THE STATE

THE FINANCIAL FOUNDATIONS
OF LEBANON

Hicham Safieddine

Stanford University Press
Stanford, California

Stanford University Press
Stanford, California

Printed in the United States of America on acid-free, archival-quality paper

Library of Congress Cataloging-in-Publication Data

Names: Safieddine, Hicham, author.
Title: Banking on the state : the financial foundations of Lebanon /
Hicham Safieddine.
Description: Stanford, California : Stanford University Press, 2019. | Series:
Stanford studies in Middle Eastern and Islamic societies and cultures | Includes
bibliographical references and index.
Identifiers: LCCN 2018049490 (print) | LCCN 2019005424 (ebook) |
ISBN 9781503609686 | ISBN 9781503605497 (cloth : alk. paper) | ISBN
9781503609679 (pbk. : alk. paper)
Subjects: LCSH: Masarif Lubnan—History. | Banks and banking, Central—
Lebanon—History. | Monetary policy—Lebanon—History. | Finance—
Lebanon—History. | Lebanon—Colonial influence.
Classification: LCC HG3259.A7 (ebook) | LCC HG3259.A7 S24 2019 (print)
| DDC
332.1/1095692—dc23
LC record available at https://lccn.loc.gov/2018049490

Cover design by Kevin Barrett Kane
Credit: Lebanese President Fuad Chehab (front center), and Banque du Liban's
first governor Philip Takla (front left) exit the central bank's newly-built
premises shortly before it opens for business in April 1964. Courtesy:
An-Nahar Research and Documentation Center.

To my late father Nazem, a labor of life,
And my mother Fatina, a labor of love

Lebanon is a big bank.

—Dhulfiqar Qubaysi, editor-in-chief of *al-Masarif*

Contents

Acknowledgments

This book is the fruit of several years of research and writing, during which I received the intellectual and financial support of several individuals and institutions.

Throughout my research, many dedicated librarians, archivists, and scholars spared no effort to assist me in locating and accessing valuable resources that constituted the building blocks of my narrative. Special thanks in this regard go to Fatmeh Charafeddine, Dr. Kaoukab Chebaro, Alberto Haddad, Claude Matar, and Hussein Mokdad at the American University of Beirut's Jafet library; Rita Chakour at Banque du Liban; Saqr Abu Fakhr at the newspaper *al-Safir*, Dr. Sandrine Mansour in Nantes, and Nabila Bitar at the newspaper *al-Nahar*. My trips to the National Archives in Washington, DC, the Rockefeller Archive Centre in Sleepy Hollow, New York, and the French Diplomatic Archives at Nantes were possible thanks in part to funds secured respectively from the University of Toronto, Rice University, and King's College London. I also had regular access to the Jafet Memorial Library of the American University of Beirut as an affiliate at AUB's Center for Arab and Middle Eastern Studies.

During the different stages of writing, in which the book manuscript evolved in historical scope, writing style, and analytical depth, I greatly benefited from a wide array of insightful commentary. I am indebted to Jens Hanssen, professor of history at the University of Toronto, for his generous and invaluable academic support and insightful feedback on earlier drafts of this work. Special thanks to University of Toronto professors James Reilly, Paul Kingston, and Mohamad Tavakoli-Targhi for their constructive criticism of those drafts. I am also thankful for the generous appraisal provided by the late Roger Owen, former A. J. Meyer Professor of History, Emeritus, at Harvard University. My sincere gratitude goes to Ussama Makdisi, Arab Educational Foundation Professor of Arab Studies at Rice University, for his unwavering academic support. Ussama,

Abdel Razzaq Takriti, associate professor and Arab American Educational Foundation chair in Modern Arab History at the University of Houston, as well as my brother Najib and my friend Dania Dandashly kindly read all or part of the book proposal or later drafts of the manuscript. They provided extremely useful suggestions on developing and improving their content and style. My heartfelt gratitude also goes to the two blind reviewers assigned by Stanford University Press (SUP), who provided the most detailed and conceptually stimulating feedback. Their reviews helped me better envision what the book is about. They opened up productive paths for revising the manuscript in creative ways. I am also grateful to Kate Wahl, publishing director and editor-in-chief at Stanford University Press, for believing in the worthiness of this project and seeing it through. Her astute editorial guidance helped me navigate the elaborate process of turning the proposal into a book. SUP's dedicated staff were also of great assistance at the different stages of production. Peter Dreyer's superb copyediting skills and incredible attention to detail made accepting edits to my work a pleasure rather than a pain. I thank him for ensuring that the manuscript was whipped into excellent shape for publication. My appreciation also goes to Nour Ibrahim, who kindly reviewed the manuscript's formatting and citations on very short notice. I am grateful for all these contributions and solely responsible for any errors or shortcomings.

Last but not least, I warmly thank all my friends who kept me intellectual company during long years of research and writing in Toronto, Beirut, Houston, London, and elsewhere. They are too many to list. My ultimate gratitude is reserved for my supportive family: my dear brothers Najib and Ali, my uncle Ghassan, Wael, Layal, Karim, Mona, Tara and most of all my caring and beloved mother, Fatina. I dedicate this book to her and to my dear father Nazem, who regretfully did not live long enough to see it in print.

Abbreviations

ABL	Association of Banks in Lebanon / Association des Banques du Liban
AUB	American University of Beirut
BCC	Banking Control Commission (Lebanon)
BDL	Banque du Liban
BSL	Banque de Syrie et du Liban
BSGL	Banque de Syrie et du Grand Liban
BCAIF	Banque de crédit agricole, industriel et foncier (Lebanon)
BIO	Banque impériale ottomane
BIS	Bank for International Settlements
BLOM	Banque du Liban et d'Outre-Mer
BNFCI	Banque nationale, foncière, commerciale et industrielle(Lebanon)
CCC	U.S. Commodity Credit Corporation (government agency)
CMC	Council on Money and Credit
CMOP	Colonial Mode of Production
EFO	Economic and Financial Organization (League of Nations)
EPDB	Economic Planning and Development Board
ERI	Economic Research Institute (AUB)
FN	file number
FRB	U.S. Federal Reserve Bank
HCCI	Higher Council for Common (Syro-Lebanese) Interests
IBRD	International Bank for Reconstruction and Development
IFIs	international financial institutions
IMF	International Monetary Fund
IRFED	Institut international de formation et de recherche en vue du développement harmonisé (Paris)
KFTCI	Kuwait Foreign Trading Contracting and Investment
LL	Lebanese Lira

M   million
MEA   Middle East Airlines
MEEP   *Middle East Economic Papers*
MESC   Middle East Supply Centre
NBER   U.S. National Bureau of Economic Research
NDIC   National Deposit Insurance Corporation
OPDA   Ottoman Public Debt Administration
SLEP   Société libanaise d'économie politique

BANKING ON THE STATE

Illusions of Financial Independence

O Lebanese [Citizen]

There can be no political independence without economic independence and no economic independence without bayt al-mal al-Lubnani [i.e., a Lebanese central bank]. Otherwise, we will see our agriculture, industry, commerce, and tourism endangered.

—petition by Lebanese political parties, business associations, and labor unions, 1953

In 1918, when British-led armies marching out of Egypt occupied Damascus, paper currency issued by the Ottoman Imperial Bank (BIO) was still in circulation. British authorities introduced sterling-tied Egyptian bank notes to finance their military expenditures in the newly acquired former Syrian provinces of the Ottoman empire. They threatened to imprison anyone who refused to accept them as payment. One year later, control of the northern part of the provinces, encompassing modern-day Syria and Lebanon, was passed on to French rule. The handover was in partial fulfillment of the Sykes-Picot agreement for the partitioning of the Ottoman empire secretly concocted by the allies during the Great War. The French chose the prosperous port city of Beirut on the eastern Mediterranean as their administrative capital. Soon enough, they found the constant buying of Egyptian pounds to finance their own military needs costly and cumbersome, and they turned to the BIO for assistance. Under Ottoman rule, the BIO was a private Anglo-French venture. Founded in 1863, it had monopolized the issue of Ottoman paper money and acted as Istanbul's financial agent. It also served as a private arm of European financial investment and capitalist expansion into Ottoman lands, with Beirut as its gateway. Under French rule, the BIO's regional headquarters in Beirut's Ain el-Mraisseh district was reconstituted as the Banque de Syrie et du Liban (BSL).[1] The new bank's first order of the day was the issue of a local paper currency dubbed the Syrian lira. Pegged to the French franc, the lira was declared legal tender to replace other currencies, including Egyptian pounds, for military and other payments. Across the mountains from Beirut, the short-lived Arab government in Damascus, which had assumed control of the city following British withdrawal in 1919, refused to acknowledge the Syrian lira. It had declared its own Syrian dinar as legal tender. The dispute was settled in favor of the lira by force of arms rather than trade when French invading forces reoccupied Damascus in July 1920.

This heated battle over currency control reflected the increasingly important role of monetary regimes in the formation of post–World War I nation-states and, to borrow Timothy Mitchell's phrase, fixing their economies. The year Damascus fell to the French, bankers and economic experts from around the world gathered at a League of Nations' international financial conference in Brussels and declared that "central banks should be created in every politically independent country *without any exception* [emphasis added]."[2] The Geneva conference two years later reiterated this belief. The Great War itself had highlighted the expediency of having a central bank ready to finance war activities. In the interwar years of hyperinflation, the need to maintain financial and economic stability granted the idea of central banking further prestige and sway. Central banking became "an entirely separate branch of banking as compared with commercial banking, investment banking, industrial banking, and agricultural banking." It developed "its own code of rules and practices" that elevated it into a "science . . . acknowledged by many."[3]

Central banks perform three major roles, which evolved over time, in the construction and consolidation of newly emerging nation-states, defined as the twin processes "of creating new sovereign entities and. . . new centres of power and control."[4] Firstly, they issue and manage a single national currency, whose circulation within national territory to the exclusion of other currencies creates a monolithic monetary space. Secondly, they act as the government's financial agent for the purposes of fiscal management and in certain cases economic development. Thirdly, they regulate the banking sector and encourage the growth and deepening of national money markets. In the early twentieth century, central banks were increasingly seen as centers of "moral authority in moments of crisis" and symbols of economic independence. They were also credited with the ability to develop sounder banking systems. In the wake of World War I, "an orgy of central banking propagation" ensued in countries that lacked central banking institutions, "based on the simple belief that it was necessary to establish a miniature replica of the Bank of England or of the Federal Reserve Bank of New York."[5] Between 1920 and 1954, close to fifty such central banks were created.[6]

The poorly examined and vaguely understood creation of central banking institutions in the modern Arab world, which lasted well into the mid-twentieth century, was highly distorted by colonial policies in the interwar period. Under European rule, Arab monetary systems, and by extension economies, were not conceived in parallel with the newly demarcated national polities and their borders. This is because French and British authorities, while expected to pave the way for eventual independence after mandatory rule, did not draft monetary policy with a view to consolidating local state power over newly charted national boundaries. Rather, they did so in accordance with the logic of colonial material interests and political expediency. This led to the formation of what I term heteronomous national economies, whereby state-instituted monetary regulatory regimes and nationally imagined markets did not overlap with territorial boundaries. The role of central banking in the mutually constitutive formation of Lebanon's and Syria's political economies is a case in point.[7]

Upon the abovementioned pacification of the Arab government in Damascus, French authorities split the newly acquired Syrian territories into four Syrian statelets and a Greater Lebanon with Beirut as its capital. All five entities were, however, declared a "single territory from the monetary and customs point of view."[8] When the Syrian statelets were eventually united into a single country in the 1930s, Lebanon retained its separate political status but the two countries continued to share a common market and monetary system. In 1943, Lebanese political leaders, led by President Bishara Khoury (in office 1943–52) and Prime Minister Riad Solh, took advantage of war-weary France. Backed by Britain, they declared the country's political independence following a fresh round of parliamentary elections. In 1946, French troops stationed in both countries withdrew. The French political and military mandate over Lebanon and Syria had ended. But the monetary mandate, embodied in the customs union and the single currency tied to the French franc and issued by the BSL, did not.

Terminating this monetary dependency on France precipitated divergent Syrian and Lebanese paths of financial regulation and economic development. Negotiations with Paris led to separate monetary agreements for Lebanon (1948) and Syria (1949), which in turn hastened the breakdown of the customs union in 1950. More significantly, central banking reform, perceived by most "Third World" nations at the time as a cornerstone of attaining economic independence, followed a different trajectory in each country. In Syria, the government unilaterally withdrew the BSL concession as a state bank in 1953 and eventually replaced it with a national central bank. The Bank of Syria acted as a primary instrument of state-assisted agricultural and industrial economic development. In Lebanon, the BSL's French director René Busson, rarely mentioned in Lebanese historiography, continued to act as a de facto financial governor of the country. BSL monetary policies furthered the creation of an open economy in which the services sector reigned supreme. The BSL concession lasted for two decades after independence, at which point a national central bank replaced it. Inaugurated on April 1, 1964, Banque du Liban (BDL) was billed by Lebanese authorities as the primary symbol of economic sovereignty and the last step towards full independence. Press reports described it as a means of projecting state power and enhancing national pride. Such proclamations were, and remain, illusions of financial independence. Lebanon's financial foundations, the subject of this book, tell a more complicated and globally connected story.

Lebanon's financial system is the product of the interaction of colonial monetary control, national institution-building, global currents of technocratic knowledge, and private business interests. These interactions took place under two historical conjunctures: French financial rule (1919–48) and Lebanese financial restructuring (1948–75). Under French rule, the BSL was the backbone of a financial regime that linked the colonial economy to the French metropole. BSL credit policies, coupled with a franc-exchange standard that pegged the lira to the franc favored French capital investment over local economic development. In the post–World War II period, Lebanese bankers[9] gradually took on the function of "strategic monitoring" of the Lebanese economy via the banking sector and constantly bargained for their share of financial power on the political stage.[10] On their watch, the country's financial foundations were reconstituted in the context of U.S. financial hegemony, large regional capital flows, and global circuits of financial know-how. American officials based in Beirut were eager to see the BSL replaced by a national central bank that would cease favoring French-tied capital over its American competitors. During this formative period, Lebanon's capital, Beirut, became the region's financial hub thanks to large flows of petrodollars and the influx of finance capital fleeing nationalization in nearby countries like Syria, Iraq, and Egypt. Between 1945 and 1960, the number of banks in Lebanon skyrocketed from 9 to 85.[11] Lebanon became a "merchant republic" where ruling elites, whose wealth largely depended on imports and financial services to the region, fiercely guarded the laissez-faire system and portrayed it as the panacea for the country's economic prosperity.[12]

The merchant republic narrative and its corollary the laissez-faire paradigm have dominated classical histories of modern Lebanon. In these works, Lebanon's laissez-faire economy is read through the lens of entrepreneurial creativity of the mercantile-financial class, informal networks of familial and sectarian relations, or structural analysis of economic sectoral growth.[13] By contrast, the institutional architecture of financial regulation and monetary policy underpinning the emergence of laissez-faire is rarely examined. Recent and insightful studies of Lebanon's post–World War II political economy have gone a long way towards dispelling these national myths and transcending the accompanying historiography. But with rare exceptions, they remain largely concerned with how the Lebanese state, in the first decade after independence, shaped the free market through full deregulation of capital flows.[14] I reverse the direction of inquiry and examine how market forces and private actors, including bankers, financial experts, and bureaucratic officials haggled over and shaped the state and its major financial institution, the central bank.[15] In the post–World War II independence era, state financial institutions like central banks were a major instrument of engineering national economies in much of the "Third

World." Lebanon, its open economy notwithstanding, was no exception. Its laissez-faire regime was the product of conscious and constantly contested state policies, top among them central banking design. The primary guarantor of the longevity of laissez-faire and banker influence was the BDL, rather than reified market forces or an entrepreneurial spirit.

BANKERS AND THE STATE

The BDL's managerial structure and monetary functions were largely dictated by dynamics of political power and financial profit rather than well-defined notions of national economic development. The central bank served rather than challenged the interests of an oligarchy of local financiers, such as the Eddé brothers, who banked on the state much more than the market to reproduce the dominance of the banking sector in the economy. The Eddés were key figures in founding the two institutional pillars that turned the country's banking sector into an organized political community largely immune to state authority. The first of these was the Banking Secrecy law of 1956. The elder Eddé brother, Raymond, the law's architect, told the press a year prior to its passing that his "greatest ambition was to turn Lebanon into the bank of the Arab world" the same way Switzerland acted as the money warehouse of Europe.[16] The law accomplished the twin objectives of attracting large sums of Gulf capital and shielding it, as well as the bankers, from state inspection and taxation for decades to come. The second pillar was the Association of Banks in Lebanon (ABL), the first of its kind in the Arab world, which was founded in 1959 under the leadership of Raymond's younger brother Pierre, who was head of Bank Beirut Riyadh at the time. The ABL's goal was to "create cooperation among its members in matters pertaining to professional affairs and furnish mechanisms for [achieving] common interests and collectively defend these interests in the form of collective representation of its members in public or other administrations."[17]

Unlike often-studied state institutions like the Chamber of Deputies, personal status courts, or religious councils, the ABL and the BDL were one step removed from sectarian politics, while simultaneously forming the deep structural basis for reproducing the economic power sustaining this sectarian system. Sectarian quotas did affect who was who at the

BDL, but mattered much less than ideological orientation and vested interests. At the time of its founding, the person most qualified to serve as BDL governor was Joseph Oughourlian, a longtime consultant to the BSL and a veteran of banking regulations. But his sectarian Armenian identity relegated him to the role of deputy governor for his long years of service. Still, he left his conservative managerial imprint at every major juncture of building the financial system, from delinking the Lebanese lira from the franc in 1948 to the 1963 drafting of the law of money and credit that created the central bank. The ABL, meanwhile, was not a nationally driven, let alone a sectarian, endeavor. Members were initially either allied with or opposed to French capital. Lebanese bank members retained a controlling vote, but founding members included local, Arab, and U.S. banks. Chase Manhattan's Beirut-based manager Julius Thomson was a founding board member.

The ABL furnished the new barons of banking with a formal and institutional, rather than familial or sectarian, framework in which to interfere in monetary policy. In the late 1950s, pressure by international financial institutions (IFIs) and local experts for setting up a strong central bank mounted. The ABL was highly successful in lobbying for a largely toothless central bank even if the bank retained a degree of managerial autonomy and state officials portrayed its founding as the culmination of economic independence. The collapse of Intra, the country's largest bank, three years later exposed the unsustainability of unfettered laissez-faire banking. The crisis was a watershed in the history of Lebanese banker power. It shook the status quo of anti-regulation to a point that threatened the laissez-faire system itself. In effect, state intervention through the BDL became both a political and a market necessity. State actors and ABL bankers returned to the drawing board. They sank Intra but saved the sector by creating new administrative structures linked to the BDL, including a U.S.-inspired deposit insurance scheme. They also agreed to regulatory measures such as minimum reserve requirements and the categorization of long- versus short-term credit institutions. This new regulatory regime, however, reinforced rather than constrained laissez-faire policies by making the system more resistant to future shocks.

LAISSEZ-FAIRE AND THE MONEY DOCTORS

The conflict over Lebanon's financial regulatory regime and economic orientation was not only of interests but also of ideas. The idea of Lebanon as naturally suited to be a free-market economy was most vociferously articulated by Michel Chiha.[18] A professional banker, prolific journalist, and influential politician, Chiha spent the better part of his adult life consolidating Lebanese nationalist ideology in word and deed. He opposed the integration of Lebanon into nearby Syria or a larger Arab state and co-wrote Lebanon's constitution in 1926 under French tutelage. Following a short stint in parliament in the 1920s, he exerted influence in the corridors of power through his close association with his brother-in-law Bishara Khoury. The latter hailed from a notable family in Mount Lebanon. After a long career serving French administration during the mandate, Khoury became the country's first post-independence president in 1943. Aside from his association with Khoury, Chiha achieved broader ideological influence through his own writings in the press and public speeches. He espoused a dogmatic form of geographic determinism, which he argued dictated Lebanon's social, political, economic, and even cultural characteristics. Lebanon was "unique in the world" due to its small size and particular nature. It was a refuge for minorities thanks to its mountainous topography, a seafaring nation thanks to its Mediterranean coast, and a natural trading route thanks to its purported location as a meeting point of three continents (Europe, Asia, Africa). Given the country's alleged lack of natural wealth, Chiha reasoned, it "must be given economic freedom."[19] In the lexicon of Chihism, the ancient merchant was reinvented as the modern entrepreneur. The Lebanese nation, Chiha concluded, was a nation of merchants at the individual level and sectarian minorities at the collective level. Most crucial for Chiha and the mercantile-financial class he represented was preserving the dominant trade and services sector at the expense of industry and agriculture.

Following independence in 1943, Chiha's views were enthusiastically incorporated by the Khoury administration into state policy and disseminated by think tanks and cultural centers into public discourse. Politically, the 1943 national pact struck between Khoury and Solh, each representing their respective elite communities of Christians and Muslims, consecrated the French-installed sectarian system, under which political office was linked to sectarian affiliation according to a set formula.[20] Economically, market regulations introduced during World War II, including capital and exchange controls, were gradually removed. In public discourse, policies of deregulation were cloaked in Chiha's laissez-faire ideology, which normalized an obsession with price stability at the expense of balanced economic growth. Newly founded research institutions like the Société libanaise d'économie politique (SLEP) and prestigious public debate fora like the Cénacle libanais acted as cultural conduits for the propagation of Chihism.

Conventional as well as critical accounts of Chihism have affirmed its legacy as the uncontested ideology of the Lebanese ruling elite during the formative years of independent Lebanon. This has reinforced the particularist and parochial narrative of Lebanon's merchant republic as a unique model of unfettered laissez-faire. Its hegemonic status notwithstanding, Chihism was increasingly confronted at the height of the merchant republic by a competing, but not contradictory, bourgeois ideology of technocratic and state-managed modernization. The latter was highly significant in laying the long-term financial foundations of the state. A group of professional economists based at the American University of Beirut (AUB) were at the center of this countermovement. Members of this group like Said Himadeh and Salim Hoss saw financial regulation, namely, the setting up of a central bank, as an institutional imperative. Their names and works populate the footnotes and figures of most political economy studies of the period, but rarely figure in the grand narrative of the merchant republic that drew on their very work for its construction. Their story highlights the ideological and institutional dimensions of the shift from French to U.S. economic and political influence, which are often overshadowed by the story of oil and Cold War geopolitics.

The AUB's developmental institutionalists, as I refer to them, played a pioneering role in the diffusion and circulation of ideas about the national economy that challenged dominant paradigms of unregulated finance. They equally contributed to the idea of Lebanon, no less than the ideology of Chihism, by giving the latter a hardwired statistical existence through their calculations of Lebanon's gross domestic product, at a time when international organizations like the UN and the IMF were struggling to distinguish Lebanese from Syrian economic data. The influence and out-reach of these economists, individually and institutionally through the Economic Research Institute (ERI) they set up in 1953, went well beyond academic and scholarly circles. They had access to Lebanese elite public opinion, including the Cénacle libanais, and penetrated the bureaucratic apparatus of the state well before the rise of the mild form of etatism associated with Fuad Chehab's presidency (1958–64).

The economic philosophy and financial expertise of these scholars were part of the global transformation of monetary policies and practices in the early to mid twentieth century. These transformations were largely driven by U.S. economic expansion abroad and the rise of Third World nation-states. In the early 1900s, U.S.-led missions of financial experts like Parker Willis and Edwin Kemmerer were dispatched to Caribbean and Asian countries under U.S. influence, like the Philippines, to "fix" currency systems and tie them to the U.S. dollar. By the 1930s, the majority of U.S. "financial missionaries," who had grown into a professional class of "money doctors," were graduates of the colonial experience. In the post–World War II period, these missions grew from enforcers and stabilizers of currency systems tied to the U.S. dollar into the initiators and overseers of elaborate schemes of financial control that encompassed all aspect of financial administration, including tax codes, private banking regulation, and currency reform.

These U.S. money doctors espoused paternalistic oversight over weaker nations like that of former imperialist powers like Britain and France. In the post–World War II period, however, some of their views on central banking reform diverged from those of their European counterparts. British and French monetary officials often resisted the creation of national central banks. Their nations having lost military and political influence, they suggested reforming existing currency boards that kept local currencies tied to the franc or the pound sterling. By contrast, unorthodox U.S. money doctors like the Federal Reserve Bank's Robert Triffin encouraged and aided the creation of national central banks. Triffin understood the necessity of supporting economic nationalism that espoused a strong central bank in former European colonies in order to reorient their economies away from the colonizing metropole—and communist alternatives—and towards the international market. Central banking reform in these "Third World" countries became part and parcel of broader discourses of the "science" of economic modernization that were adopted by thousands of Arab and other "Third World" professionals trained in the United States, thus exerting U.S. economic power abroad.[21]

In Lebanon, U.S.-educated money doctors on the faculty of the American University of Beirut called for financial reform inspired by modified versions of Keynesianism and economic institutionalism that they argued were better suited to underdeveloped money markets. Their empirically oriented economic philosophy offered financial solutions without undermining the ideological basis of laissez-faire. This allowed their competing doctrine to gain a footing in the state and in public discourse in the merchant republic era. But it also reduced the question of social control to developing the statistical machinery of the state and its administrative apparatus in order to rationalize rather than radically change the uneven economic structure of Lebanon's service-dominated economy. Under such a configuration, local development was more easily geared to the interest of global capital and its local agents, rather than the benefit of the broader domestic population. The AUB institutionalists had thus struck a Faustian bargain with the West. Their "deal" aided, even if belatedly, the incorporation of Lebanon's financial system into the international monetary order in the hope of securing a long-term future of balanced economic growth. But thanks to the entrenchment of the local interests of the mercantile-financial class, there was little economic development to show. The country remained dependent on a hyperinflated services sector and external capital inflows for its economic survival, and subject to foreign interference for its political viability.

FINANCIAL SOVEREIGNTY AND STRUCTURAL DEPENDENCY

The reliance of Lebanon's mercantile-financial class on external markets for economic profitability and on foreign interference for political viability can easily lend itself to narratives of a "comprador class" doing the direct bidding of its class counterpart in Paris, Washington, DC, or some other Western capital. The conflict over Lebanon's financial system after independence, however, paints a more complicated picture. At certain historical junctures, Lebanon's top bankers and monetary bureaucrats found themselves in an antagonistic position vis-à-vis foreign officials whom they otherwise looked up to for economic support and cultural inspiration. When the IMF sent missions in the 1950s to push for banking regulation, for example, Michel Chiha and veteran bankers like the future BDL deputy governor Joseph Oughourlian scoffed at these experts' purported incapacity to understand the uniqueness of Lebanon's economy. Chiha defended the laissez-faire economic order against reform, irrespective of whether it was liberal or socialist.[22]

Chiha and his protégés were not seeking to protect the Lebanese economy from further integration into the global financial order. Quite the contrary, they sought further dependency on global markets and Western political patronage to compensate for the loss of French patronage and to counter socialist forces on the rise in the region. But they did not want to erode their advantageous position as intermediaries between global and regional markets, which was secured by unfettered financial practices. Ultimately, the Intra crisis pushed them to accept further structural adjustment to suit international banking practices without fully jeopardizing their privileged position locally. Seen in this light, Lebanon's post–World War II financial dependency was, to invoke Mahdi Amel's formula, the dependency of "a structure of relations of production to another structure of relations of production, not a dependency of one class on another."[23]

Examining structural forms of financial dependency sheds further light on the intertwined relationship between economic nationalism and sovereignty in the Middle East. The "Third World" variety of economic nationalism is often invoked in relation to the question of "national" versus "foreign" ownership of capital, or in relation to the pursuit of economic activity like industrialization aimed "at developing the country's resources with the minimum of help from foreign countries."[24] Economic sovereignty, on the other hand, is largely concerned with questions of autonomous state and government decision-making in the sphere of economic policy. Financial autonomy is essential for economic sovereignty. It is compromised by sovereign lending, especially from a foreign source, and by lack of control of capital flow and regulation of credit relations within the domestic money market (usually dominated by banks in underdeveloped markets).²⁵ Sovereign lending and credit controls are both handled by central banks. The construction of the Lebanon's central bank thereby offers insight into the applicability and operation of sovereignty in Lebanon. It does so, not merely in relation to external actors, that is, other states, but internally in relation to local actors such as bankers.

The emphasis on structural rather than class dependency also challenges the binary of "national" versus "foreign" capitalists. In the post–World War II period, Lebanese bankers selectively deployed this binary to call for state intervention in order to protect their share of the money market, rather than protect the national economy at large. What mattered was whether banks were confined to local markets or had access to international branches they could draw on for support in times of crisis. The classification of post–World War II banks along foreign versus national lines fails to accurately reflect the type of transnational partnerships, regional business networks, and political patronage that shifted the French-dominated structure of capital ownership and financial flows in favor of U.S. and Arab markets.

Local and international actors steering this shift were not operating in isolation from one another. U.S. diplomatic channels and IFI fora often acted as major interfaces of the local and international spheres. Cooperation should not, however, be confused with even power relations. U.S. supranational policy networks enjoyed superior bargaining positions compared to local or regional actors. These networks involved men who straddled the world of finance and foreign policy, like Paul Parker, an Intra bank advisor and former U.S. Treasury representative in the Middle East, and the former World Bank president Eugene Black, who was a Kuwaiti financial consultant. Both men played pivotal roles in resolving the Intra crisis as the U.S. sought speedy financial reform in Lebanon to avoid the collapse of a free-market economy that was a "living refutation" of Arab socialism.²⁶ This tilted the outcome of resolving financial crises like the Intra affair in U.S. favor. Local Lebanese elites chimed in to protect their own interests at the expense of Intra.

The new financial regulatory regime installed in the wake of the Intra crisis fortified the bankers' stranglehold on the local economy. When civil war broke out in 1975, the central bank, unlike many other state institutions, was not severely destabilized or readily coopted by warring factions. By the end of the war in 1990, Lebanese bankers—top among them the central bank's governor, emerged as the self-designated guardians of the state's stability. Today, more than quarter of a century later, they have managed to monopolize the founding myth of Lebanon's laissez-faire economy. But there is a rich, untapped archive that tells a different story. It includes U.S. and French diplomatic cables, IMF reports and directives, old annual reports of the BDL and the Association of Banks in Lebanon, unpublished treatises by AUB economists and state technocrats on Lebanese central banking, local and international newspapers and magazines, Lebanese central and private banking laws and decrees, and the diaries and biographical accounts of Lebanese politicians and bankers. It is this well-documented yet suppressed history—its conflicts, contradictions, compromises, and contingencies—that this book aims to bring to light.

CHAPTER 1

Colonial Finance

The Long Monetary Mandate

To this day I do not know how Monsieur Busson agreed to a text rendering his bank subject—immediately and in the future—to Syrian legislation.

—Khaled al-'Azm, former prime minister of Syria

The Banque impériale ottomane (BIO) was a government bank of one state, the Ottoman empire, owned by private capital of two others, France and Britain.[1] The French historian Jacques Thobie describes the late Ottoman era of its establishment as "proto-colonial," and Emmanuel Monik, one of the BIO's long-serving managers, quipped that it was "très originale."[2] On one hand, Ottoman decision-making was increasingly subject to the dictates of European interests and doctrines of state modernization. On the other hand, Istanbul retained a substantial margin of independence, lacking in regions under direct colonial rule like British India. Edicts and policy measures aimed at extensive restructuring of the Ottoman state and society issued in the course of what is called the Tanzimât (Reorganization) period reflected this proto-colonial conjuncture.

The Tanzimât reforms are often invoked in relation to civil and minority rights, land tenure, commercial regulation, military modernization, and administrative organization. Ottoman historians of financial reform largely restricted themselves to questions of fiscal policy and public debt. Public debt, also referred to as sovereign debt, lay at the heart of the empire's vulnerability to European intervention. The conventional story of Ottoman public debt begins with the first foreign loan granted by European creditors to Istanbul in 1854 to help finance its participation in the Crimean War. The story reaches a climax with the empire's bankruptcy in 1875. It concludes with the establishment six years later of the Ottoman Public Debt Administration (OPDA), a European committee officially entrusted with managing the empire's finances. The OPDA was tasked with streamlining revenue to prioritize foreign debt payment over other national expenditures. Its mandate and member composition were a clear violation of Ottoman sovereignty.[3]

This story seldom explores the impact of BIO policy in detail, despite the fact that the bank long acted as an instrument of foreign financial control and prolonged Western capitalist expansion into the empire. Well before Istanbul's mounting sovereign debt became a crisis in the mid 1870s, British officials in Istanbul had envisaged an Ottoman bank as an instrument of financial reform. Up until then, foreign debt had been celebrated as the cure for, rather than the cause of, financial disarray.[4] The BIO had a broad financial mandate and wide economic outreach in its dual capacity as state and commercial bank. Under its 1863 founding charter, it was granted three privileges. The first was a monopoly on issuing paper currency. The second was the exclusive right to act as the Ottoman treasury's financial agent. The third was its designation as the state's lender of first resort.[5] Its "orderly system of short-term credit," it was hoped, would replace the disorderly and chaotic dealings of the Porte with local money changers concentrated in Istanbul's Galata district.[6]

The high expectations pinned on the BIO's role in overhauling the empire's finances failed to materialize. Despite its monopoly of currency issuance, currency unification in Ottoman lands did not take place until 1916. The bank failed to stem the tide of financial collapse that hit the empire in the mid 1870s. As the debt crisis reached its zenith in 1874, the bank prioritized its private interests over state demands. It adopted a policy of refraining diplomatically from advancing new loans to the government.[7] This paved the way for the introduction of a more specialized and intrusive instrument of debt management, the OPDA.

The BIO's waning role in financial restructuring at the state level did not hinder its waxing role at the market level. By the turn of the century, the bank's credit relations were extended well beyond those it wove with the Ottoman treasury. The BIO spearheaded the financing, creation, and operation of large-scale projects in transportation infrastructure (railways, ports), resource extraction (mining), cash-crop production and distribution (tobacco), and maritime trade (silk).[8] The BIO's failure to "fix" the finances of the empire must not therefore be conflated with a failure to produce and reproduce an increasingly dependent capitalist economy tied to European finance.

In the Syrian provinces, the BIO furnished French capital with a state-linked institutional advantage before any French troops set foot in the region at the end of World War I. The bank's Beirut office was set up early in 1856 as a branch of the Ottoman Bank that merged into the BIO. It was the first to open in the empire's Arab provinces and served as the BIO's regional headquarter.[9] During World War I, the BIO's loyalty to British and French political interests became more pronounced.[10] When the Ottomans entered the war on the side of Germany, the Entente powers sought to deprive Istanbul of any financial assistance. The BIO was in a unique position to implement such a policy. Despite its designation as the government's bank, the BIO declined the Ottoman government's request for much needed loans. The Porte stopped short of insisting that the money be dispensed, fearing that such a step would lead to the confiscation or freezing of its assets in London and Paris.[11] This stood in sharp contrast to Anglo-French attitudes during the Crimean War. Back then, London and Paris backed Istanbul against Saint Petersburg, and as a result facilitated the financing of Ottoman military expenditures via loan guarantees. These foreign loans, the first undertaken by the Ottoman empire, had set the stage for the founding of the BIO itself.

After the victory of the Triple Entente in World War I, the BIO's successor in the interwar period, the Banque de Syrie et du Liban (BSL), became the primary institutional guardian of a long monetary mandate over Lebanon and Syria. Colonial authority guaranteed BSL legitimacy and its privileged position within an emerging national space. In return, BSL policies reproduced the dominance of French capital in the money market. More broadly, mandatory financial regulations, including BSL policies, played a central role in the formation of a new monetary space stretching from Lebanon to Iraq that underpinned the emergence of what are best described as heteronomous national economies.

HETERONOMOUS NATIONAL ECONOMIES

The victorious European powers justified their mandatory economic policy by framing their administration of the former Ottoman territories as a mandate of "advanced nations" over people "not yet able to stand by themselves under the strenuous conditions of the modern world." As Mohamed Ali El-Salih points out, the mandatory authorities thought that like political rule, economic development should not be left entirely to colonized peoples.[12] French and British authorities tried to reconstitute economic relations in ways that appeared independence-oriented but aimed at tying these regions, either directly or indirectly, to their own interests. Three major tenets of this policy were: the incorporation of the mandated regions into the world economy, further exploitation of their natural resources, and the administration of economic surpluses and revenue as a system of compensation for mandatory expenditures. This created considerable friction between Anglo-French authorities keen to preserve their privileged position and local actors bent on securing eventual independence. As a result, economic management was subject to competing legal and political norms.[13]

The scope and impact of competing claims to management of the economy varied over time and across mandatory territory. Contestation took place at the state and market levels in ways that overlapped and interacted with broader material realities and social structures. The conflict over financial regulation, including the impact of the BSL on the banking sector and the broader formation of the political economy of Lebanon, was part of this process. It is best understood within the context of other, corollary mechanisms that created heteronomous national economies. These mechanisms included national market formation, fiscal policy, and the professionalization of the administrative management of public and private enterprise.

In terms of national market formation, territorial partition coupled with new tariff policies created new barriers between the countries that had hitherto been part of a single Ottoman market. The presence of two separate powers, French and British, across this erstwhile single market meant that market divisions suffered from the double threat of market fragmentation within the same mandatory region (Syria and Lebanon) and across mandatory regions (Syria and Palestine). Syrian nationalists struggled to reconcile the need to foster a Syrian national market within French-set borders, on the one hand, with the ambition of preserving a regional market in line with pan-Arab visions of an Arab market that included British-held areas like Iraq and Palestine, on the other. New forms of corporate organization emerged to counter some of these challenges. These forms were seen as an integral aspect of nation-building. Leading Syrian entrepreneurs and national figures like Lutfi Haffar and Shukri Quwwatli recognized the need for joint-stock rather than familial forms of ownership to launch competitive large-scale industry. Haffar invoked corporatism as a leitmotif of national integration.[14] In the late 1920s and 1930s, joint-stock companies in different branches of industry like cement production, food preserves, and textile were set up. A self-declared pan-Arabist, Quwwatli made a point of capitalizing his newly founded Syrian Preserves Company at the Arab Bank in Palestine and Bank Misr in Damascus.[15] Over time, however, the development of small-state economies further weakened the pan-Arab appeal for economic unity.[16]

French fiscal and administrative policies further contributed to the heteronomous character of the mandatory economies. The customs union between Syria and Lebanon was a stark example of the incongruence of territorial borders with national economies. Another was France's creation of a dual budgetary system within the Federation of Syrian States. Local state budgets were issued alongside a centralized common-interests budget controlled by the French high commissioner. Revenues of the common budget were earmarked for mandatory military expenditure, civil administration, and remittances to Paris.[17]

Increasingly complex structures of administration and accelerated urban development were accompanied by professionalization of technical knowledge within the bureaucracy and in relation to private enterprise.[18] In the field of corporate finance, as was the case with commerce, accounting firms operated within a precarious regional-national space that simultaneously transcended and was curtailed by national and mandatory boundaries. In Lebanon, competing French and British accounting practices produced a new generation of hybrid accountants, like Iskandar Semaan and William Mitri, who were educated in French missionary schools and trained in British accounting firms. The reverse occurred with the founder of the first Arab accounting firm. Fuad Saba studied in French Beirut—albeit at the American University—and set up shop in British Palestine. His firm, Saba and Partners, would later expand to Baghdad, Amman, Aleppo, and Beirut.[19] Despite Saba's pioneering efforts, modern professional accounting remained the unregulated domain of small circles of business under the mandate. Like accounting, local banking was not regulated as a separate sector or profession. But with its roots dating back to the Ottoman era and its economic function much broader than accounting, it had a critical impact on the formation of heteronomous national economies via the production of mandatory monetary spaces.

MONETARY SPACE FORMATION
AND BSL DOMINANCE

Under the mandate, the emergence, spread, and mediocre success of local banking in Lebanon was intimately tied to the role of the BSL in the engineering of monetary space formation, a key component of the construction of heteronomous national economies. Interwar monetary space formation involved the creation of new financial regulatory regimes. This included the introduction of new currencies, setting up monetary institutions like government banks and currency boards, and legislating for financial regulation. The outcome was highly influenced by the structural characteristics of the political economy of each country and the colonial power in charge. Prior to World War I, the Ottoman empire's single market of goods and people did not correspond to a single currency area. Increased market incorporation by European capital raised demand for foreign currency, while private but state-propped banks like the BIO expanded the Turkish currency area. Ottoman currency dominated as a medium of exchange, particularly in the regions closest to the center of empire, like Syria and northern Iraq. But other currencies, like the Indian rupee and the Maria Theresa thaler, featured prominently in southern Iraq and the Arabian peninsula respectively. In short, foreign currencies moved along circuits of trade that permeated the Ottoman imperial economy.

The currency map of the region was abruptly and drastically altered under British and French occupation. Nonmarket forces played a crucial role in this formation. Old currencies were legally outlawed and new ones imposed. French and British monetary policies differed in some respects and converged in others. Single countries were rarely granted their own individual currency or regulator authority. For the most part, under the British, boards in London issued local currencies in the mandatory region, whereas the French opted for state-linked private banks like the BSL. Both mandatory powers, however, sought to peg newly minted local currencies to their own. Currency boards thereby acted as mere offices of exchange control rather than arbiters of monetary policy. Government-linked banks played a similar function, but had the extra leverage of conducting commercial business in addition to their regulation of currency. As a result, monetary spaces emerged along colonial rather than national lines. When countries were grouped into a single monetary space, colonial considerations were a more important determinant than geographical proximity or common economic interests. French Syria and Lebanon, for instance, were part of a single monetary space with French Algeria and Tunisia, rather than nearby British-controlled Palestine and Iraq, which belonged to a sterling area that included Egypt, Transjordan, and far-flung countries outside the Arab world. The British added an extra ring in the chain of currency dependency by declaring the Indian rupee to be legal tender in Iraq and retaining the Egyptian pound as the national currency of Palestine until 1928. Meanwhile, among Gulf sheikhdoms and across the Arabian peninsula, "currency chaos" persisted till World War II.[20] In the cases of Syria and Lebanon, financial institutions like the BSL were indispensable instruments for the production, management and differentiation of monetary space through nonmarket mechanisms ranging from political legitimation to currency regime regulation to credit control.

Political Legitimation

The first step towards introducing a new monetary regime in Lebanon and Syria via state edict took place in October 1918. After occupying Damascus, the British proclaimed the Egyptian pound, tied to sterling, to be legal tender in Syria, with refusal to accept it in payment subject to penalty of imprisonment. The decree did not designate acceptable currencies as such, but those that must be accepted in payment for military expenditures. In addition to the Egyptian pound, acceptable currency for such payments included the British pound, the Indian rupee, the French franc, and Turkish silver and gold coins. Turkish paper money, a symbol of Ottoman sovereignty, was not acceptable.[21]

When French authorities took over the administration of Syria in the fall of 1919, their search for an alternative currency to the Egyptian pound was also initially motivated by military concerns. Continually having to buy Egyptian pounds to meet the expenditures of the 70,000 French troops stationed in Syria was "extremely inconvenient and expensive," the French high commissioner Robert de Caix explained many years later.[22] A new paper currency issued by the BSL was thus introduced.[23] This monetary switch reflected the new complex arrangement of heteronomous national economies. On one hand, the Syrian lira, thanks to its name and distinct design, looked like a local national currency. On the other hand, it was pegged to the French franc, at a fixed rate of 1 Syrian lira to 20 francs, making it the franc in disguise.[24]

The short-lived Arab national government set up by Syrian notables and headed by the Arab revolt leader Faisal bin Hussein refused to acknowledge the Syrian lira as "official exchange" and issued its own currency, the dinar.[25] In an ultimatum to Faisal on July 14, 1920, however, General Henri Gouraud, the French military commander, demanded acceptance of the lira and facilities for its circulation, and on August 9, two weeks after the fall of Damascus, he proclaimed it legal tender throughout the Syrian interior, or "east zone."[26]

The influence of nonmarket forces on monetary space formation and the legitimation of new heteronomous national economies was also evident in the founding of the BSL. In early January 1919, the BIO's management in Paris set up the Banque de Syrie as a subsidiary based in Beirut to account for the new political reality of mandatory rule. The different bank bargains struck to establish the BIO in 1863 and Banque de Syrie in 1919 reflect the difference between proto-colonial and mandatory, or late colonial, political economies. These differences left their mark on each bank's managerial organization and financial functions.

The BIO had been the outcome of negotiations among European governments, the Ottoman imperial regime, and private European investors, whose general committee, sitting in London and Paris, retained full independence over the bank's investment strategies, while day-to-day operations were managed by its executive headquarters in Istanbul.[27] The Ottoman government was accorded a nominal supervisory role to give "the *appearance* [emphasis added] of an official Ottoman element in the hierarchy of the country's state bank." More significantly, Ottoman courts were granted full legal jurisdiction over the bank's affairs and the currency issued bore Ottoman insignia.[28]

By contrast, Banque de Syrie was an exclusively French affair.[29] In its first incarnation, its financial mandate was outlined via an accord in Paris in April 1919 between the newly constituted bank and the French Ministry of Finance—with the approval of the Ministry of Foreign Affairs. Under this accord, the bank was split into two independent departments: currency issue and commercial. During later correspondence between the bank and Paris, the French finance minister cited the "uncertain political situation in Syria" for not having "permitted" the newly created Syrian states (Syrian statelets and Greater Lebanon) to take part in the convention that had granted the bank its monopoly of issuing paper money. Given that local governments were not to take part in such an agreement, the minister's colonial logic led him to conclude that these governments were in no position to "receive a legitimate share in the profits derived from the issuance [of notes]."[30] Bank officials were equally dismissive of local authorities even as they sought their nominal recognition of the bank's privileges. In a letter dated August, 22, 1922, the bank asked the French Finance Ministry whether it thought that the "moment has arrived" to "fix the links that unite [the bank] to the new states." The "most rational" course of action would be for the French government to confirm these privileges and rights. Newly formed states should not be excluded from negotiations, but the bank could not "be too concerned . . . with their respective points of view."[31] On January 23, 1924, representatives of Banque de Syrie and local governments, including that of Greater Lebanon, signed a French-approved convention that confirmed the bank's concessionary privileges granted by the French military rulers in 1920. Like the BIO, the Banque de Syrie secured a monopoly over banknote issue and government financial dealings. Unlike the BIO, which was subject to Ottoman law, however, the Banque de Syrie was governed by French law. As a nominal gesture, the bank's name was changed to Banque de Syrie et Grand Liban to account for the newly created Greater Lebanon. Despite demands to the contrary, Syrian (and Lebanese) officials were granted only a minority share of seats on the board of directors, and a token share of the bank's capital, 16 percent, was offered for purchase in the local market.[32]

The Failed Franc Exchange Standard

Formal recognition of the Syrian lira did not lead to its swift transformation into a dominant currency of exchange in Lebanon and Syria. The financial regime introduced by the French involved a labyrinth of decrees and edicts over a number of years. It instituted certain denominations while annulling others. Reduction in the number of economic spheres in which other currencies were deemed legal tender was gradual.[33] This unstable process of introducing a new currency was exacerbated by the time-dependent nature of credit relations. Debts in Egyptian pounds now fell due in Syrian lira. General Gouraud's decree no. 129 ordained that everyone accept the Syrian lira as payment "for all operations, whatever may be the cause or object," but additional decrees had to be issued prescribing grace periods and exchange rates for settling debts contracted prior to decree no. 129 in other currencies. The complexity of the currency system made it unintelligible to the majority of the population. With multiple, unstable exchange rates and market unit pricing, merchants were no longer able to properly assess their financial standing based on registered prices. It took more than ordinary bookkeeping skills to keep proper tabs on costs, revenue, and net profit. Tax and fee calculations in Syrian currency turned into a burdensome accounting process.[34]

It was not until 1928 that all public accounting and pricing was required to be, once and for all, in Syrian lira. But even when this regime of currency control managed to settle into a well-defined juridical structure, it was persistently undermined by economic and social forces beyond the control of the mandatory powers. Paper money remained largely confined to urban centers, specifically those in coastal areas. Much of the interior retained its mistrust of bank notes and dealt in specie. Economically, the extreme fluctuation and overall depreciation of the French franc for much of the 1920s made the Syrian lira—which was pegged to the Franc—an extremely unattractive currency to hold. Coastal cities with strong links to external economies, like Beirut, suffered from these fluctuations the most.[35] As late as the mid-1930s, Syro-Lebanese paper money remained a minor part of the region's monetary stock, the larger part of which consisted of Turkish gold and silver coins, mostly in use in Damascus and Aleppo. Syrian and Lebanese citizens were obliged to use paper money for dealing with the state, but they preferred Turkish specie for private transactions and transmittances. Even in Beirut, where bank notes were the principal currency, many people continued to express an attachment to Turkish gold money and preferred it as the denomination of choice for writing up commercial contracts.[36]

The full integration of the currency system was thus more of a legal chimera than an existing practice. On the ground, there were two unconnected major standards of money and pricing. The first was official, designated by the Syrian lira, while the other was customary, predicated on the Turkish gold pound. With different standards adopted by different people in different places, credit became a lot less mobile, and the economy a lot more disarticulated. The BSL's contribution to the disarticulation of the Lebanese and Syrian economies towards greater dependency on France was not restricted to its management and preservation of the franc-exchange standard. It was exercised through market-based operations ostensibly guided by the mandatory mission to develop nascent national economies. In practice, however, these policies supported the private interests of state-favored enterprises like the BSL to the detriment of developing local money markets.

Underdeveloped Money Markets

The mapping of mandatory monetary spaces was grafted onto existing money markets that had emerged in the nineteenth century as a result of increased intrusion of European capital, which led to the expansion of the Ottoman empire's "economic frontier" into hitherto peripheral regions like Transjordan.[37] Attempts to incorporate this frontier into the Ottoman economy led to an increased demand for coinage, which was met by moneylenders in Damascus, Beirut, and the towns of Palestine, who became major creditors of merchants and farmers across the Jordan.[38] Beirut's leading role in this money market formation was aided by its long-standing ties to European capital.

The spread and growth of moneylending houses in Beirut tied to French capital was directly linked to the silk trade. Throughout the second half of the nineteenth century, and up to World War I, French capital enjoyed the lion's share of a burgeoning silk industry in the Syrian provinces producing for French markets.[39] As a capital-intensive horticultural industry affected by seasonal cycles of harvest, silk production was highly dependent on credit. Historically, it was common for silk traders, particularly exporters, to act as moneylenders or bankers. Local banking houses acted as financial intermediaries between foreign banks and local merchants or producers who sought to secure capital sums too large to be raised in the local money market. Several money-exchange houses in Beirut financing the silk trade engaged in commercial banking. These included Elias and Ibrahim Sabbagh, Hakim Bros., Jirjy Trad & Sons, Rabbat & Co., Musa de Freij, Michael Trad, and Nakhle Tueni, as well as Faroun and Chiha. In the southern port city of Saida, Hannah Audi set up a moneylending and exchange house in 1830 that lent money to farmers and later acted as an agent of foreign banks. Bank Audi was revived by Hannah's descendants in the twentieth century and is today one of Lebanon's largest and most powerful banks.[40]

The absence of an active stock market prevented the expansion and deepening of Beirut's local money market beyond commercial financial mediation. The creation of a Beirut bourse by the French in 1920 did little to change the situation. The bourse, whose founding committee included Michel Chiha and the BSL's director, was envisioned as a stock or produce exchange market. Several factors, however, led to its quick deterioration into a market for gold and foreign currency. Unstable political conditions led many traders to prefer gold over stock as a means of exchange. Additional decrees by the French governor in 1921 and 1922 placed tight controls on foreign currency and gold exchange respectively, which some citizens saw as attempts by colonial powers to siphon off gold out of the Lebanese market.[41] The major institutional impediment, however, lay in the mandate's corporate law. From its inception in 1920 until its restructuring in 1943, bourse regulations prohibited the formation of Lebanese limited companies. This meant that no Lebanese stock was traded. Government securities, which would have stimulated the credit market, were not traded at the bourse either. All treasury bonds were deposited at the

BSL as partial guarantee of note issue.[42] In addition to depriving the bourse from trading in government bonds, the BSL effectively employed its newly consecrated powers of its 1924 charter to dictate the path of economic development, or lack thereof, throughout the interwar period.

Disarticulated Development and Foreign Banks' Domination

Decree no. 129 of 1920 confined the BSL's public role to issuing paper money, but the 1924 convention went further, explicitly stating the principal objective of the bank to be "the promotion of the economic development of Syria and Greater Lebanon." There is little evidence, however, that the bank's vision or policies were designed to fulfill that purpose.[43] Quite the contrary: the BSL's state privileges were employed to advance the bank's own economic vision and business interests. Thanks to minimal reserve ratio requirements, monopoly of note issue, and a long history of financial dealings in the region dating back to the BIO, the BSL had political and economic leverage that surpassed any other competitor. The bank organized a number of economic missions that attempted to map the Levantine states' agricultural, commercial, and energy resources, facilitating the infiltration of French capital, with little investment in building the capacity of local syndicates and companies. Economic planning and organization on a national scale remained a marginal element of the bank's operations.[44]

The setting of discount rates was another instance of prioritizing profit over public interest. Central banks are expected to set discount rates to mitigate business cycle fluctuations by encouraging borrowing when the economy is sluggish and encouraging saving when it is overheating. The BSL's credit policy, however, did the reverse. It encouraged borrowing when the economy was heating up and earned high margins in that respect at the expense of long-term monetary stability.[45] By 1932, close to half of the bank's deposit holdings had, moreover, been invested in French bills and securities—in effect, an involuntary loan of resources to the French government by the Syrian people at a time when, as the economist Edmund Asfour later argued, Syria "needed them badly for its own economic development."[46]

BSL policies payed off for its stockholders. The BSL's share in the interwar capital market in Lebanon and Syria rivaled that of the rest of the entire banking sector, both local and foreign.[47] The mandate period was one of expansion for the bank, with seven of its fifteen branches in Syria established in less than fifteen years of its operation.[48] BSL growth coincided with accelerated French capital penetration of Syria and Lebanon during the interwar years, three quarters of which was invested in the banking sector.[49] Banking institutions with a history in colonial banking were encouraged to invest in France's eastern Arab colonies. By 1934, four out of the five major foreign banks doing business in Syria and Greater Lebanon—the BSL, Banque française de Syrie, Crédit foncier d'Algérie et de Tunisie, and Compagnie algérienne—were French. The fifth was Italy's Banco di Roma.[50]

Some of these large banks, such as Crédit foncier d'Algérie et de Tunisie, were involved in the establishment and financing of public utilities industries and infrastructure projects in Lebanon and Syria, but most of their operations were in commercial banking. They financed foreign commerce and traded in foreign exchange. Local governments seeking to meet the demand for industrial and agricultural credit, needed for business growth and national economic development, tried to set up an industrial bank, but the project was disapproved by the French authorities. Agricultural credit was available, but only to government entities.[51]

World-economy dynamics gave foreign-based banks additional advantages over their local counterparts. Foreign banks operated through a system of branch banking and were linked to wider networks of foreign capital via their home offices. This enabled them to draw on a relatively unlimited reserve of cash. By contrast, local banking was a decentralized system of "unit" banks. Each local bank operated in a confined geographical space and served the direct interest of its community. The vast majority of houses were individual-owned, family-owned, or at most partnership-based. They lacked specialization, with bankers often acting as merchants, industrial agents, or real estate owners. Their business was highly concentrated on financing domestic trade, foreign imports, and foreign-exchange dealings. As a result, local banking capital was largely immobile, of limited value, and dependent on the banker's own resources.

Several factors, however, managed to keep these local banks running amid the encroachment of international capital. For one, the branching out by international banks was relatively limited compared to the spread of local bankers and moneylenders over much of Syria. Borrowing culture also played a role in the survival of local banking. Local bankers tended to be less formal and strict in their dealings with their customers. They maintained the practice of open accounting, in which the credit relation was a long-term one, subject to adjustment, and based on community reputation and trust rather than strict calculations of collateral and credit history. Intimate knowledge of customers' credit ratings was another factor, making local bankers intermediaries between risk-averse international capital and local borrowers. Corporate organization was virtually absent among these financial houses. The Cairo financier and nationalist figure Mohamed Talaat Pasha Harb's Bank Misr in Egypt was a pioneer in the creation of joint-stock banking ventures with cross-Arab ownership and regional outreach. In 1929, Talaat Harb teamed up with a Tripoli businessman, Wasif Izzidine, and Lebanese and Syrian investors to set up the Banque Misr-Syrie-Liban, based in Beirut, with branches in Tripoli and Damascus. Although modeled on the Egyptian Bank Misr, it failed to produce comparable results in financing industry.[52]

By the late 1930s, some of these advantages turned into structural weaknesses, particularly during times of crisis or assertive colonial control. The Great Depression and the global financial crisis of the early 1930s took their toll, with many local banks declaring bankruptcy. The crisis in local banking triggered calls for major legislative reforms and internal restructuring of the sector. Small-scale initiatives to organize the profession were launched, but they were eventually drowned by the ground swell in mass-mobilization politics that defined much of the 1930s and 1940s. The relationship between colonial authority and local elites, including its financial linchpin, the BSL, was in for another round of contestation.[53]

WORLD WAR II FINANCIAL DISORDER
AND BSL COMPLICITY

The 1930s saw the rise across the Arab world of more assertive, mass-based movements for national independence. State institutions became a more heated site of contestation between the colonial powers and urban elites.[54]

Britain's declaration of Egypt's and later Iraq's formal independence fueled similar demands in French-ruled Syria and Lebanon. Talk of impending war in Europe put more pressure on Paris to protect the mandatory status quo by concluding treaties of "friendship" with Syria and Lebanon. These treaties, signed in 1936, sought to devolve certain powers to national elites, while guaranteeing France's vital geopolitical and economic interests. The French colonial policy of treating Lebanon and Syria as separate political entities under a single economic administration complicated the devolutionary process. Structural limitations were exacerbated by the divergent attitudes of Lebanese and Syrian ruling elites to what constituted sound, independent economic policy. The conflict over the economic future of the two countries began in earnest with the BSL's concessionary privileges due to expire in 1939. The dispute over their renewal evolved into a turbulent and complicated process of financial disorder during World War II, which culminated in the delinking of Lebanon's and Syria's local currencies from the French franc, in 1948 and 1949 respectively, and the collapse two years later of the customs union between them, spelling the official end of Syro-Lebanese economic unity.[55]

Renewal of the BSL's Concession

The BSL's privileges, including monopoly of note issue, had to be formally negotiated between the local governments of Syria and Lebanon on one hand and the bank on the other. In practice, however, the BSL's vital role in maintaining the currency peg and managing the Syrian and Lebanese economies as a single unit meant that its powers were fought over through formal as well as informal channels of political pressure and maneuvering. The outbreak of World War II and the increased instability of the French franc further blurred the lines between the legal, political, and economic forces at play. The BSL concession granted in 1924 was due to expire in 1939. Haggling between the BSL and local governments to extend it kicked off in tandem with negotiations over the 1936 "friendship" treaties. Leaders among Syria's main political coalition, the National Bloc, dreaded the BSL concession's renewal, fearing that it might be interpreted by the Syrian public as a further capitulation to French dictates. Negotiations between Damascus and the BSL were therefore arduous and unpopular.

Issuance of a draft convention in 1938 led to the resignation of the then Syrian prime minister, Jamil Mardam, and the draft was never ratified by the Syrian parliament. By contrast, Lebanon's political establishment was quick to extend the concession for another twenty-five years from its date of expiry. Lebanon's finance minister, Hamid Frangieh, was hailed by the local French daily *Le Jour* for his "systematic and enlightened mind." Frangieh, who at the time chaired the finance and justice parliamentary committees, billed the renewal as "taken for granted," a "necessary" measure, coinciding in duration with the Franco-Lebanese friendship accord.[56]

The new Lebanese BSL convention reached in 1937 failed to significantly alter the institutional relationship between the government and the BSL. Lebanon and Syria remained a single customs unit under the franc exchange standard. There were, however, nominal changes through which the Lebanese ruling elite further inscribed Lebanon in the public imagination as a national entity independent of Syria. Under the 1937 renewed concession, the Banque de Syrie et du Grand Liban (BSGL) became the Banque de Syrie et du Liban (BSL). The new convention introduced a new insignia on paper notes destined for Lebanon. These notes had a "form special to Lebanon," with the word "Lebanon" emblazoned on them. They were declared the sole currency of legal tender in Lebanon. There were slight improvements in the terms of the concession to the benefit of the Lebanese state. The bank's gold reserve was raised from 5 to 10 percent of the money supply, and the seigniorage (the difference between the cost of printing money and its monetary value) that accrued to the government was made proportional to the bank's profit. The ceiling on amount of paper money issued was removed, however, allowing the BSL to engage in potentially reckless—but highly profitable—printing of bank notes.[57]

To justify the unilateral signing of the convention, Lebanese elites invoked this nominal differentiation of the Lebanese pound from the Syrian lira as one more step towards independence, but their claims to increased monetary autonomy were short-lived. As the drums of war began beating in Europe, French authorities sought to return to the status quo ante, gains by local elites were rolled back, and colonial policy was enforced in a top-down manner. Syria and Lebanon were once again to be ruled by French decree and whim, as had been the case after World War I. The monetary arrangement was among the first casualties of this approach. The high commissioner invoked war exigencies to rescind, amend, or selectively apply monetary laws, including those applying to the BSL. Two days before the 1924 accord expired on April 1, 1939, he issued a decree unilaterally renewing the BSL convention in Syria. Four months later, locally elected governing bodies were suspended in both countries. In December of the same year, an *office des changes* attached to the BSL was established to regulate capital flows, especially those seeking to exit the franc bloc. The BSL's reserve ratio requirements were altered to facilitate the printing of larger amounts of paper money to finance war expenditures. In June 1941, the Vichy government depleted official gold reserves by shipping six million liras worth of gold to France.[58]

Wartime economic regulation was not restricted to finance. It encompassed the collection and distribution of foodstuffs, the introduction of price controls, and the restriction of foreign trade and commerce for nonmilitary purposes. Moreover, the war would redefine relations between the mandatory powers. To recover French mandated territories under Vichy control, General de Gaulle's Free France (France Libre) had increasingly to rely on Britain's support, and British forces moved into French mandatory Lebanon and Syria, imposing a new, short-lived Anglo-French monetary regime, whose institutional embodiment was the Middle East Supply Centre (MESC). Engineered and spearheaded by the British, with U.S support, MESC activities were a critical factor in the reorganization of state-market relations, as well as colonial-local ones.[59]

Multiple Currency Regimes

News of a prospective Anglo-French monetary order in Lebanon and Syria fell from the sky on June 8, 1941. French fighter planes dropped pamphlets that among other things conveyed a promise by the Free French commander in chief, General Georges Catroux, to incorporate the Syro-Lebanese lira into the sterling area. Following the successful ouster of Vichy forces from the region, France tried to renege on its commitment to a currency tied to the pound sterling. But the odds were stacked against her. By 1943, Lebanon and Syria had attained formal political independence. The Syrian government reminded the French of the Catroux declaration of June

8. Public opinion, distrustful of the franc exchange standard and its fluc-
tuating legacy, was equally unsympathetic. War developments reinforced
these sentiments. A sharp increase in money circulation due to high military
and other war expenditures placed extreme inflationary pressures on the
local currency and the franc, further galvanizing public opinion against a
reinstatement of the franc-exchange standard. Faced with persistent depreciation of the franc, the French succumbed to mounting pressure from
all sides. On January 25, 1944, an Anglo-Franco-Syro-Lebanese monetary
accord was signed in Damascus suspending the franc-exchange standard.

The accord indirectly linked the local currency to the pound sterling
via the franc. Rather than allow the BSL to hold sterling as a cover for
the Syria-Lebanese lira, the French treasury was to replenish franc deposits by as much as they depreciated against sterling. The lira would retain
its exchange value vis-à-vis sterling, but the revaluation process was in
the hands of the French authorities and the replenishment in French currency. Keeping French francs as the currency of choice for BSL reserves
had a stabilizing psychological effect on the franc money market. No mass
selling of francs would take place, and future reserves continued to be invested in French treasury bonds. The difference now was that whenever
the franc lost value relative to the pound sterling, the French government
had to deposit francs at the BSL as bank-note cover, so that the total new
amount of francs corresponded to the same amount of sterling they had
been equivalent to prior to the depreciation, thereby preserving the lira-
to-sterling ratio. By attaching itself to sterling, the Syro-Lebanese lira thus
ceased to be a masked denomination of the French franc, but only through
the creation of a multiple-currency regime.[60]

The 1944 monetary arrangement reflected the unstable nature of the
transition from a late colonial to a national order. The agreement had no
time limit, but in 1946 the French government decided to stop honoring
its obligations under it. Having concluded a separate agreement with the
BSL, in a manner reminiscent of Paris's dealings with the bank in 1919,
the French Ministry of Finance matter-of-factly informed the Lebanese
government of its unilateral termination of the link to sterling.[61] The fact
that this took place as late as 1946, the year French troops withdrew fully
from Syria and Lebanon, and three years after both countries gained their

political independence, showed that monetary decolonization was far from complete—the relationship between the two newly independent colonies and the metropole remained one of subordination.

The franc-sterling debacle and the ensuing currency crisis—its origin, evolution, and rationalization by France—also revealed the deep-rooted links between financial dependency and war economies in a colonial context. Inflation in Greater Syria was produced by allied military spending there during World War II, much of it financed by borrowing from the BSL in Syro-Lebanese liras, which had to be backed by increasing BSL reserves, overwhelmingly secured by the bank in francs drawn on the French treasury. These in turn were guaranteed against sterling under the understanding of 1944. In short, military relations during the war congealed into unsolicited and elaborate sovereign debt relations subject to dispute.[62]

France invoked the military relations that exacerbated the 1946 crisis to rationalize its unwillingness to honor the 1944 Anglo-French treaty. The French delegation argued that the reduction of military operations—now that the war was at a close—eliminated the need for the sterling monetary order put in place to sustain them. The Lebanese government, however, considered the move a form of "illicit gain for the French treasury." Unlike the termination of French political authority and military presence in Greater Syria in 1943 and 1946 respectively, the responses of third parties like the United States and Britain to Lebanese calls for intervention in the monetary dispute were lukewarm. Appeals by Lebanese officials to the United States, Britain, Egypt, and Saudi Arabia to support the lira were turned down. Lebanon and Syria were left to face off this institutional form of colonial control on their own.[63] The crisis paved the way for the Franco-Lebanese monetary accord of 1948, which delinked the lira from the French franc once and for all. It, simultaneously, led to a political confrontation between Beirut and Damascus, culminating in the termination of the economic union they had enjoyed under French rule.

THE SYRO-LEBANESE ECONOMIC SPLIT

Lacking international patronage, and without a clear political or legal framework to handle the fallout over the franc-sterling agreement with Paris, the Lebanese and Syrian governments sought expert financial advice.

Paul van Zeeland, the top consultant, a former Belgian prime minister, saw the alternatives before them as either to contest France's unilateral abrogation of the 1944 accords at the newly formed International Court of Justice or to negotiate and sign a new treaty with Paris—the course he recommended and the one the Lebanese and Syrians opted for.[64]

Negotiations kicked off in Paris on October 1, 1947. France insisted on linking the termination of the franc exchange standard to settling its overall debt to the Lebanese and Syrian governments which it had largely incurred as a result of its military spending during the war. Syrian delegates opposed this omnibus approach. The Lebanese conceded to it.[65] French authorities presented detailed estimates of military equipment and French property left behind, as well as the cost of maintaining a native military force called the Troupes spéciales du Levant and demanded that they be deducted from the total amount owed.[66]

Lebanese delegates sought expert financial assistance from Beirut to counter these claims and assess the overall costs and benefits of the deal. Reliance on financial expertise took on an ambivalent nature in the person of René Busson, the BSL's director general. Busson's role reflected the problematic relationship between emerging national governments and state financial institutions that were still tied to the former colonial power. In his capacity as head of the BSL, the powerful Busson occupied the simultaneous role of a guardian of the interests of French capital and the arbiter of Lebanon and Syria's monetary policy. Busson's dual loyalties did not seem to ring alarm bells among members of the Lebanese ruling elite, who shared the veteran banker's economic vision and in some cases private financial interests. Frangieh sought to keep Busson at his side in Paris for consultation, but Lebanon's president, Bishara Khoury, recalled Busson to Beirut and involved him in all steps of planning and formulation of policy vis-à-vis Damascus and Paris.[67]

By contrast, there was no love lost between Busson and Syria's foreign minister and head delegate at the Paris currency negotiations, the veteran politician and Damascene businessman Khaled al-'Azm, who had had previous dealings with Busson and private links with the BSL.[68] During the 1944 franc-sterling accord, Busson acted as a representative of the French government in both official and unofficial capacities. He also took part in the drafting of memos of understanding between the Syrian and French sides. According to al-'Azm, Busson at the time feigned loyalty to Damascus. Despite his French nationality and his position as head of a French bank, he allegedly told al-'Azm that he, Busson, considered himself Syrian and favored the interest of the country he worked in. But Busson would "show his true colors" a few years later during the franc-exchange-standard negotiations, al-'Azm commented in his diaries.[69]

The estrangement of Syrian officials with Busson over franc-exchange-standard negotiations was not simply a matter of his personal role as mediator with French authorities. The Syrian government was exasperated after the Lebanese delegation in Paris signed a unilateral agreement with the French in 1948, putting Syria and Lebanon on a collision course. The BSL played an active role in accelerating the crash. In the days leading up to the official signing of the Franco-Lebanese treaty on February 6, 1948, confidence in the Syrian currency fell, with Syrian merchants seeking to exchange Syrian liras for gold in Beirut. With news of the imminent signing of a Franco-Lebanese monetary agreement to the exclusion of Syria, the Sursuk market in central Beirut, where gold and currency exchange shops were located, went calm, with Syrian traders roaming around with puzzled faces. Even small shopkeepers reportedly refused to accept Syrian liras as payment for things like cigarettes. Busson added fuel to the fire. The BSL issued a communique, "in its capacity as the issuing institution," declaring that "no currency but the Lebanese will have purchasing power" and set February 2 as the deadline to exchange Syrian bank notes for Lebanese ones. The BSL measure caused capital flight from Syria, with gold smuggled from Syria into Lebanon and large numbers of Lebanese rushing to exchange Syrian liras for Lebanese ones. Damascus called on Beirut to fix the exchange rate to avoid further depreciation of the Syrian lira, but to no avail. Instead, and under French influence, the BSL froze Syrian funds it had accumulated during the withdrawal process. The Syrian government took several measures to stem the collapse of its currency including the closure of BSL branches outside Damascus. The crisis triggered calls in Damascus for the creation of a new currency and the establishment of a Syrian national central bank.[70]

The currency crisis had a ripple effect on the overall political and economic relation between the two neighboring countries. The 1948 Franco-Lebanese accord was the final straw that broke the back of economic unity between them. It also created an irreconcilable wedge between Syria's ruling nationalists and their Lebanese primary ally, Riad Solh. In the run-up to Lebanon's political independence in 1943, the nationalist ruling blocs in Beirut and Damascus had forged an alliance that tried to reconcile political independence with joint administration of economic affairs embodied in the Higher Council for Common Interests (HCCI). This institutional framework remained controversial and provisional. It was constantly subject to readjustment by Beirut and Damascus and criticism by Lebanese ultra-nationalists like the Maronite Patriarch Antoine Arida.[71] Following the 1948 Franco-Lebanese monetary accord, Syrian authorities accused their Lebanese counterparts of conspiring with the French to pressure Syria into remaining bound to French monetary tutelage. Lebanese officials tried to downplay the impact of decoupling the currencies on the ability to sustain economic cooperation between the two countries. But it was too little too late.[72]

The volatile nature of the economic union between the two nascent states was stoked by the divergent national economic visions of the ruling parties of each country. Damascus opted for a state-centered and centrally planned approach that favored agricultural production and industrial development while protecting the interests of its urban merchants from Lebanese competition. Beirut pushed for the reinstatement of laissez-faire economics that prioritized free trade and the services sector. Agreeing to fiscal policies such as taxation and custom dues that reconciled these two approaches proved impossible. By 1948, economic unity was hanging by the thread of a common currency. The Franco-Lebanese monetary treaty cut that thread. Economic cooperation became a practical nightmare. Complicated plans were devised to set up separate BSL accounts in different denominations for each country. Estimates of how much Damascus owed Beirut because of the withdrawal of the Syrian pound from circulation varied. Disputes arose over acceptable forms of payment and revenue collection and redistribution within joint agencies like the HCCI. According to al-'Azm, the Lebanese government ignored the findings and recommendations of joint committee of experts from the two countries. Damascus called for both currencies to be declared legal tender in both countries, which was turned down by Beirut. The use of economic sanctions by Damascus in retaliation and the political mudslinging that ensued culminated in the dissolution of the joint customs union, thereby dashing any hopes of economic unity harbored by Arab nationalists on both sides of the border.[73]

The parting of ways between the Syrian and Lebanese liras spelt the end of economic cooperation and political partnership between the two countries. More significantly for our story, it charted a divergent path of financial organization within each country. Bad blood between the BSL and the Damascus government persisted after the subsequent signing of a monetary agreement between Syria and France in February 1949 under which the BSL concession became subject to Syrian law. For the first time since its creation, the BSL's concessionary status and regulatory framework now fell under of the Syrian legislature, al-'Azm gleefully pointed out in his memoirs, commenting: "To this day, I do not know how Monsieur Busson agreed to a text rendering his bank subject—immediately and in the future—to Syrian legislation. Gaining his approval and the approval of his government was a manifest victory, since any provision of the bank concession or those of other French companies, [which had hitherto] been conditional on the consent of the bank or the company in question, became subject to amendment the moment a Syrian piece of legislation is passed."[74]

A few months after the conclusion of the Syro-BSL treaty, Busson pounced on the opportunity offered by an unexpected military coup in Syria to bypass the legislative process. He got the coup leader, Husni Zaim, to renew—via decree—the BSL's concessionary status under more favorable terms to the bank. But an equally swift countercoup in August of the same year scuttled Busson's plans. His nemesis, al-'Azm, was back in power, this time as prime minister. The seasoned al-'Azm was now determined to terminate the BSL's standing as a state bank monopolizing bank-note issue.[75] Severing Syria's last vestige of financial dependency on France required a series of legislative maneuvers and practical administrative measures that gradually stripped the BSL of its powers. The first step took place on March 11, 1950, when a new Syrian monetary law was promulgated by government decree. In addition to unifying preexisting monetary edicts into a single piece of legislation, a new amendment stipulated that bank-note issue was a prerogative of the Syrian state, which could assign it to a private institution if it so decided. The BSL objected, arguing that the amendment violated its concessionary rights. The Syrian government acknowledged the BSL's concession, but upheld the amendment and affirmed that unlike the day-to-day management of bank-note issue invested in the BSL, the Syrian state's *right* to issue bank notes was a basic principle accepted by all countries and is not subject to compromise.[76] With the legal justification in place, the Syrian government sought a smooth transition with little disruption to money markets. A department was created at the Syrian ministry of finance with the legal power and material resources to issue currency. This included paper money without BSL markings, designed and printed in England after seven months of planning, that could be circulated in the event that the BSL abruptly decided to withhold bank notes in retaliation for ending its concession. The new bank notes were nonetheless held for safekeeping in the BSL's vaults, the keys to which had been copied for the government.[77]

Three years after the 1950 decree, an updated monetary law provided for the creation of a national central bank. The law was drafted by the Syrian ministry's French financial advisor François Cracoux following consultations with Belgian, French, and Arab financial experts like Said Himadeh based at the American University of Beirut (AUB). A stately celebration under the title of The Festival of Monetary Independence was held at the University of Damascus's amphitheater. Syria's military strongman and de facto ruler at the time, Adib Shishakli, told the attendees that this decree "which undoubtedly ushers in our economic liberation, following our political liberation, is the greatest legislative event in Syria's modern history." The decree, Shishakli added, turned the page on the last trace of foreign rule. It would release the country's productive powers and allow for the economic and social renaissance Syrians hoped for.[78] A similar ceremony was held three years later to celebrate the inauguration of the new central bank's operations. Syria's president, Shukri Quwwatli, and prime minster, Sabri Assali, praised the creation of a national institution to issue bank notes as a milestone in achieving monetary independence. To the ire of France's chargé d'affaires in Damascus, Christian d'Halloy, the bank's first governor, Izzat Traboulsi, thanked Belgian but not French experts for their contribution. Traboulsi concluded his speech by suggesting that the new Syrian central bank might one day issue the bank notes of a future pan-Arab state.[79]

Faith in Future Economies

Switching to a fully sovereign monetary regime, however, required more than political declarations or the transfer of administrative control from the privately owned BSL to a state-run equivalent. Without guarantees from France or other financial powers, long-term currency stability and financial independence could only be sustained through a strong economy that would generate its own gold and hard currency reserves through a positive balance of payments. In short, it required a leap of financial faith in the future potential of the national economy and the taking of concrete steps to develop its infrastructure and productive sectors. Syrian officials exhibited such confidence, not only towards the country's own economy, but even towards Lebanon's. In the course of trying to dissuade their Lebanese counterparts from signing the 1948 Franco-Lebanese monetary accord, Syrian officials argued that Lebanon's economy, with Syrian assistance, could absorb the shock of weaning the Lebanese lira off the French franc. Their Lebanese counterparts were not convinced, or saw their interests elsewhere. For the Syrian government, removing the franc exchange standard was a matter of untying "a knot in the series of chains of the French mandate" and refusing to commit to a "new monetary mandate" after it had cast off the political and military ones. The key to Syrian long-term financial independence was the ability to provide sufficient alternative coverage of the new Syrian lira to the one previously supplied by francs, largely drawn on the French treasury, in the form of gold and hard currency. The latter, Syrian officials hoped, would be secured through boosting agricultural exports, paid for in hard currencies, while placing strict controls on foreign-exchange market transactions to prevent capital flight. This economic sovereignty stance contrasted with the currency-centric one clung to by Lebanese officials. The ruling clique in Lebanon gave priority to the "value and stability of the Lebanese currency." It sought foreign financial guarantees as opposed to relying on economic levers like local development. The Lebanese obsession with stabilizing the currency as opposed to gaining economic independence fit well with the narrow interests of the mercantile-financial class whose fortunes derived from the import trade and unfettered capital flows.[80]

Another key element that contributed to the viability of Syria's de-linking scheme was the emergence of a new global monetary order. The Bretton Woods system put in place in 1944 provided an internationally sanctioned currency exchange system for Syria to fall back on. Damascus had become a signatory to the IMF and the IBRD Articles of Agreement in April of 1947, that is, two years prior to settling its monetary and credit relations with France. During this two-year period, Syria and Lebanon were technically under three regimes of currency control: the mandate-instituted franc exchange standard, the war-driven and sterling-guaranteed exchange system, and the U.S. dollar-mediated and IMF-regulated financial order. The overlap of these monetary systems reflected the complicated and intertwined nature of financial decolonization. But it also presented emerging national governments with the possibility of charting different post-independence financial arrangements as was the case in Syria and Lebanon. In both instances, financial decolonization through a negotiated settlement led to a structural transformation of currency regimes. In Syria, this change led to a further harmonization of its national monetary space. The foreign and privately owned institutional apparatus in charge of regulating this (the structural dimension), the BSL, was replaced by a state-controlled public bank.

The end of BSL's role as an instrument of financial dependency and control in Syria breathed new life into its authoritative role in neighboring Lebanon. Having become persona non grata in Syria, Busson lost a prized colonial privilege in one zone of influence while consolidating it in another. His allies among the Lebanese mercantile-financial class were much freer now to pursue their laissez-faire policies unencumbered by pressures from the Syrian big brother next door. The waning threat from the Syrian East, however, would soon be supplanted by unexpected calls for change from the American West. If Syrian pressure emanated from the conventional quarters of a decolonizing periphery eager to assert its own sovereignty and localize its finance capital, the Western winds of change blew from the new global monetary order of Bretton Woods. With the

Bretton Woods system increasingly governing the global economy, the concessionary privilege of the French-linked BSL came under increasing criticism from various stakeholders. Calls for institutional reform and the creation of a central bank "proper" in Lebanon became more pressing. These calls were not restricted to international actors, such as the IMF. They were voiced in scholarship and public opinion in Lebanon as part of an emerging discourse on national economic planning and central bank reform by a circle of U.S.-educated Lebanese economists based at the AUB. Through institutional and bureaucratic channels, they challenged the dogmatic laissez-faire paradigm that served as the ideological foundation of the currency-centered monetary regime realized in the BSL's modus operandi, through which Lebanese bankers' power was reproduced.

CHAPTER 2

Central Bank Reform

Ideas and Institutions

The last mistake one should make here is to imitate countries where Lebanon's special case is unknown as a model for taxation and finance.

—Michel Chiha, *Propos d'économie libanaise* [On the Lebanese Economy]

In the first decade of Lebanon's formal independence, the director general of the Banque de Syrie et du Liban, René Busson, emerged as the country's most powerful financial figure. Busson exerted significant control over Lebanon's postwar economy through the BSL. In addition to helping precipitate the Syro-Lebanese split, he used his post to steer the bank's investment priorities and monetary policy in favor of French capital and its local Lebanese partners. These partners included an increasingly powerful circle of businessmen and politicians associated with President Bishara Khoury. They exercised their economic power through the Société d'études et de réalisations industrielles, agricoles et commerciales (SERIAC), a BSL-sponsored, state-favored business consortium.[1] Thanks to its pro-French and partisan policies, however, the BSL was an object of vociferous criticism by local anti-Khoury forces and American officials eager to undermine the dominance of French capital in Lebanon.

Laissez-faire advocates close to President Khoury, like his brother-in-law Michel Chiha, were not opposed in principle to replacing French with U.S. patronage or shifting Lebanon's business ties beyond French markets.[2] But they were adamant that the foundation of their laissez-faire system and the key to their private wealth, namely, a stable currency overvalued in favor of the import trade, remain intact. They therefore lobbied—contrary to IMF and U.S. financial advice—for a heavily gold-backed currency with full deregulation of the exchange market. By 1952, all the regulatory measures that had been put in place during World War II had been rolled back, and the merchant republic of Lebanon was officially born.

The story of successful deregulation and the rise of the merchant republic has often ignored the conflict over the BSL and its impact on economic development and state-building following independence. Studies of Lebanon's post–World War II political economy largely focus on the informal and corporate networks woven by Lebanese elites with French and later U.S. capital under a regime of unfettered economic freedom. The narrative that emerged portrayed a triumphant "merchant republic," in which the ideology of laissez-faire reigned uncontested during a well-marked period (1952–1958), and the subsequent presidency of Fuad Chehab (1958–64) was the "only 'developmental' period in the history of Lebanon" that had "explicit objectives of building and consolidating state institutions in order to promote economic and social development." Prior to the rise of "Chehabism," the Lebanese political leadership rarely if ever debated economic theory, Carolyn Gates claims.[3]

The making of Lebanon's central bank, both as an idea and an institution, challenges these assumptions about the political economy of the merchant republic. Elite circles passionately debated economic development during this period. Banking regulation and the fate of the BSL was a central theme. Furthermore, these debates, and the gradual but impactful institutional change they precipitated, shed light on a hitherto unexamined, but significant, dimension of U.S. influence on the formation of post–World War II states that espoused laissez-faire like Lebanon. The shift from French to U.S. economic and political influence under the merchant republic is well documented. U.S.-funded development projects were well under way by 1952, and Washington's political sway reached a crescendo with military intervention in 1958.[4] Little, however, is made of the institutional and ideological dimension of American influence. In the postwar world, Keynesianism informed U.S. aid policy and structured the process of incorporating emerging national economies like Lebanon into the world capitalist system. While the Keynesian version of modernization theory was hostile to socialism, it could not be easily reconciled with Lebanon's unfettered system of laissez-faire. Financial regulation was particularly a sore point of disagreement.

Eager to preserve their social status and material interests, governing Lebanese elites had to grapple with this influx and influence of new ideas of economic development. Ideologues like Michel Chiha invoked the paradigm of laissez-faire and Lebanese exceptionalism to resist Keynesian-inspired financial reform that undermined their privileged position in the market. Chiha, Khoury's brother-in-law and close advisor, who sat on the board of the BSL, warned against seeking foreign financial expertise. Foreign technocrats, Chiha argued, did not—and could not—understand the supposedly exceptional character of Lebanese history and geography that dictated the country's adherence to laissez-faire.[5] Statistical computations and economic studies by Gabriel Menassa, who headed the Société libanaise d'économie politique (SLEP), a Chiha-backed research institution, gave Chiha's polemics the appearance of scientific validity.

In practical policy terms, these efforts bore fruit with full deregulation by 1952. But a series of contingencies and deeper structural transformations undermined the stability of this order as soon as it had been established. For one thing, its main proponents, like Busson and Chiha, left the stage. Busson departed the BSL in 1951, and Chiha died in 1954, two years after his ally President Khoury was forced to resign in favor of the Anglophile Camille Chamoun. These developments made calls for central banking reform all the more threatening to the paradigm of laissez-faire. Busson had acted as laissez-faire's financial guardian of last resort in the absence of direct French political patronage. U.S. officials foresaw the decline of French influence in Lebanon in the wake of his "bombshell" resignation. They hoped that Lebanon's Ministry of Finance would become more autonomous vis-à-vis the "[French-]controlled, semi-monopolistic, unregulated" BSL and thereby more willing to implement financial reforms that better incorporated Lebanon into the global financial system of Bretton Woods.[6] Chiha's death silenced the most vocal and authoritative proponent of unfettered laissez-faire. Chihism remained a dominant ideological force well after his death, but his less charismatic protégés had to contend with countercurrents of economic thought in Lebanese elite culture that could not be readily dismissed as "foreign." The U.S.-friendly Chamoun presidency furnished a welcoming if not always enabling environment for these countercurrents, particularly at the American University of Beirut. The ideas and institutions that fed them, which contributed to a complex process of financial acculturation in Lebanon, are best understood in the broader context of pre– and post–World War II U.S. financial reform.

U.S. MONEY DOCTORING:
THE COLONIAL CONNECTION

In the first half of the twentieth century, influential U.S. financial advisors like Parker Willis, Charles Conant, and the latter's student Edwin Kemmerer developed their theories and best practices of financial reform in colonial contexts like the Far East and the Caribbean.[7] Willis was the first president of the Philippines National Bank. Kemmerer, who became head of the American Economic Association, saw Egypt as a model of progressive colonialism.[8]

Following World War I, with hyperinflation sweeping over Europe and governments going off the gold standard, European finance was as much in need of "fixing" as its colonial counterpart. Money doctoring became a universal practice. Kemmerer became the most sought after money doctor in the interwar period and led missions to Poland, South Africa, China, and Turkey.[9] Attempts were made to organize financial management at the international level via the League of Nations. Amid the political turmoil and the social upheaval that marked this period, a near consensus emerged within influential circles of financial experts, including top U.S., British, and German central bankers, concerning the recipe for financial reform: restore the global order of free international trade. Two other institutional fixes in that regard were the privatization of public finances and the independence of central banks from political authority, particularly the treasury.[10]

The interwar recipe was more of the same classical liberal order that preceded World War I. It took the Great Depression and a second world war to upset this consensus. The construction of the post–World War II global monetary order, as envisioned at Bretton Woods, followed a different formula, shaped by the ideology of "embedded liberalism." In lieu of preaching gold standard discipline that prioritized the stability of world markets, embedded liberalism took its cue from Keynesianism. In attempting to reconcile an international system of free trade with increasingly assertive notions of national economic sovereignty, it prioritized the role of national governments in pursuing domestic economic growth and employment within a multilateral world economy. As Eric Helleiner points out, the role of "southern countries" in the construction of this new order has received less attention compared to that of "northern countries" despite the dramatic monetary reforms that took place among the former. These reforms, as Helleiner shows, were backed by unorthodox U.S. money doctors, notably the Federal Reserve Bank's Latin Section chief, Robert Triffin, who, although aware of the geostrategic value of not opposing the rising tide of economic nationalism, was committed to "embedded liberalism."[11]

Unlike Kemmerer, Triffin indirectly endorsed capital controls and in some cases want as far as advise against dollarization. Paraguay, South Korea, and Sri Lanka (Ceylon) were among the nations in the global south visited by Federal Reserve Bank missions.[12] Assistance ranged from counsel to direct intervention. In the case of Ethiopia, the United States went as far as secretly print new national currency notes and supply the first central bank governor at the country's behest. Powerful central banks were deemed an indispensable tool of state building, a symbol of national sovereignty, and a necessary condition for economic freedom. The course of central banking reform, as well as the form, extent, and impact of U.S. influence, varied according to the extent that these southern countries fell within the sphere of British or French financial influence. British and French governments were generally hostile to the creation of national banks. They advised reforming existing structures like currency boards, common in ex-British colonies and the CFA bloc in French West Africa. Leading nationalists in countries like Ceylon saw currency boards as financial appendages of colonialism. Breaking from the sterling area or the CFA, however, had serious economic consequences, particularly for local elites tied to the European metropole. Consequences included structural constraints like the loss of European markets as well as aid and security protection provided by their colonial masters. But as Helleiner points out, ideological motivations also determined whether national elites chose to remain within these economic zones or create new independent institutions. While some elites feared separation, others facing identical structural consequences, like the anti-colonial leaders of Mali and Guinea, opted to leave. Guinea's first president, Ahmed Toure, went as far as declare that creating a central bank and a national currency were equally if not more important than demanding immediate independence in 1958. At times, ideology also motivated those opposed to embedded liberalism. Acting as an international entrepôt and keen to preserve its monetary stability, Singapore maintained its currency board and backed its currency with 100 percent reserves. Most of Singapore's decision-makers of the time, according to its finance minister, held anti-Keynesian views.[13]

The interplay of structural constraints and ideological motivations produced equally diverse results in the Arab world. The struggle over central banking reform in Lebanon provides a compelling example of the complicated nature of such interplay and the wide range of institutional and individual actors involved. These included international financial institutions like the IMF, nongovernmental U.S. aid groups like the Ford and Rockefeller Foundations, and U.S.-educated money doctors based at the American University of Beirut (AUB). In the heyday of the merchant republic, all these actors challenged the ideological hegemony of unfettered laissez-faire and the institutional primacy of its financial system in different yet interconnected ways. The first palpable challenge came in the form of increasing international pressure to conform to IMF financial rules concerning exchange-rate regulation and national accounting practices.

IMF RULE(S) AND BSL INTRANSIGENCE

In the Bretton Woods system, central banks acted as the national nodes of an increasingly integrated system of global finance. They produced or validated national accounting data key to the calculation of IMF fund quotas and oversaw capital controls and exchange-rate stabilization necessary for smoothing out trade relations among nations. When the French-installed BSL proved highly inadequate in that respect, central bank reform in Lebanon—which had joined the IMF in 1946—became an IMF demand. At the time, IMF officials complained of their inability to construct a satisfactory statistical representation of the Lebanese economy. Such data would have enabled them to estimate Lebanon's quota in the Fund, evaluate its currency's par value, and determine whether Lebanon's foreign-exchange policies were justified or not. Up until the Syro-Lebanese economic split, the lack of reliable data was compounded by the two countries' economic union and single currency system. Data from the BSL's balance sheets did not treat Lebanon and Syria separately.[14] Research personnel at the Fund pointed out that the BSL acted as a bank of issue and fiscal agent of the government, but had "no central banking functions."[15] Balance-of-payments figures published by the BSL differed substantially from those in IMF reports and were seen as "tentative estimates." Other sources were thus sought. These included UN national income estimates, reports by Syria's Ministry of National Economy, the monthly bulletin published by the joint Syro-Lebanese High Commission of Common Interests (HCCI), older reports issued by the French mandatory powers, the Lebanese press, and U.S. economic missions to Syria.[16] Despite the absence of independent economic data for Syria and Lebanon, IMF staff recommended that separate Fund quotas be implemented for the two countries and devised the IMF's own formula to calculate each quota.[17]

The delinking of the Lebanese currency from its French and Syrian counterparts in 1948 and the promulgation of Lebanon's first monetary law in 1949 further paved the way towards the conceptualization of the Lebanese monetary system as a separate entity on the IMF's books. But it gave rise to a new dilemma: a lack of statistics due to Lebanon's full deregulation of the capital and exchange markets. In the four years following the delinking of the lira from the franc, a series of Lebanese government decrees and legislative acts had officially recognized the free exchange market and then gradually lifted any restrictions on market sales and purchases of gold and foreign exchange. At the BSL, new reserve requirements for currency issuing were set in place. Gold and hard foreign currencies would replace the franc as backup reserves for the Lebanese lira. The BSL pursued an aggressive policy of gold purchases, raising gold reserves to nearly 100 percent of note cover. These measures embodied the triumph of laissez-faire and its national manifestation, the merchant republic. The BSL's policy of maintaining an overvalued official rate for the Lebanese lira created multiple exchange rates in the black market. IMF officials debated whether these rates violated IMF rules and undermined the fragile foreign-exchange system IMF rules tried to establish.[18]

By 1952, the BSL's reluctance to interfere in Beirut's exchange-rate market prompted Fund officials to ponder the country's lack of central bank powers, and U.S. embassy dispatches noted that they made explicit reference to the BSL's foreign identity.[19] Lebanese government intervention in the economy, as a general policy, also became an explicit topic of discussion among IMF officials. In 1953, questions of how to finance large-scale economic development and how to gauge capital inflows into the country pushed the subject of regulating the banking sector as a whole to the fore. Fund officials lamented the "paucity of information in regard to banking and money." Private banks, they pointed out, neither published statements of their activities on a regular basis nor were required to supply such information to a central monetary agency. The absence of such an agency, they argued, posed a "considerable problem" for the collection of banking and monetary statistics.[20]

Lebanon's exchange system and gold purchase was another source of friction.[21] Lebanese officials invoked cultural and financially flimsy excuses to delay shipments of gold to the IMF in order to evade meeting their obligation of restocking Lebanon's gold subscription quota. They told their IMF counterparts that the Lebanese people were "extremely gold conscious and distrust instinctively paper money," and any such transfer would undermine public confidence. They also complained of the lack of U.S. dollar reserves, given the absence of exchange controls and pending receipts of transit fees from oil companies like the Trans-Arabian Pipeline Company. Lastly, they suggested that the gold be set aside for the IMF at the BSL. Once Lebanese authorities received U.S. dollars, they would be used to purchase the equivalent amount at the Federal Reserve Bank and place it at the IMF's disposal.[22] Unable or unwilling to enforce the Fund's own regulations, IMF officials took a conciliatory route. They sought to provide Lebanon with the "technical assistance" necessary to effect a speedy transition. They offered unsolicited low-key missions. At first, the Lebanese government turned down such overtures.[23] The tide turned in 1954. Lebanon's Economic Planning and Development Board (EPDB), a state organ overseen at the time by the AUB economist George Hakim, invited the IMF to send a technical mission devoted to banking reform. The new mission's head, F. A. G. Keesing, was a high-ranking advisor at the IMF's exchange restrictions department and spent several months in Lebanon. With the assistance of an IMF legal expert, Keesing produced a detailed roadmap for regulating banking.

Keesing submitted his report, titled "The Monetary and Banking System of Lebanon," on May 10, 1955.[24] His attack on laissez-faire and his recommendation for a comprehensive reform of the banking sector ran contrary to the basic interests of the mercantile-financial elite standing guard at the gates of the merchant republic. Joseph Oughourlian, who at the time was a highly influential BSL official, railed contemptuously against the report and its author, writing in Beirut's French daily *Le Jour*:

ANOTHER EXPERT!

ANOTHER REPORT!

MEDIOCRE, this report by Mr. F. K. of the IMF on the banking and monetary system of Lebanon . . . we speak our mind in a straightforward manner because the matter at hand is serious . . . it is regarding currency, in other words regarding the fortune and the fate of this country.[25]

At the heart of Oughourlian's disdain for Keesing lay the latter's critique of "dogmatic" laissez-faire, which, Keesing argued, stood in the way of devising a sound monetary policy and measured government control. Keesing's call for a middle path between extreme liberalism and dirigisme, or planned economy, was dismissed by Oughourlian as an instance of what John Stuart Mill termed "sophisms of observation."[26] That some form of state intervention was required was self-evident, but the methods of intervention and whether they aligned with the politics of liberalism or a planned economy were not, and Keesing explained neither point, according to Oughourlian.

Oughourlian equally derided Keesing's lamentation of the absence of national economic and budgetary statistics. The BSL advisor ostensibly shared Keesing's "keenness," as he put it, for data. But Oughourlian pointed out that the very structure of laissez-faire, with the preponderance of invisibles among economic transactions, posed difficulties in this regard that might only be overcome with time. Keesing had argued that the inability to take stock of invisibles, that is, service transactions, meant that any attempt to devise an appropriate economy policy was doomed to fail. But the ability to comprehend reality in its specificity and complex totality, something Keesing purportedly lacked, was more important than transforming economic activity into "battalions" of "precise figures," Oughourlian pontificated.

To Oughourlian's horror, Keesing extolled Syria's regulation of banks, both quantitatively and qualitatively, and cited the Syrian monetary system as a "ready-made" model to emulate, with some modifications. Although he praised Lebanon's banking system, he proposed setting up a council of money and credit—which Oughourlian sarcastically called a "solemn device"—to regulate it. In Oughourlian's eyes, Keesing's "summary" analysis and "fragile" conclusions were "useless" and reflected the IMF official's lack of confidence in his own recommendations. Such recommendations, Oughourlian proclaimed, were bound to lead to misfortune. Keesing was guilty of the faux pas of wanting to have it both ways, to deal out liberalism with the cards of dirigisme.

Oughourlian had hoped the debate would end then and there. "For the love of Lebanon and the renowned intelligence of the Lebanese," he pleaded at the closing of his *Le Jour* diatribe, "Mr. K.'s report must be shelved." And so it was, Oughourlian boasted decades later. But that was not entirely accurate. Keesing's recommendations would become part of the debate between proponents of unfettered laissez-faire and those of planned economy that lasted well into the early 1960s. The IMF official's major recommendation of setting up a currency board was implemented a few years after his visit. The genie of government planning and monetary reform was out of the bottle, and Keesing wasn't its only advocate. An intergenerational group of economists at the American University of Beirut (AUB) were at the forefront of this debate. Their ideological and institutional intervention to reform central banking posed a more fundamental, if less direct, challenge to unfettered laissez-faire and corresponding financial policies.

THE AUB INSTITUTIONALISTS: FIXING THE LEBANESE ECONOMY

The ideas and activities of the AUB economists are best theorized in terms of how they "transformed the intellectual environment of economics, and . . . altered the terms of political discourse in such a way as to legitimate a variety of policies and make new combinations of political forces possible."[27] AUB institutionalists altered the terms of political discourse and government action in three different capacities: as state technocrats directly involved in policy-making; as academic institution-builders and educators linked to American and international networks of knowledge production; and as active participants in shaping public opinion through writing in the press and participating in prestigious public debating fora like the Cénacle libanais . Their contributions spanned three generations of scholars, reaching a high point in the late 1950s and early 1960s. Each successive generation built on the work of the preceding one in constructing a fuller representation of Lebanon's national economy and refining its theses on economic development and financial reform.

Institutional Genealogies

At the base of this three-tiered edifice of knowledge lay the work of the AUB economics professor Said Himadeh, later dubbed the "dean of economic studies in Lebanon,"[28] who explicitly called for banking reform two decades before Keesing broached the question. A Columbia University graduate, Himadeh headed several "pathfinder" studies in the interwar years aimed at mapping the economic organization of Arab countries in a national framework. They included a specialized study of the monetary and banking system of Syria, in which Himadeh was assisted by the financial expert Henry Parker Willis, professor of economics at Columbia.[29] Himadeh upheld the "structural theory of economics and politics" and privileged the role of institutions in his writings. Another important contemporary was the economic department's "sharpest wit" George Hakim, later head of Lebanon's Economic Planning and Development Board (EPDB) and minister of national economy.[30] Himadeh and Hakim constituted the nucleus of the first generation of AUB institutionalists. Their influence extended well beyond the confines of the classroom into Lebanese state policy, public discourse, and regional as well as international diplomacy. Himadeh was a longtime member of the Lebanese economic delegation handling economic relations with Syria after independence. The local Arabic press solicited and published his expert opinion on controversial monetary questions of the day, and he had the ear of the U.S. Department of the Treasury.[31] Gabriel Menassa referred to his intellectual rival Himadeh as "notre ami." Menassa quoted the latter's advice when it fit the laissez-faire paradigm and opposed him when such advice ran contrary to laissez-faire.[32] In 1947, it was Himadeh, not Menassa, who delivered the first lecture on fixing the postwar Lebanese economy at the

Cénacle libanais.[33] Hakim also graced the stage at the Cénacle forum twice to sing the praises of economic development.[34] At the government level, he was closely involved in planning and executing Lebanon's monetary and economic policy during the height of the merchant republic era.[35] Under Chamoun, Hakim held several prestigious ministerial portfolios including those of national economy, finance, foreign affairs, and agriculture.[36] Earlier, between 1949 and 1952, he was appointed Lebanon's governor at the IMF, with the BSL official Joseph Oughourlian as his deputy.[37]

The efforts of Himadeh and Hakim to shape public discourse and state policy on economic development experienced a major institutional leap with the establishment of the Economic Research Institute (ERI) under the auspices of influential second-generation AUB members like Albert Badre, Paul Klat, and Yusif Sayigh.[38] The professional careers of these second-generation policy advisors also straddled the world of higher education, private business, and state bureaucracy. Badre and Klat occupied high-ranking posts within international institutions such as the UN and the IMF as well as the Lebanese civil service, including the EPDB.[39] Klat was also close to Lebanon's top bankers. In 1961, he was appointed to the country's first Keesing-style Credit and Money Council, which drafted the Law of Money and Credit discussed in chapter 5.

Badre, a student of business administration and later a professor of economics, played a leading role in conceiving and setting up ERI. In his 1950 memorandum to the AUB's Board of Trustees, Badre envisioned a permanent statistical and research institute that would supplant existing practices of specialized technical assistance under which local governments draw on the temporary advice of international, usually UN, consultants with little long-lasting impact. According to Badre, the lack of extensive and reliable statistics of the region, the high incompetence prevalent among public service employees, and the absence of centralized gathering of data handicapped the work of these specialists and prevented any meaningful follow-up by local government agencies. In addition, a workable solution in one country may not apply, as international experts sometimes eagerly assumed, in a different country. A regional and permanent institute, Badre argued, would serve as the ideal venue for collecting, compiling, and analyzing statistical data. It could also provide training programs for Arab government officials to reform public administration and modernize state bureaucracies in relation to concrete problems. To avoid interstate rivalries and ensure its success, Badre suggested that the institute be nongovernmental and attached to a local yet highly regarded university like the AUB. Two years later, an AUB-sponsored funding proposal submitted to the Ford Foundation drew on Badre's memorandum. The project for an institute was framed in relation to broad questions of economic development and had explicit political overtones. Its chief architects, who included Badre and his two colleagues Said Himadeh and A. J. Meyer, asserted that mass poverty resulting from the extreme underdevelopment of the Arab world's physical and human resources was "a menace to world peace and security." Without increased output and better distribution of wealth, "inroads of anti-Western doctrines" would be harder to resist. The institute would provide a "sound foundation of economic knowledge about the Near East," without which plans for growth are unlikely to succeed. Studies produced by the institute, the authors pointed out, would be of value to local governments, private enterprise, foreign aid missions, and international agencies. They also hoped that the institute would graduate a corps of young Arab-speaking economists willing to return to their countries and carry on developmental projects along the lines of what they learned.[40]

Upon securing a $200,000 grant from the Ford Foundation, the ERI was set up as an affiliate of the AUB's Economic Department under the directorship of the dynamic Badre.[41] In the decade that followed, the institute carried out quantitative studies on national income, balance of payments, and capital formation, as well as surveys of rural and urban development, tourism, and entrepreneurship. In addition, the ERI expanded already-existing AUB initiatives, also funded by the Ford Foundation, for regional capacity building. The AUB's Public Administration Department invited top government officials from various Arab countries, including Syria, Egypt, Libya, Jordan, Iraq, and Sudan, to the first Arab conference of its kind to develop strategies for reforming administrative practices,[42] and the ERI oversaw the training of more than a hundred junior government officials from across the Arab world in statistical methods at Beirut's International Statistics Education Centre (ISEC), established by the

International Statistics Institute with Lebanese, American, British, and French collaboration. Instruction was of a practical and applied nature.[43]

The ERI augmented its personal capacity building projects with initiatives to encourage research publications up to international scholarly standards. In 1954, the ERI launched its annual peer-reviewed journal *The Middle East Economic Papers* (*MEEP*). In the foreword to its first issue, Badre told its readers that the ERI was part of the long-felt need for "an organization which devoted itself to a *systematic* [emphasis added] study of the economic problems of the Middle East." Badre hoped that the ERI would also weave "close professional ties among scholars residing in the different countries of the region."[44] *MEEP* facilitated the production, analysis, dissemination, and preservation of accumulated knowledge in the field. Submissions were diverse but had to relate in some manner to the question of economic development in the Middle East. The journal acted as a catalyst for the creation of international currents of intellectual exchange and influence within the Arab and Muslim Middle East that spanned Karachi, Tehran, Baghdad, Istanbul, Cairo, and Khartoum.[45] Collaborative studies mapped the economies and human resources of the region with the aim of developing the oil sector, dominated by American companies.[46]

The ERI's long-term regional impact is hard to assess. The rise of Arab socialism in the late 1950s and early 1960s in countries like Egypt, Iraq, and Syria checked U.S. influence. A 1959 regional tour by Yusif Sayigh, then acting director of the ERI, to recruit participants in a conference on economic education reform convinced him that given political considerations and government regulations, there was scant prospect of this succeeding.[47] By contrast, the ERI had a profound and long-lasting impact on the construction of Lebanon's national economy both as a concept and an organized set of state and market relations. Under the direction of Badre, the second generation of AUB institutionalists at the ERI produced the most comprehensive and authoritative quantitative study of Lebanon's national income.[48] This is Badre's main claim to fame. The study made the ERI internationally known, and the Lebanese economist Georges Corm referred to Badre at the Cénacle libanais as the "founder of [Lebanon's] national accounting."[49] Beirut-based U.S. officials who had been independently and persistently trying to generate data on the Lebanese economy described the study's monographs as possibly "the most careful national income estimates ever attempted in the Near East," next to those conducted by mandatory powers in Palestine. By the end of the 1950s, national income time series had been generated by the ERI and the Economic Division of the U.S. embassy in Beirut respectively. Badre's estimates, which differed from the embassy's and covered more years, were more widely adopted, figuring in international reports like the UN's *Yearbook of National Accounts Statistics*, Food and Agriculture Organization (FAO) country studies, the IMF's *International Financial Statistics*, and Lebanese government data publications.[50] Future research on Lebanon's political economy, including that by the mission of the Paris-based Institut international de formation et de recherche en vue du développement harmonisé (IRFED) under President Chehab, relied on AUB-generated employment figures.[51] The significance of computing a national income went beyond its statistical value. It consolidated the very idea of Lebanon. One of the obstacles to national accounting had been the lack of statistics specific to Lebanon under the economic union with Syria. By creating a distinct numerical representation of the Lebanese economy, the notion of the separateness of Lebanon was reinforced at the epistemological and psychological level by these second-generation economists in ways subtler yet possibly more effective than the anti-Syrian rhetoric of radical Lebanese nationalists.

Third-generation AUB institutionalists carried on with charting the specificity of Lebanon's economic configuration. The question of finance in general and central banking in particular took on a salient character and a sense of urgency. Leading scholars of this group included Salim Hoss, Talha Yaffi, and Elias Saba. Like their predecessors, these economists made important interventions in public discourse and government policy beyond their academic circles. Yaffi received his first professional training at the IMF in the 1950s. Hoss began his career as an accountant with the U.S. Trans-Arabian Pipeline Company. The following decade, Hoss—and to a lesser extent Saba—played leading roles in the restructuring and regulating of the Lebanese banking sector precipitated by the crash of Bank Intra. Saba served as minister of finance under President Suleiman Frangieh in the early 1970s. In 1967, Hoss was appointed as the first head of Lebanon's newly created Banking Control Commission.

Seven years later, he became prime minister under President Elias Sarkis (himself a former governor of the BDL).[52] The financially focused work of this third generation emerged in the broader context of the economic doctrines honed by all generations of AUB institutionalists into a school of economic thought best described as developmental institutionalism.

Developmental Institutionalism

The writings and pronouncements of the AUB technocrats affirm their institutional rather than state-centered approach. The theoretical underpinnings of their ideas largely derived from the U.S.-based institutionalist movement in economics that emerged in the first half of the twentieth century.[53] At the time of its inception, two main attributes distinguished American institutionalism from Eurocentric economic thought. The first was a strong sense of realism critical of orthodox economic theory. The latter was deemed too abstract and incapable of explaining and resolving the social conflicts produced by industrialization and market expansion. Theory had to be based on axioms derived from economic "realities" that were testable. Institutionalists thus adopted an empirical and investigative approach that involved the application of natural science methods to economics. The movement's co-founder, Wesley Mitchell, saw the "statistical laboratory as the closest approach to the methods of physical science." Quantitative methods became a hallmark of institutionalist economics. The second characteristic of this school of thought was its emphasis that economic systems were institutional rather than natural in character. The economy was largely constructed by a set of evolving legal conventions and social norms rather than fixed and natural laws to be discovered. This meant that economic problems ranging from unemployment to class conflict to business-cycle fluctuations were a product of the failure of markets—or of relevant institutions—to direct economic activity in a manner consistent with the collective interest of the system and of society. At the core of institutionalism lay the epithet that social control in the service of public interest, whether state-led or privately driven, is best achieved through institutional reform.[54]

According to A. J. Meyer, an ERI associate, institutionalism dominated the interwar period in the Middle East.[55] The imprints of institutionalism are present through much of the writings of the AUB economists including Said Himadeh, a student of Wesley Mitchell. Economic organization and monetary management were primary objects of Himadeh's pioneering economic studies and analyses of Greater Syria.[56] The two main characteristics of institutionalism, namely, a preoccupation with quantitative methods and statistical inquiry coupled with an emphasis on institutional reform, became the sine qua non of second- and third-generation AUB economists. These characteristics were reflected in the mandate, constitution, and operation of the ERI.[57] AUB institutionalism was not, however, a copycat of its American counterpart. Institutionalists in the two countries were grappling with different problems, specific to the historical period and sociopolitical context they worked in. U.S. institutionalists like Mitchell devoted much of their attention, including the application of quantitative methods, to the question of business cycles and how they led to economic and social crises. Pecuniary institutions were distrusted and partially blamed for economic disorder. In the books of institutionalists, social control was about mitigating or eliminating these crises in the interest of the public good.

In the case of the AUB-based group, statistical studies sought to calculate data such as national income, population increase, and balance of payments in an "underdeveloped" context. Social control and financial regulation were about expanding the economy and increasing its productivity levels. Institutional reform was thus more of a catalyst for accelerating market forces at work. Tenets of developmental economics such as central planning and macroscopic aggregate accounting were pivotal to the economic philosophy formulated by these thinkers. With the rise of the second generation of AUB institutionalists, Keynes's *General Theory of Employment, Interest and Money* and novel economic concepts such as "gross economy" merged with institutionalist and structuralist approaches. In line with Keynesianism, second-generation institutionalists tolerated public debt as a way of financing development. They were also critical of the imbalance among Lebanon's economic sectors with two thirds of national income accruing from trade (mainly imports) and the tertiary sector (banking, transport, tourism), resulting in a chronic deficit. Yet mainstays of Keynesian-inspired economic development embraced by Third Worldism, such as import substitution, inflationary fiscal policy, nationalization of vital economic sectors, and exchange-rate control, were *not* advocated by the AUB institutionalists.[58]

In the Lebanese context, the AUB institutionalist blueprint for development came close to policy favored by the Société libanaise d'économie politique (SLEP), whose director Gabriel Menassa helped promote liberal ideas of growth in Lebanon's post-independence period that rationalized Michel Chiha's privileging of trade at the expense of industry: expand import and transit trade, improve and modernize government services, and enhance the balance of payments account by developing the agricultural sector and specialized industry "suited" to Lebanon's resources (e.g., the food industry), rather than heavy industry.[59] The AUB's Yusif Sayigh equally emphasized agricultural development as an engine of growth in underdeveloped countries.[60] Both camps, the AUB institutionalists and Menassa's SLEP, held similar views on the role of the state vis-à-vis private enterprise in this process. SLEP's master plan for reconstructing the post–World War II Lebanese economy, published in 1948, opposed the full state control and planning that took hold during World War II. But it also explicitly refrained from calling for a full return to laissez-faire. AUB Institutionalists advocated a middle path. The state was seen as a coordinator and guide for the national economy through various forms of indirect intervention. Major reforms of its administrative and technical apparatus along modern lines were required. Laissez-faire had to be rationalized.[61]

Rationalizing Laissez-faire

The emphasis by AUB institutionalists on economic modernization as the rationalization of public administration has often been overshadowed by the way in which the laissez-faire under the merchant republic has become a point of reference against which ideological currents and political allegiances are measured. Within this binary framework, public actors including economists are generally categorized based on their support for or opposition to laissez-faire, which is often treated as synonymous with resistance to or advocacy of state intervention in the economy. Such a classification obscures rather than illuminates the intellectual trends that AUB scholars upheld. AUB economists stressed the *institutional* character of intervention in the economy as opposed to its state-led nature. In line with laissez-faire rhetoric, the institutionalists, especially those of the second generation like Badre and Sayigh, celebrated free trade and the Lebanese entrepreneurial spirit. But the "miracle" of the Lebanese economy was quantified by computations and historicized by attributing its prosperity to changing economic and social structures.[62]

The prominent Lebanese economist Georges Corm attributed the invocation of Chihist tropes by "reformists" like Badre to the latter's desire for an audience drawn from the elite Lebanese circles among whom the hegemony of Chiha's economic liberalism was uncontested.[63] A more convincing explanation, borne out by the academic corpus and public speeches of these scholars, was the prevalence of their institutionalist approach to political economy. It is worth noting that at the time of Badre's Cénacle libanais lecture in 1960, laissez-faire's hegemony, in its crude merchant republic form, had been challenged by Chehabism. Badre had little incentive to cater to laissez-faire, but he conceded that it had brought "great gain" and "prosperity" to the Lebanese economy. He saw the problem in the attempt to depict the success of laissez-faire as a product of some ahistorical and unfathomable force not to be tampered with, and he invoked an institutionalist worldview of the economy in his rebuttal of such attempts. He blamed the state of affairs on two illusions that had attained the force of truth among the Lebanese educated class. The first pertained to the very concept and nature of economics in general. Contrary to the widely held implicit assumption that the economy possessed deep-rooted, universally comprehensive, and constant principles that applied to all countries and in all epochs, Badre proclaimed that the "science of economics is a science of means not a science of ends." This "science of means" was capable of devising a variety of methods and policies for reaching a single objective. This goal was not permanent either, but subject to the development of a society's capabilities and openness. It followed that the logic and nature of economics dictated a constant revision of the policies, objectives, and indeed the entire economic system in place. Laissez-faire, Badre told his audience, was no exception in spite of the halo bestowed on it by the educated class. This halo was an illusion specific to the Lebanese that was canonized in an alleged remark by the former Belgian prime minister and financial consultant Paul van Zeeland to the effect that "there is a deep secret behind the Lebanese economy accessible to a select few of Lebanon's shrewd sages that work out of sight and in silence for the public good and are careful not to divulge this secret and give away the elegant tricks that drives the Lebanese economy from one gain to another."[64]

The Lebanese economy, Badre asserted, was not an unsolvable riddle. It was subject to scientific rationalization, something he set out to show by qualitatively and quantitatively historicizing and contextualizing its success. For Badre, state intervention was not necessarily the right thing to do. The splendid economic activity that Lebanon witnessed post–World War II was largely due to the individual efforts of the Lebanese, which reached their full potential due to a state policy of nonintervention. The success of that policy was, however, dependent on a set of political and economic conditions, including the flow of petrodollars in the post–World War II global order. These conditions, Badre pointed out, had become increasingly untenable by the late 1950s. The lopsided economic structure favoring the tertiary sector made Lebanon extremely vulnerable to external shocks, something Badre demonstrated with ample reference to statistical data. Moving forward, future success was dependent on economic planning that addressed these facts and evolved with time and a changing environment, rather than policies that invoked past success to justify outdated philosophies. State intervention had become a rational necessity, Badre said. He enumerated six conditions that had contributed to Lebanon's economic success and "dazzling activity" in the 1950s—and justified its laissez-faire policy—but were no longer necessarily true in the early 1960s. These were Lebanon's large holdings of foreign currency at a time when European countries were experiencing a post–World War II construction boom; the weak commercial links between the Arab world and the rest of the world, allowing Lebanon to act as intermediary; the flood of capital into Lebanon from Arab Gulf oil revenues; the growing desire of Western countries to engage in commercial and financial dealings with Arab countries, and the suitability at the outset of Lebanese as middlemen; the laxity of some countries in implementing plans for economic self-sufficiency, thereby facilitating triangular trade; and the laxity in uprooting illegal commercial transactions prevalent in Lebanon, including drug trading and prostitution.[65]

This a priori indifference to state intervention allowed for the near consensus between AUB developmental institutionalists and SLEP advocates of state-managed laissez-faire when it came to reforms of budgetary practices, fiscal policy, administrative reorganization, and even agricultural and industrial development. But consensus stopped short at the gates of finance and the future of the Lebanese economy after its delinking from France. Economists in the two camps disagreed regarding issues such as the full adoption of the new international and IMF-regulated financial order, mechanisms for funding development, organizing the banking sector, and the future of the BSL. Third-generation AUB institutionalists took this debate one step further by focusing almost exclusively on central banking reform.

FINANCE WITHOUT FRANCE

Contrary to conventional wisdom upheld by AUB institutionalists, Menassa praised the French mandatory monetary regime, claiming that pegging the Lebanese lira to the French franc prevented rigging and other currency problems. France had also acted as a "super-state," unifying the Lebanese and Syrian economies and regulating their exchange. Following the breakup of the customs union with Syria in 1950, Lebanon lost both unhindered access to the Syrian market and substantial currency reserves to back the lira. While AUB economists conceptualized the role of the Lebanese state in post–World War II economic development in terms of a generalized scientific doctrine of economic growth dictated by modernization theory, Menassa did so in relation to reviving Lebanon's prewar economic organization. In Menassa's eyes, state intervention during World War II had been a transient phenomenon, dictated by the exigencies of war. It had to be reversed without causing a decline in living standards. Lebanon thus needed to regain its role as a "natural intermediary" of exchange that could rapidly grow into a large financial center and a haven for capital flows. Menassa outlined what he saw as the new consensus for the reconstruction of a healthy global economy. Its four pillars were: economic liberalism, stable international money, freedom of access to primary resources, and increasing the purchasing power of the masses.[66] In the absence of unilateral economic links to France, Menassa advocated multilateral trade with Arab states to compensate for the loss of the Syrian market. Currency backing, however, was a more complicated issue. In Menassa's view, the 1948 monetary agreement with France provided a provisional solution that should be held on to until a satisfactory monetary arrangement among Arab countries was concluded. It was only in the long run that international cooperation, including the adoption of the common formula of note cover adhered to by the IMF, was in the interest of Lebanon.[67]

Menassa acknowledged that adopting the IMF financial framework was in the interest of Lebanon. Unlike AUB institutionalists, however, he did not express the same confidence in the ability of IMF rules to secure currency stability. Menassa doubted that IMF interventions would be timely enough to handle unpredictable economic crises. Seeking full gold cover would be much preferred, despite the difficulty in securing the hard currency to buy it. As a first measure, Menassa saw no harm in replacing surrogate France with the United States and soliciting commercial credit from the latter to the tune of U.S.$75–100 million, which would be largely reimbursed, he surmised, once French note-cover assets were liquidated as stipulated by the 1948 monetary agreement with Paris.[68] In the long run, laissez-faire measures would solve the problem of hard currency and gold reserves, according to Menassa, who called for expanding imports while simultaneously citing a lack of hard currency. This flew in the face of his ostensible pursuit of currency stability and betrayed his primary allegiance to the vested interest of the mercantile-financial class. These measures included abolishing foreign-exchange control and restrictions on the flow of gold, liberalizing legislation to repatriate capital in all its forms, and even authorizing the opening of bank accounts in gold and foreign currency.[69] Many of these measures were implemented between 1948 and 1952 and formed the basis of the merchant republic.

Menassa did not dispute the essential role of a central bank in implementing these measures and providing the desired level of cover for note issue. But he saw no justification in setting up any such independent organization and devoted little space to discussing central and private banking reform and regulation. A central bank was a question for the distant future. According to Menassa, the right to issue bank notes, even during a transition phase, was best vested in a currency board rather than the BSL. The latter should remain the government's bank, however, and be represented on the currency board. In Menassa's opinion, BSL collaboration was irreplaceable rather than inadequate. Its private ownership was lauded as a safeguard against government financial imprudence rather than a bulwark in the face of monetary reform.[70]

By contrast, AUB institutionalists consistently advocated a major overhaul of the unregulated banking sector, promoting monetary policy that was largely aligned with the tenets of embedded liberalism, including its prescriptions for central bank reform. Himadeh had broached the subject as early as the 1930s. For the second generation, it was overshadowed by the broader question of economic development that dominated post–World War II economic thought, but it resurfaced with third-generation institutionalists. The BSL concession was due to expire in 1964, and Talha Yaffi, Salim Hoss, Paul Klat's student Yahya Mahmasani, and George Medawar pondered the fate of the BSL at length, reviving the question of banking reform.[71]

The Ideal Central Bank

Blueprints of the ideal central banking arrangement proposed by third-generation money doctors tackled three broad themes of banking reform. The first was the regulation and reorganization of Lebanon's banking sector independently of its direct relation to the central bank. This included the introduction of legislation governing commercial banking, the reorganization of banks' ownership structures and business practices along modern corporate lines, and the facilitation of interbank cooperation through more formal channels. The second theme was the search for the ideal institutional arrangement that constituted a theoretically sound basis for the operation of a central bank in a developing economy (including its direct relation to banks). The third theme pertained to the best practical institutional arrangement to be adopted in the Lebanese setting. Such a practical arrangement would have to take into account the fate of the BSL, as well as political and other extra-economic considerations prevailing in Lebanon at the time.

At the level of theoretical models, third-generation institutionalists identified credit control (the countercyclical expansion and contraction of the money supply) rather than economic development as the primary function of a central bank. The bank would contribute to developing the economy and growing national income, but indirectly. It would guarantee government loans earmarked for developmental projects, supervise other credit institutions created for this purpose, and influence the propensity to invest through its primary function of manipulating the size and direction of credit flow. Its primary function of credit control, however, was itself framed in relation to theories of underdevelopment. The ideal institutional arrangement in this regard was one that would best achieve efficient credit control in an underdeveloped economy like Lebanon's. Himadeh recognized this fact and AUB's third-generation financial economists reached conclusions similar to his. But third-generation economists couched them in more theoretical terms, derived from emerging literature that specifically dealt with central banking in the context of developing countries.[72]

Two main influences in this regard were A. F.W. Plumptre, University of Toronto professor of political economy, and S. N. Sen, lecturer in economics at the University of Calcutta. While Plumptre focused on central banking in the British dominions, Sen broadened the scope of his study to include developing countries in general.[73] Both, however, raised the question of how newly established central banks can assert their authority and efficiently fulfill their mission of credit control. They conceded that all central banks must be guided by public interest rather than the pursuit of profit. Central banks were expected to perform universally accepted duties such as maintain currency stability and act as a government bank and bank of last resort. The specific institutional organization of a central bank and the techniques it employed to achieve such goals were not deemed universal, however, but determined by the financial space they were operating in, namely, the degree of development of the money market.[74]

Sen argued that an underdeveloped money market rendered central banking more complicated. Mature Western money markets reflected a highly organized banking sector and robust credit structure. Under such conditions, central banks had attained a dominant financial position over many decades, if not centuries. They would be able to directly affect credit flow through open market operations (sale and purchase of securities) or indirectly through the changing of discount rates at which other banks can buy and sell bills to the central bank. In developing countries, these two conditions—an integrated and deep money market and an experienced and dominant central bank—were often absent.[75] Unable to exercise sufficient authority in the money market, the central bank's most effective option would be to impose minimum cash reserve ratio requirements on commercial banks and to vary them as needed. Such a statutory-based technique could not be employed as frequently as open market operations or variation in the interest rate, but it provided the central bank with direct means of forcing unwieldy market agents (regular banks) to abide by central bank policy. The additional right to inspect the books of private banks and demand information on a regular basis would greatly enhance the power of the central bank to make sound judgments in this regard. As Sen put it, such information constituted the "raw materials of control."[76]

AUB third-generation institutionalists endorsed the assumptions and conclusions of Sen's analysis. They lamented the underdevelopment of Beirut's money market; assigned secondary importance to economic development compared to credit control; identified cash reserve ratio requirements and their variation as the favored means of such control; and stressed the need for the inspection of bank books and the collection and regular publication of banking data.[77] In their assessment, the existing institutional arrangement, embodied in the BSL, failed on all counts. Even at the apogee of its influence in the mid-1930s, Himadeh had pointed out that the BSL lacked the ability to control and regulate credit in the money market and did not adopt a clear policy of public interest.[78] By the late 1950s, the BSL's precarious status as a central bank was attacked on practical performance and not just on purely theoretical grounds. Yaffi cited the BSL's unwillingness to act as a central bank and promptly intervene to control credit during crises such as the Korean War and the Suez conflict. Even if it possessed the will, Hoss pointed out, it was under no "legal obligation" to control the money supply, and its lack of "jurisdiction" over other banks was a serious handicap.[79]

The BSL's continued amalgamation of statistics regarding both its commercial and state assets, as well as those of government deposits in Lebanon and Syria, further impeded the implementation of an effective fiscal policy. Such concerns were raised by Hoss and Mahmasani. Yaffi also pointed out that the BSL's influence in the private money market was declining. BSL figures cited by AUB institutionalists indicated that the proportion of the BSL's private deposits to the total amount of Lebanese bank deposits was steadily shrinking. It had slipped from 38 percent in 1951 to 9 percent in 1959. BSL business had become more and more dependent on its government banking, whose deposits at the bank had increased from LL145M in 1955 to a whopping LL247M in 1960. Should the government deprive it of that privilege upon expiry of its concession in 1964, it was likely to become one of the smallest banks in the country.[80]

AUB institutionalists proposed several alternative arrangements to the BSL. Back in the 1930s, Himadeh's ideal solution was a central bank modeled on the U.S. Federal Reserve Bank (FRB) but financed by "native" bankers. Himadeh, however, surmised that political instability of Syria at the time, and the need to decommercialize the BSL, would render the FRB option impractical. These political, rather than economic considerations, led Himadeh to suggest that the BSL be transformed into a full-fledged central bank along the lines of the Bank of France, which did commercial business in addition to its central banking functions. Should the BSL refuse that option, Himadeh—who was writing in the run-up to the expiry of the BSL's concession in 1939—suggested a short-term (ten-year) renewal of its concession until political circumstances in Syria changed. In the meantime, national influence could be achieved by increasing the proportion of "natives" on the bank's board and boosting the authority of the government representative.[81]

Conditions in Syria developed more quickly than Himadeh had anticipated. As noted, Syria never officially renewed the 1924 concession but opted instead for setting up a state-owned central bank. By contrast, Lebanon renewed the BSL's concession for another twenty-five years. Time, however, was not on the BSL's side. Theories of monetary regulation and regimes of credit control had undergone fundamental transformations in favor of empowering central banking authorities. World War II and the subsequent rise of developmental economics endowed these banks with greater prestige and authority. They had become a necessary staple of self-government and economic as well as political independence. The BSL's position became increasingly untenable in light of Lebanon's developing monetary conditions under the new global order.

Third-generation proposals for central bank reform reflected these transformations. The government was expected to take initiative in this regard. Yaffi, seconded by Mahmasani, listed four options: extending the BSL's concession, "Lebanonizing" the bank by acquiring at least 51 percent of its joint stock, fully nationalizing it, or creating an altogether new state-owned central bank. The fourth option was favored by the institutionalists. The EPDB, on which Yaffi and several other members of the group served, shared that view. The EPDB adopted it as a policy recommendation and estimated the necessary capital for its launch to be LL5M.[82]

The question of state ownership of the central bank would acquire an overtly nationalistic tone in the early 1960s. Mahmasani explicitly accused the BSL of providing French-owned banks all the assistance and help they desired and thereby representing "foreign interests." Quoting Sen, Mahmasani reiterated that a central bank represented a country's economic independence. Setting up such a bank demonstrated Lebanon's "ability to manifest its authority in the monetary and banking system and to play its role in the development of the economy without any foreign influence or pressure."[83] For these third-generation institutionalists, calling for a nationally owned central bank did not imply a wholesale embrace of etatism. Managerial autonomy, private-public partnership, and independent technocratic expertise all remained central to the scheme. In emulation of existing international practices and in accordance with IMF recommendations, institutionalists suggested that a council of money and credit take charge of managing the bank. The council's board members would be appointed by the president of the republic but would retain operational autonomy. In order for this board to represent the various segments and interests of the national economy, it would be composed of a mix of politicians, high-ranking civil servants, and a majority of technocratic experts.[84]

References by AUB institutionalists to nationalism and state supervision were not inspired by prevalent discourses of Third Worldism, anti-imperialism, or state socialism. On the contrary, they sought to conform to U.S.-inspired notions of financial management and economic planning. Himadeh warned against peasant revolts, which "we detest," while Badre described imperialism as a benign, even beneficial, set of institutional relationships between more developed and less developed countries.[85] In terms of state sovereignty over central banks, Yaffi cited the growing international consensus that controlling money had become a fundamental exercise of sovereignty while third-generation members often reduced the question of economic underdevelopment and dependency to that of underdeveloped money markets rather than economic dependency on Western countries. Calling for public ownership of institutions like the central bank was in line, as Mahmasani put it, with a worldwide tendency to shift ownership from private to public. What really mattered, Yaffi stressed, was management, not ownership. Government management was assumed to be inefficient and subject to political pressures. In response, institutional safeguards such as the granting of managerial autonomy to experts had to be put in place.[86]

AUB institutionalist ideas were therefore reformist and liberal. They posed little threat to the overall structure of the Lebanese economy and its capitalist foundations. Their institutionalist intervention in public debate around the economy writ large could be reconciled to the doctrine of economic liberalism that many of these elites professed. Their affinity to mainstream economic currents of thought, however, made them more menacing in one particular quarter, the banking sector. When it came to the field of finance, AUB institutionalists advocated drastic restructuring of the financial system and regulation of the banking sector. Yaffi put it quite bluntly when he wrote that monetary policy "will not only manage and regulate the composition of the cover and notes in circulation—assets and liabilities—of the currency-issuing department, *but also* [his emphasis] the management and regulation of the assets and liabilities of the *whole* [emphasis added] banking system."[87] Furthermore, the preferred central banking technique for such control advocated by the institutionalists (the cash reserve ratio requirement) implied the direct subordination of private banking activity and policy to constant adjustment by a central authority. This in turn required better access to banking data. The specter of inspection was added to that of authority. The fig leaf of laissez-faire was no longer able to hide the parochial interests of Lebanon's top financiers and bankers. By the late 1950s, the case for a central bank had made inroads into the bureaucratic apparatus of the state. By the early 1960s, Chehabism was in full force in the country, and the BSL's concession was about to expire. In the long-drawn-out battle to set up a national central bank for Lebanon, the Lebanese bankers were the last frontier.

CHAPTER 3

Barons of Banking

The Untouchables

The central bank might find that cooperation with the Association of Banks is the ideal method to prevent distortions, through understanding instead of coercion, and persuasion instead of written provisions.

—Pierre Eddé, president of the Association of Banks in Lebanon, 1963

While AUB money doctors sought to promote the idea of a central bank among elite circles and state officials in Lebanon, another AUB alumnus was giving similar advice in Washington.[1] In September 1953, the prominent Princeton University historian Philip Hitti suggested creating a central bank in Lebanon as a means of "solving some of the pressing economic problems that beset the land" in a letter to U.S. Assistant Secretary of State Henry Byroade.[2] Hitti argued that the central bank would be able to regulate currency and act as the best guarantee against both inflation and deflation. Three months later, Hitti passed on news of a popular petition back in Lebanon calling for the immediate founding of such a bank. Signed by over a dozen mainstream political parties, grassroots social organizations, and prominent commercial, industrial, and agricultural syndicates and published in prominent Lebanese newspapers including *al-Nahar* and *al-Hayat*,[3] the petition addressed the Lebanese public ahead of the first parliamentary elections to be held under the presidency of Camille Chamoun:

O Lebanese [Citizen]

There can be no political independence without economic independence and no economic independence without *bayt al-mal al-Lubnani* [i.e., a Lebanese central bank]. Otherwise, we will see our agriculture, industry, commerce, and tourism endangered.

Dear Citizen—Demand that your candidate commit to establishing *bayt al-mal al-Lubnani*, provided that it is administered by nationals under the supervision of the Lebanese government without any foreign interference.[4]

The petition's content, reach, and the scope of its signatories indicate the extent to which the call for central banking was a matter of debate beyond elite circles like the Cénacle libanais and specialized technocrats like the AUB economists. Public demands for a central bank came at a time when state-led development had become a fundamental tenet of economic growth and national independence.[5] The absence of financial institutions as signatories to the petition may suggest that positions were split between merchants and industrialists on one hand, and the bankers on the other. But the fault line was drawn within the banking sector. While the BSL-led consortium saw a central bank as a threat to its financial dominance, emerging rival banks—largely linked to U.S., Latin American, and Gulf capital—were eager to gain an upper hand in the money market via a state-sponsored central bank. Several start-up bankers like Michel Saab were strongly in favor of a central bank. Wealthy Lebanese émigrés had been pushing for a privately funded national bank with currency-issuing powers since World War II. They sought security guarantees of their investment against "unjust" taxation or state nationalization. In 1950, Lebanon's foreign minister, Philip Takla, following a tour of Latin America, gave such proposals serious consideration, only in the end to deem them "impractical" in light of the long-term concession held by the BSL and suggest a purely commercial venture instead.[6]

The strategies of the pro and anti-BSL camps evolved over time. The BSL consortium's first line of defense, as articulated by SLEP's chief economist, Gabriel Menassa, was to dismiss the urgent need for such a bank.[7] In the 1950s, calls for state-led economic development through a central bank became harder to oppose. BSL supporters chose to vouch for state-sponsored development banks as the lesser evil. The shift in the stance of the emerging anti-BSL bankers was more drastic. Up until the mid 1950s, when their market share was low and their influence minimal compared to that of the BSL, start-up bankers actively campaigned in favor of a central bank or state-sponsored development banks. But following the restructuring of state-sector relations in favor of the banking sector under the 1956 Banking Secrecy law, which led to a banking boom, these new barons of banking realized that a central bank might also jeopardize their own financial power. The two camps found themselves fighting a common enemy: state regulation under Chamoun's successor, Fuad Chehab. In the final years leading to the BDL's creation, the joint strategy of both camps changed from protesting against to cooptation of the institution-building process.

The shifting trajectory of this interbank rivalry was integral to the much-emphasized rise and rule of Lebanon's mercantile financial class during the merchant republic phase under Chamoun. Yet classical historiographies of this class's evolution have little to say about the formation of its financial wing and the mechanisms through which it contributed to the domination of the class as a whole. In these historiographies, the hegemony of the merchant-financial class is largely ascribed to the triumph of traders over industrialists in determining the path of state policy, which is summed up as the full deregulation of markets in line with the laissez-faire principles that underpinned the merchant republic. The question of credit control and financial regulation is mentioned in passing. Bankers are subsumed within the broader commercial community. When singled out, they are either romanticized or vilified. There was little study of them as a social group and in relation to merchants, industrialists, and other business professions.

Yusif Sayigh's pioneering study of entrepreneurship in the context of a developing country like Lebanon touched on certain aspects of Lebanon's banking community, but failed adequately to map out the ownership and operational structures of the banking sector and resorted to the tropes about business dynamics cited above. Sayigh surveyed several hundred business leaders, managers, and owners in the sectors of industry, agriculture, finance, and services. His study was informed by Joseph Schumpeter's work on economic development and entrepreneurship, which gained currency in the late 1950s.[8] Schumpeter posited the banker as the modern entrepreneur par excellence given his key mediating role in credit distribution. Sayigh found Lebanon's financial sector to be very restricted and credit allocation lacking in innovation. Determining real ownership was challenging. In several cases, Lebanese citizens or residents owned shares but the real authority lay with foreigners. Of Sayigh's chosen pool, only one bank supplied medium- and long-term nonmercantile credit.[9]

Rather than creativity and stability, the Lebanese economy's bias in favor of the trade and services sectors created a business culture of "cleverness" (*shatarah*), Sayigh observed. Short-term gains and high-risk but profitable speculative practices were valued more than long-term investment and reward. More than two-thirds of respondents to Sayigh's survey noted the shortage of credit facilities for medium- and long-term loans.[10] Rather than digging into the causes of this shortage to explain the modest presence of entrepreneurial initiative in Lebanon, Sayigh fell back on worn-out Chihist tropes and invoked the so-called Phoenician "heritage of adventure, trade, and brisk business."[11] According to Sayigh, contemporary social fragmentation[12] and political competitiveness turned the Lebanese into a "die-hard" person and produced "entrepreneurial resilience and intense drive in economic pursuits." Material success was a compensation for the limitations and rigidity of Lebanese sociocultural formations and political factions. Economic sectors that required little or no partnership. such as trade and services, were thus preferred to other sectors. Sayigh partly attributed the "free" environment in which Lebanese economic actors operated to "an innate revolt against control and regulation and a genuine love of freedom."[13] In his final theoretical analysis, he argued that unless the definition of an entrepreneur—marked as a key factor of development—was relaxed beyond "epoch-making innovation," little business activity in Lebanon and other developing countries would be identified as entrepreneurial.[14] To survive as a category outside the industrial core, Sayigh reasoned, the entrepreneur must be identified as a strategic factor in development but *not* its initiator.[15]

Despite resorting to unconvincing explanations, Sayigh rightly linked this environment to the lack of an adequate institutional framework able to provide a more conducive environment for innovative enterprise. This institutional gap included the lagging behind of business legislation, the paucity of research, and the inadequacy of credit for agricultural and industrial development, the latter normally provided by specialized and state-sponsored banks.[16] The making of the central bank and the drive for development banks under Chamoun were key elements in fostering this gap, something Sayigh doesn't dwell on or link to class formation. Bargaining over these financial institutions impacted state-led developmental policy, including the price, access to, and allocation of credit among trade, agriculture, and industry. It also shaped the *institutional* transformation of the banking community. It affected the sector's capital size and owner-ship structure, triggered its political self-organization, and required the deployment by different actors of paradigms of laissez-faire and economic independence to project and protect the privileged position of bankers vis-à-vis market and state. The institutional outcomes constituted the in-frastructure of the mercantile-financial class's cohesion and hegemony. Their evolution took place amid a transnational boom of capital that saw American and Arab Gulf investments compete with and threaten French capital dominance in the Lebanese market.

DEVELOPMENT BANKS AND TRANSNATIONAL CREDIT COMPETITION

Prominent Lebanese bankers have depicted the 1950s banking boom in Lebanon as the rise of national banking after the dominance of foreign banks between the mid-nineteenth century and the post–World War II era.[17] Petitioners cited above equally articulated their demands for a cen-tral bank in relation to national independence and foreign interference. In his conversation with Henry Byroade cited earlier, Philip Hitti pointed out that the central bank would protect "native" capital while attracting foreign investment, particularly from Lebanese emigrants. U.S. officials also adopted the binary of foreign and native banks to understand the Lebanese financial market.

In reality, the perceived rise of national banking was more accurately the rise of new and the reconfiguration of old, local agents of transna-tional capital, which increasingly contained a heavy American and Gulf rather than French component. These agents included wealthy Lebanese emigrants seeking to repatriate their foreign-earned capital, aspiring re-gional entrepreneurs like Michel Saab capitalizing on new opportunities to break into the market, veteran local businessmen like Michel Doumit willing to strike new partnerships to capture incoming investments out-side their BSL-linked networks, and merchant-notables like Saeb Salam and Husayn Uwayni who were eager to tap into U.S., Gulf, and Lebanese expat capital for greater influence at home.

A close examination of U.S.-government classification of bank ownership in Lebanon reveals this complex web of partnerships behind many so-called Lebanese banks. In 1958, American officials identified "ten principal Lebanese banks" with head offices in Beirut. But at least half of those—including self-identifying Lebanese banks such as Intra Bank and Banque Sabbagh—were partnerships with foreign, Arab, and at times European, capital.[18] An earlier tally of top banks classified the institutions in question as either foreign, mixed, or Lebanese. But even this nuanced tally falsely identifies certain banks, such as the prominent Banque du Liban et d'Outre-Mer (BLOM), with exclusive "native" capital.[19] BLOM was the fruit of a partnership that extended from Beirut to Jeddah to France and all the way to Brazil.[20] Its founders and directors included Hussein Uwayni, several times prime minister; the future Central Bank governor Philip Takla; and the latter's father-in-law, the Brazilian businessman Georges Maalouf. These men wore several hats as leading businessmen and powerful politicians whose accumulation of wealth rarely originated from, or was limited to, the Lebanese market.[21] BLOM's chair and its public face, Uwayni, embodied Saudi capital and political interests as he much as he did Lebanon's.[22] Well-established French capital was also partner to the venture.[23] Saudi and Kuwaiti Gulf capital flows were not restricted to the deposit of money in Lebanese coffers. Gulf investors actively participated in the co-founding of new banks like the Bank Beirut Riyadh, drawing on Lebanese expertise and political patronage to secure a dominant position in the market. Incorporated in March 1958 with an authorized capital larger than that of any other Lebanese bank at the time (LL25M), Bank Beirut Riyadh's capital was reportedly 55 percent Lebanese and 45 percent Saudi. The bank boasted Saudi royalty among its investors, and the well-connected Lebanese politician and banker Pierre Eddé as its first manager.[24]

Some of the privately driven banking ventures, including those tied to French capital and ostensibly wedded to laissez-faire, explicitly invoked the discourse of Third World economic development to push their financial agendas. They took advantage of a growing American appetite for large-scale investment projects in the Arab region to raise the required capital and solicit foreign patronage. Michel Chiha's banking partner and brother-in-law, the Lebanese tycoon Henri Pharaon, and Michel Khoury, son of the country's first president, called on the U.S. embassy

in Beirut in 1959 to solicit corporate American funds for the establishment of a development bank, which, they told U.S. Ambassador Robert
McClintock, would finance large-scale construction projects in Lebanon
and the Arab world, including the building of merchant ships, silos, and
warehouses.[25] An "almost identical" proposal to Pharoun's and Khoury's
was presented by the Beirut banker and embassy informant Sami Shoucair. A third project was circulated by the Lebanese expatriate Mansour
Zanaty, a wealthy Alabama attorney who was a leading delegate at the
1959 overseas convention of the National Association of the Federations
of Syrian and Lebanese American Clubs held in Beirut. Zanaty did not
seek direct financial assistance from Washington. His scheme relied instead
on Lebanese and Syrian expatriate investment.[26] The Beiruti notable Saeb
Salam preferred American capital. In 1952, he reportedly visited the Chase
National Bank in New York and managed to persuade it to open the first
U.S. bank office in Beirut.[27]

In their diplomatic dig for U.S. greenbacks, Pharaon and Khoury availed
themselves of all the "cleverness" that Sayigh ascribed to Lebanese entrepreneurs.[28] They argued that the scheme "would be meeting a genuine desire
on the part of private enterprise[s] in the West to associate themselves with
the efforts of their respective governments in the aid which must be given
to under developed countries and particularly Lebanon," where the U.S.
hoped "to raise the standard of life of the Lebanese quickly." The purely
private nature of the proposed bank would "safeguard it from political
or confessional interference and intrigue." The bank's self-effacing brokers promised to entrust its management to a neutral Swiss. "[Given our]
meagre means," they wrote to the ambassador, "it would only be honest
on our part, in appealing for help, to entrust the execution of this work
to groups and men better equipped than we are." Pharaon, who served
on the BSL board of directors, and Khoury, a future governor of the BDL,
reasoned at the time that the development bank's board of directors had
to be "exclusively composed of Lebanese," however, to enable the company to enjoy the full rights of Lebanese companies and gain easier access
to the Arab world. U.S. corporate shareholders, the duo argued, did not
need to worry about the integrity of these board members. According to
Pharaon and Khoury, "the personalities chosen to sit on this board . . . ,

with their prestige and influence, will be able to facilitate the work of the Bank without trying to make any personal profit or handicap its progress."[29] Ambassador McClintock was not impressed. He wondered about the benefit of yet another scheme for a development bank at a time when other development-oriented schemes were in the air, and when the Lebanese government was about to seek U.S. loans for setting up the Banque de crédit agricole, industriel et foncier (BCAIF), a private-public development partnership sponsored by the Lebanese government.

Unlike private ventures, plans for large-scale state-sponsored projects like the BCAIF were deeply enmeshed in the struggle over access to cheap transnational credit, the delay in central bank reform, and the restructuring of the Lebanese economy in line with the contemporary push for industrially based economic growth. Hitti, for instance, had reported in his 1953 letter to Byroade that president Chamoun preferred to delay the establishment of a Lebanese central bank by citing the government's decision at the time to set up a development bank to finance agriculture and industry. Hitti countered, however, that there was no conflict between the two projects reports in the Lebanese press indicating that "native" banks in Beirut had expressed their readiness to invest the entire necessary capital to realize such a "vital project." Hitti's source on Chamoun's stance was the Tehran-based Lebanese businessman Michel Saab. In his own letter to Byroade, Saab billed the Lebanese central bank as a first step towards the realization of Byroade's own proposal for an Arab development bank.[30] Saab's brother, Joseph, "violently opposed to the BSL and considers it the agency which thwarts the development of Lebanon for its own profits," led a popular campaign for a central bank.[31] In 1951, the Saab brothers had partnered with the Beiruti notable Sami Solh, who became prime minister under Chamoun, to found the Federal Bank of Lebanon.[32] The Saabs, the dispatch claimed, hoped their bank would be among those that won the concession for setting up a national central bank.

Proposals for state-sponsored development banks by pro-French and pro-American groups alike began circulating in earnest after Chamoun's election. In November 1952, the government approved the incorporation of the Banque nationale, foncière, commerciale et industrielle (BNCFI), funded by prominent Lebanese businessmen, including the gold broker

Michel Doumit and the prominent politician Najib Salha, which began operations in late 1953.[33] Discreet enquiries by the U.S. embassy found links between the BNFCI and the BSL. Two of the latter's brightest officials were put at the "disposal" of the BNFCI. Some financial circles believed the BSL was hoping that the BNFCI would take over as bank of issue once the BSL's concession expired in 1964.[34]

The BCAIF emerged in 1953 following a request by the Lebanese government that the International Bank for Reconstruction and Development (IBRD) outline its vision for founding a state-sponsored development bank. During a three-week stay in Beirut, IBRD special consultant Harold Johnson held a series of meetings with Lebanese government officials including President Chamoun and the then minister of national economy—and AUB money doctor—George Hakim to test the waters for such a possibility. Johnson envisaged a trilateral partnership. Arab-Lebanese banks would supply the BCAIF's share capital of LL5M, the IBRD would furnish it with a foreign-currency line of credit of LL10M, and the Lebanese government would supply an equivalent amount and exempt the bank from taxation for five years.[35]

In line with contemporary doctrines of economic development, Johnson and Hakim proposed that the bank be solely devoted to financing industrial projects, albeit small-scale ones "commensurate" with the resources and capabilities of the country. With the assistance of Hakim, Johnson was able to secure the written commitment of seven Arab banks, including Intra Bank, the Arab Bank, and Saab's Federal Bank, to subscribe the full LL5M. The Saab brothers were key in securing private bank participation.[36] Johnson also received the backing of technical members of the Lebanese government's Economic Planning and Development Board (EPDB), including the second-generation institutionalist Paul Klat, who was called in by Chamoun to study the case. Chamoun's counterscheme differed from Johnson's in two main respects. The first was regarding the kind of development projects the bank was authorized to fund. Despite acknowledging that credit conditions for agricultural development differed from those of industry, Chamoun thought it was "politically necessary" that any financing scheme for industry must also simultaneously provide credit facilities for agriculture.[37] The second disagreement was over the source and composition of loan capital and founding share capital. Chamoun proposed to split the founding share capital 40/60 between the government (LL2M) and private investors (LL3M) rather than the latter investing the full amount. As for loan capital, Chamoun deemed IBRD interest rates for loans too high. Instead, the entire loan capital (estimated at LL25M) would be borrowed from the BSL against treasury bills at a rate of 1 percent compared to the estimated 4 percent rate offered by the IBRD.[38]

BCAIF was incorporated in 1954 and opened its doors the following year. The U.S. chargé d'affaires, Armin Meyer (not to be confused with the economist A. J. Meyer), described the final arrangement as a "compromise between the President's proposal for a single institution and the theory advanced by an IBRD mission and the Economic Development Board favoring separate institutions for agriculture and industry."[39] Calls for separate institutions were ostensibly assuaged by dividing BCAIF into three autonomous departments and apportioning funds to each department based on a fixed formula (2/5 for agriculture, 2/5 for industry, and 1/5 for real estate). There was less of a compromise, however, in the realm of share and loan capital. IBRD-facilitated international capital was excluded. BSL influence was secured, with the BSL designated as the sole lender of loan capital. The 40/60 public-private ownership proposed by Chamoun also prevailed.[40] The bank's charter stipulated that four of the twelve members of the board of directors be appointed by the government. But government representation was about clientalism rather than technocratic oversight: all four—the industrialist Toufic Ghandour; Georges Rayes, the manager of the Bristol Hotel; and the agricultural engineers and merchants Fuad Najjar and Fouad Saade—were from the private sector.[41]

In short, Chamoun opted for an inflationary policy of financing development via BSL-issued public debt. He also chose a public-private ownership, rather than a purely private yet internationally backed, scheme. Chamoun's two choices contradicted the fundamentals of laissez-faire. The fact that they were adopted as policy during the heyday of the merchant republic demonstrates that the Lebanese ruling clique largely saw laissez-faire in a functional fashion. They used the state as a source of cheap and very profitable credit. In return for their LL3M contribution, private shareholders were gaining access to almost eight times that amount from government funds at the cheap rate of 1 percent. They were then able to lend it out as short-, medium-, and long-term credit to industry and agriculture at rates ranging from 4 to 7 percent. The BSL was also guaranteed control of financing the bank in its capacity as primary lender.

Up until the end of the Khoury presidency, state-linked and large-scale credit control had been largely mediated by the BSL through consortia like the Société de crédit agricole et industriel du Liban (SCAIL). Set up by the BSL in 1936, SCAIL was the country's major credit facility, lending to businesses and landowners close to Lebanon's first president, Bishara Khoury, but largely avoiding industrial projects that required long-term investments.[42] By securing a stake in BCAIF to the exclusion of the IBRD, the BSL scuttled attempts to wrest significant control of credit flow out of its hands. Talk of founding a central bank under Chamoun threatened this monopoly, and a development bank reduced the threat. The compromise reached was also a blow to the doctrine of development as a conceptual framework for government policy. BCAIF's single-institution-serves-all-sectors approach challenged the emerging paradigm of privileging the industrial sector for development.[43] The BSL consortium paid the price for fending off this international attempt to restructure Lebanon's banking sector on the local stage: the radius of local beneficiaries, typically restricted to the BSL consortium, was widened to include new financial rivals like the Saabs' Federal Bank and Intra Bank.[44] Over time, the capital share and political clout of BSL rivals grew exponentially and placed the entire banking sector on a path to securing the dominance of this sector in Lebanon's economy. The rapid rise and longevity of banker power had less to do with market forces or entrepreneurial acumen than with the legislative and lobbying activities led by Raymond and Pierre Eddé.

THE EDDÉ BANKING BROTHERS

The Eddé brothers were ideally situated to defend the privileges and protect the gains of Beirut's financial elite. They were the products of a marriage of money and politics. Their mother Laudi Sursock belonged to one of the city's wealthiest merchant and landowning families. Their father Émile, a shrewd lawyer who became Lebanon's president in 1936 under French tutelage, was a scion of Ottoman-era scribes and dragomans. He fell out of grace in 1943 when his political archrival, and former legal office trainee, Bishara Khoury spearheaded the push for independence from France and became president. Émile Eddé's political career never recovered. His sons, however, managed to enter the political fray as part of the rising tide of opposition to Khoury in the early 1950s. Pierre and Raymond Eddé won parliamentary seats for the first time in 1951 and 1953 respectively. Under Khoury's presidential successor Chamoun, the Eddé brothers became prominent politicians and ardent defenders of the merchant republic and its economic engine, the banking sector.[45] The elder, Raymond, who succeeded his father as party leader of the National Bloc, was the architect of the Banking Secrecy Law of 1956, which secured large flows of capital from oil-rich Arab nations and renegotiated the power relations between the state and the banking sector in favor of the latter. Raymond's less well-known brother Pierre was three-time finance minister under Chamoun,[46] and he left his institutional imprint on the consolidation of banker power after he left office in 1958. Through his newly acquired prestigious position as head of the Bank Beirut Riyadh, he spearheaded the first successful collective effort by Lebanese bankers to self-organize. Establishing the ABL furnished the new barons of banking with a structural and sustainable framework to measure up to the BSL initially, and eventually interfere in and override state policy in defense of the interests of the entire sector.

Banking Secrecy and State Authority

Between 1950 and 1962, Lebanon's national income nearly doubled, with an annual average increase of 4.5 percent. The financial sector reaped the lion's share of this growth at a staggering rate of 200 percent. Close to 95 percent of this financial sector was banking, including foreign-exchange operations.[47] The growth of the banking sector was expressed both in terms of total capital flow and number of banking institutions. Between 1950 and 1961, bank deposits increased more than fivefold. The number of banks in Lebanon shot up from nine in 1945 to eighty-five in 1962.[48]

Different forces, both external and internal, contributed to the early phase of the Lebanese banking boom. Externally, three major forces were at play. The first was the 1948 establishment of a Zionist state in Palestine.

With the diversion of trade between Arab countries and the West from Haifa's port to Beirut's, the latter boosted its status as an entrepôt between Europe and the rest of the Arab world. The Palestinian bourgeoisie expelled by Zionist forces into Lebanon brought along sizeable capital and entrepreneurial skills that directly contributed to the growth of the banking sector.[49] The second factor was the emergence of an oil economy in the Gulf region, which generated an influx of hot capital into the international market including nearby Beirut. The third force, whose significance came to fruition in the early 1960s, was the gradual shift into planned economies in neighboring countries such as Egypt and Syria. Nationalization schemes in these countries further channeled free-enterprise capital into Lebanon's liberal economy.[50] Locally, Lebanon's laissez-faire policy of free trade, deregulation of currency exchange, unrestricted capital flow, and total absence of any banking regulation were hailed as the engines of this growth. In practice, banking "regulation" in the form of the Banking Secrecy Law of 1956 was an equally, if not more important, driving force.[51]

Without banking secrecy legislation, it is doubtful that the banking sector would have sustained such a high rate of growth well into the late 1950s and early 1960s. In 1964, Lebanon boasted over eighty banks. A caption in the sector's magazine of record, *al-Masarif,* exclaimed that banks were being founded as frequently as restaurants and cabarets.[52] By then, most of the external forces sustaining the banking boom, as the AUB economist Albert Badre pointed out, were beginning to wane.[53] This was especially the case regarding start-up banks with little else than the advantage of promising secrecy to attract capital thanks to legislation introduce by Raymond Eddé in 1956. The aim behind the legislation, Raymond pointed out ahead of its passage in parliament, was to "render Lebanon a refuge for foreign capital and Lebanese expatriate moneys."[54] The joint report on the draft law prepared by two of Lebanon's parliamentary committees reiterated Eddé's claims, adding the purported objective of providing finance for "the possibility of anticipated grand projects."[55] On July 26, 1956, the proposal received a near-unanimous yes vote in parliament. President Chamoun signed it into law on September 3 of the same year. Two months later, it went into effect.[56] The law ushered in a "golden period" of expansion. Between 1955 and 1961, the number of total banks in Lebanon jumped from thirty-one to seventy-three. Most of this expansion was by locally based banks. Between 1955 and 1962, the number of foreign-registered banks remained virtually constant at around seventeen, while the number of Lebanese-registered banks increased fourfold, reaching an estimated sixty-eight institutions.[57]

Praise for the Banking Secrecy Law was largely framed within the laissez-faire paradigm. Raymond Eddé couched his rationale in typical Chihist tropes about Lebanon's geographic position and stability vis-à-vis its environs during the 1950s. Invoking secrecy laws in Switzerland completed the metaphor. The elder Eddé admitted, albeit in passing, that the Banking Secrecy Law was also intended to "prevent the flight of Lebanese capital to avoid inheritance tax."[58] The shielding of bank accounts from tax inspection, inheritance included, restructured the relation between the state, the banks and their clients. Lebanon's 1944 income tax law had explicitly decreed that professional secrecy could not be invoked by any institution or administration to prevent the inspection of commercial accounts and documents by the Ministry of Finance. Bank officials of all ranks were subject to penalties if they refused to divulge information about clients contrary to the latter's objection. Under the 1956 Banking Secrecy Law, they became subject to fines and even imprisonment if they divulged any such information, unless they had obtained the consent of the client or his or her heir, there was litigation between the client and the bank, or, in bankruptcies, peculation was involved The duty not to divulge information applied to requests by "any person, be they an individual or a public authority, whether administrative, military or judicial." The state was also barred from freezing assets or deposits without the written consent of the owner.[59]

As a result of the new Banking Secrecy Law, bank depositors became largely immune from any form of public prosecution, taxation or even inspection. Their monetary transactions were above the law in relation to the state, *not* the banks. Banks were allowed to exchange information about their clients among themselves to conduct cross credit checks. Banks were also granted the right to open numbered accounts for clients with the names of owners known strictly only by the bank's top managers. In effect, bank directors held the key to who was who in the world of business to the exclusion of lower-ranking bank employees and the entire apparatus of the state.[60] Banks came first, clients second, and the state third. Two years after the Banking Secrecy Law was enacted in 1956, the enhanced power of individual banks became, thanks in large part of Raymond's brother Pierre, the entrenched power of a sectorwide interest group, the Association of Banks in Lebanon (ABL).

THE ABL: A FINANCIAL FRATERNITY

The rise of banker power in the second half of the 1950s and the first half of the 1960s was not an isolated phenomenon in the changing landscape of Lebanon's associational life. The hold of the professional class as a whole on the reins of power became more apparent over time as the percentage of businessmen and professionals in parliament rose compared to the dwindling number of traditional landowners.[61] Business interest groups became increasingly active in exerting direct influence on government economic policy. The majority were based in the Greater Beirut area where the highest concentration of businesses lay. Beirut's wealthy merchants were the first in the country to found a professional association to defend their business interests. Established in 1921, the Beirut Trader's Association (BTA) grew from a small collective in the early mandate period into the sector's peak association in the post-independence era. The association expressed its demand in laissez-faire lingo, promoting "free trade" as "the basis of the Lebanese economy" and defending the banking secrecy act. Its lobbying for the lifting of import restrictions after World War II put it on a collision course with the Association of Lebanese Industrialists (ALI), a national, multi-confessional interest group founded in 1943. Following independence, the ALI fought to protect the gains of industry thanks to wartime measures that increased production and expanded local markets. Despite disagreements between the two associations over protectionist measures, their relationship was not always antagonistic, as Sami Baroudi has shown. It involved cooperation as much as it did conflict, even if the BTA often gained the upper hand. Merchants branched out into industry and industrialists took part in trade deals. The BTA actively encouraged export industries that did not compete with their import trade but resisted the expansion of production for the local market. The two associations

were in agreement in opposing labor demands for higher wages and social benefits. As the ALI gained more clout in the 1960s, its president, the
wealthy businessman Boutros Khoury, set up al-Hay'at al-Iqtisadiyyah,
an informal forum for commercial and industrial associations to consult
each other on economic policy and when possible coordinate their actions.
The Chamber of Commerce, Agriculture and Industry was another and
more formal associational platform where rivalry and cooperation played
out between the two sectors.[62]

Bankers are either largely absent in these accounts of the tango and
tussle between merchants and industrialists, or lumped with the former.
The bankers, however, formed a powerful and distinct, even if porous,
interest group among Lebanon's business community. Their financial fraternity left an indelible mark on Lebanon's economic orientation during
the merchant republic era and beyond, not least in the making of central
bank and financial regulation. The successful establishment of the Association of Banks in Lebanon in 1959 stood in sharp contrast to earlier failed
attempts by local bankers to self-organize. Calls for a banking organization dated back to the interwar period. During the years of the Great Depression, dozens of Lebanese commercial enterprises declared bankruptcy,
and several local banks collapsed. Lax bankruptcy laws and the lack of
credit regulation were largely blamed for the snowballing crisis. Local
bankers convened to discuss possible remedies and formed delegations to
meet with government officials. According to contemporary press reports,
a group of bankers met on December 31, 1931, and agreed to submit an
official request for a permit to form an association of banks modeled on
the Association of Exchange Agents in Paris.[63] A few years later, the AUB
economist Said Himadeh recommended the creation of a "native" bankers'
association as one of several means of developing "native" banking along
modern lines.[64] Neither project saw the light of day. Local bankers continued to exert a powerful influence on policy well into the post-mandate
period. They rose in numbers and wealth during the 1950s, but their ability to act collectively was contingent and informal. As late as 1956, when
the Banking Secrecy Law was proposed, bankers met with Deputy Prime
Minister Fuad Ghosn in the presence of Raymond Eddé in an ad hoc manner when they persuaded the Lebanese government to amend the law.[65] It

was not until after the nationwide financial crisis of 1958 that sustainable self-organizing by bankers as a lobby got off the ground.

The 1958 presidential succession crisis was a watershed in the institutional development of the banking sector and its relationship to state authority. Two months into the armed rebellion that erupted in early May of that year, Pierre Eddé, who was then finance minister, publicly warned against speculation on the exchange market. Eddé pinned his hopes for recovery on the country's banks, which until then had "demonstrated exceptional understanding."[66] In July, the landing of thousands of U.S. troops in Beirut four days after Eddé's statement put further pressure on the foreign-exchange market, with the BSL doing little to stabilize the Lebanese lira.[67] The subsequent election of Fuad Chehab on July 31 brought calm to the money market but did not immediately resolve financial disputes between banks and their clients arising out of nonpayment of debts. In October, the newly appointed prime minister and minister of finance, Rashid Karame, summoned banking officials and instructed them to continue cooperating with nonpaying clients lest markets collapse.[68]

With Chehab in office, Pierre Eddé's political career came to an end. Karame took over his ministerial portfolio, and he lost his parliamentary seat in the 1960 elections. Eddé's timely appointment as head manager of Bank Beirut Riyadh shortly before the outbreak of the 1958 crisis allowed him to continue to play an influential role in financial regulation, however, albeit as a lobbyist for the private banking sector. Under Chehabism, debt settlement turned out to be a secondary problem for banks compared to the specter of state-led regulation of the banking profession. Following long but fruitful consultations with a handful of equally concerned fellow senior bankers, Eddé presided over the establishment and expansion of the ABL, the first association of its kind in the Arab world, licensed by ministerial decree on November 6, 1959. The ABL's founding members met twelve days later and appointed its first board of directors, with Eddé as president and Anis Bibi of the National Union Bank as his deputy.[69]

While the BTA and ALI billed themselves as exclusive Lebanese business clubs, the ABL's membership was not "native," as Himadeh had wished it to be. As its name indicated, it was an association of banks *in* Lebanon. Foreign banks with branches in Lebanon were allowed to join, and their members were eligible to serve on its executive board.[70] This reflected the transnational character of Lebanon's evolving banking sector and the prominence in it of American and Arab, rather than French, capital. The branches of the three major U.S. banks in Lebanon joined as founding members. Chase Manhattan's Julius Thomson served on the association's first executive board. By contrast, Lebanon's three large French banks, including the BSL, did not register as chartered members and opted for observer status instead.[71] The country's largest local bank, Intra, was also absent from the roster of founders due to the rivalry between its founder, Yusif Beidas, and Eddé.[72] Despite early misgivings by Beidas and the French group, the ABL eventually imposed itself as an indispensable umbrella institution for any bank operating in Lebanon. In less than five years, its membership more than doubled, jumping from twenty-four banks in 1960 to fifty-eight in 1962, and it became the sole representative of the Lebanese banking community as a whole.[73]

Banking associational life was felt beyond the workplace. It impacted various aspects of Beirut's urban space and social culture. Hamra Street grew into a financial hub that competed with downtown Beirut's Street of Banks.[74] Several factors further contributed to the consolidation of what was perceived as a modern banking community. Social institutions solely dedicated to banking were founded in the spheres of the press, education, entertainment, and union activism. The profession's "soft" feminine face was celebrated.[75] The monthly, and later biweekly, periodical *al-Masarif*, which published its first issue in July 1963, quickly became the banking sector's magazine of record, reporting on the professional, legal, financial, and social aspects of Lebanese banking life and the people behind it. A prominent banker was chosen as character of the month for each issue, with a brief bio accompanied by a caricature sketched by Pierre Sadiq. News of "People of the Banks" including hotel banquets, travel plans, and other entertainment activities were also highlighted. The first training school dedicated to banking studies, Muassasat Lubnan, was established in 1963 by Sami Seikaly.

The ABL played a formative role in the emergence and structuring of this community. Led by its dynamic and well-connected president, it wove institutional links among its member banks through regular management get-togethers and the planned and standardized socializing of its labor force. Four consultative committees were set up to oversee this process of professional and social bonding.[76] The ABL also wove financial networks and formal as well as informal affiliations between its members and important financial actors abroad. Bridges were built with European banking associations, Arab Chambers of Commerce, and the World Chamber of Commerce in Paris, as well as potential investor partners in developing African markets.[77]

Half a century after its creation, the ABL's official narrative cited the growth of the banking sector and the need to "organize, immunize, and develop the banking profession" as the main motives behind the association's founding.[78] But based on the association's first two annual reports, the priority was collective advocacy against perceived threats to the sector, both external (state regulation) and internal (union activism). As the second article of the association's founding statutes clearly indicated, the ABL's goal was to "create cooperation among its members in matters pertaining to professional affairs and furnish mechanisms for [achieving] common interests and collectively defend these interests in the form of collective representation of its members at public or other administrations."[79] The ABL was highly successful in these aims, evolving in record time into one of the country's most powerful lobbying groups. Its executive directors and growing number of subcommittees kept abreast of bank-related developments in the country and abroad. In its first year of operation, it issued circulars to member banks on laws related to finance, ended a bank employees' union strike, opposed a draft law on social security at home, and petitioned to prevent the nationalization of its member branches abroad in the United Arab Republic. A four-day strike by bank employees demanding a pay raise ended with a joint statement by the ABL and the employees' union. Five of the country's French-affiliated top banks, which were not members of the ABL, expressed their support for ABL efforts and adopted the joint statement.[80] In the fall of 1964, the association went so far as to conclude a gag-type agreement with the Lebanese Press Syndicate to silence criticism of banks.[81]

By the ABL's own admission, the rapid growth of its membership in 1961 was thanks to its increased activity and "defense of the rights of the profession and. . . its effective contribution, alongside authorities, to all matters concerning the economy, currency, and investment."[82] The most important challenge faced by the ABL in its formative years, however, was the state-led campaign to regulate the banking sector via a central bank. Thanks to the association's negotiating stance towards the drafting of the Law of Money and Credit by the newly constituted Council on Money and Credit (CMC), almost all Lebanese-based banks had become members by 1963.[83] The Law of Money and Credit outlined banking regulations and the statutes of the proposed central bank. ABL lobbying efforts to influence the process of drafting the law through the CMC resuscitated old rivalries among the different banking factions over control of the central bank and altered the central bank's evolution. ABL pressure ensured that central banking regulation did not undermine what Pierre Eddé called the "untouchable" foundation of the banking sector: the Banking Secrecy Law.

THE "UNTOUCHABLE" FOUNDATION
OF LEBANESE BANKING

Frans Keesing's 1955 report for the IMF on "The Monetary and Banking System of Lebanon" was one of the first high-profile official calls for the creation of a credit and currency board to regulate Lebanese banking. Ministerial departments like the Economic Planning and Development Board (EPDB) had seconded such recommendations and drafted bills for the collection of statistics while political parties publicly demanded that a national agency be created to issue bank notes.[84] During his presidency, Camille Chamoun managed to keep the movement for change at bay. With the date of expiry of the BSL concession in 1964 drawing closer, however, there was less room for maneuver by vested interests opposed to the project. The flurry of administrative reforms initiated by Chamoun's successor, Fuad Chehab, dealt a final blow to hopes of evading the matter. The Council on Money and Credit (CMC) was one of many bureaucratic bodies set up by Chehab in 1959. Acting as a special committee within the Ministry of Finance, the CMC's officially decreed mandate was fairly broad. The council was expected to draw on its own statistically informed studies in order to advise the ministry on its credit and monetary policy and to draft legislation for organizing the banking profession. The decree

establishing the CMC did not stipulate that the second task, namely, banking regulation, required the setting up of a central bank. At the time of its
creation, cooperation between the CMC and the BSL was an acceptable
future framework for such an organization.[85]

The decree setting up the CMC remained a dead letter for two and a
half years. Published accounts of the committee's history and activity are
silent or speculative as to why its actual formation got delayed,[86] but U.S.
diplomatic cables indicate that vested interests fighting over control of the
CMC were responsible. Efforts to influence the council were ultimately
aimed at influencing the drafting of the legislation to create the proposed
central bank. According to Sami Shoucair, a prominent Lebanese banker
"well-known" to the U.S. Department of State, three major powerful business groups were jockeying for favorable positions vis-à-vis the central
bank, given the "tremendous power" to be gained by controlling such
an institution.[87] The first group, which sought a central bank "free from
foreign influence"—"foreign" largely referring to French influence, embodied in the BSL—included Shoucair himself; the ABL's president, Pierre
Eddé; Rashid Karame, prime minister and minister of finance; and the
AUB second-generation economist Paul Klat, who was also a government
financial consultant. The second group stood for French interests embodied in the BSL. The bank's prominent member of the board of directors,
Henri Pharaon, and its financial councilor, Joseph Oughourlian, formed
this second front by teaming up with the increasingly powerful politician
Pierre Gemayel, leader of the right-wing Kataeb party. The third group
reportedly represented British interests and was headed by Yusif Beidas,
founder and head of Intra Bank. The "dynamic and ambitious" Beidas
had figured that the best way to control the proposed central bank was
by winning a contract to manage it. He acquired shares in the Pharaon-
linked al-Ahli bank and formed a covert joint front with the French-allied
group. Beidas also tried to win over Klat by offering him a tempting sal-
ary as an advisor to Intra. Klat, who was close to Pierre Eddé, declined.[88]

The Klat-Karame forces, as the U.S. confidential memo described the
first group, pushed for the promulgation of the CMC decree in the summer
of 1959 when Prime Minister Karame also held the finance portfolio. But
the BSL-backed Gemayel managed to stall the council's formation once

he became finance minister in the two successive cabinets formed by Saeb Salam. As finance minister, Gemayel signed a deal in August 1961 with the BSL's Oughourlian to head a committee that would issue recommendations on founding a central bank, but Karame cancelled the contract after he returned to power in November of the same year. The finance portfolio was also back in Karame's possession, which made him the ex officio president of the CMC.

The dilly-dallying was finally cut short by decree on December 15, 1961, when representatives of all three groups were appointed to the Council on Money and Credit.[89] In addition to Karame (president) and Klat (member), the BSL's Oughourlian was appointed vice-president. During the CMC's first meeting, held at the Ministry of Finance, Karame declared that the purpose of the council was not only to prepare legislation on banking regulation but to establish a central bank. The clandestine rivalry between the three groups continued, however, now in the form of tensions among council members over the drafting of the Law of Money and Credit.[90]

Bank of Issue, Not Bank of Banks

The Law of Money and Credit promulgated in 1963 was a turning point in the history of banking regulation in Lebanon. For the first time, Lebanese banks were treated as a distinct type of corporation subject to its own laws, as opposed to the Commercial Code. Under the new law, banking institutions were banned from directly conducting any type of commercial, agricultural, or industrial business. Their ownership had to be along corporate lines, and a bank's paid share capital was set at a minimum of LL3M. Failure to abide by the law's provisions or a private bank's own statute meant risk of being crossed off the list of banks sanctioned by the central bank, whose founding had been decreed by the same law.[91] The barons of banking objected little to these basic regulations. Their misgivings lay elsewhere. Unlike the BSL, the prospective BDL was empowered by the draft Law of Money and Credit to act as a bank of banks, not simply a department that issued bank notes. In practice, this was tantamount to regulating the banking sector via three instruments: the collection and publication of banking statistics, the classification of banks, and cash reserve ratio requirements. The Association of Banks (ABL) challenged all three.

In its initial draft, the Law of Money and Credit required private banks to submit their balance sheets or profit-and-loss statements to the BDL as instructed by the Council on Money and Credit (CMC). This was a direct threat to the confidentiality granted them by the Banking Secrecy Law of 1956. Prior to 1956, attempts by Lebanese state authorities to gather banking data and statistics were met with very limited success. Data collected by the government's General Bureau of Statistics as early as 1942 were, as U.S. officials complained, "very vaguely worded, and [asked] merely for deposit, loan and notes discounted figures."[92] In 1954, the Bureau of Statistics introduced a new questionnaire allowing for the distinction between national and foreign capital, but it later reverted to the old form.[93]

These attempts posed little threat to private banking interests keen to keep their operations in the dark compared to CMC instructions issued in September 1962. The latter were extremely detailed and sought a full standardization of data gathering both in form and content. Private banks were instructed to fill out newly designed statistical forms in typewriting and mail them to the CMC, or the central bank upon its founding, on a monthly, quarterly, and annual basis, with set deadlines, in envelopes marked "Statistics—secret."[94] Monthly submissions had to include the bank's assets and liabilities, and yearly submissions had to provide the institution's annual budget and its credit portfolio, based on the resident status of debtors and the economic sector involved. Bank secrecy was upheld, but access to information expanded to include central bank staff. The instructions also granted the proposed central bank the right to publish or share aggregate statistics regarding the budgets, profits, and losses of both the banking sector as whole and individual banks if necessary.[95] Such information would have allowed the central bank to gain a better understanding of the money supply and credit volume in circulation and enable external parties to evaluate the performance of the central bank and the banking sector.

The CMC went to great lengths to ensure that the central bank's prospective authority over the banks would not violate the Secrecy Law of 1956. The control department in charge of gathering statistics was granted independent status and its staff sworn to secrecy even against other central bank employees. These measures failed to gratify critics of regulation within the banking community, suggesting that the objection of bankers was more about the privilege of their institutions than the privacy of their clients. Towards the end of 1962, and upon completion of the draft Law of Money and Credit, the CMC invited the ABL and the EPDB to comment on it. The EPDB's feedback was largely cosmetic. The ABL's response, however, was more substantial and went beyond the question of data collection. Sensing the urgent need to formulate a collective position on the new proposed law, the association's board met a record thirteen times and held four General Assembly meetings and two extraordinary ones.[96] ABL members objected to the very principle of regulating the banking profession by any government entity, including a central bank. The latter, they argued, should not be a bank of banks but merely a bank of note issue.

The ABL's distinction between currency issuing and banking regulation was justified by a laissez-faire logic dressed up as a matter of national security and prosperity. In its first memorandum addressed to Prime Minister Karame on February 12, 1963, the association took the position that "note issue is a symbol of state sovereignty and the Central Bank is a mere government institution, while banking regulation is concerned with a liberal profession and as such is of concern to private initiative."[97] Contrary to its ostensible acknowledgement of the need to organize the profession, the ABL also tried to delay the issuing of banking regulation legislation, claiming that priority should be given to replacing the BSL as an institution of issue. It recommended that the draft law be split into two distinct pieces of legislation. The first and more urgent one would deal with currency and the central bank, while the second handled banking regulation. The ABL's memorandum also stressed the primacy of the Secrecy Law of 1956 as the governing principle of banking in Lebanon and the source of its prosperity and stability against capital flight during political crises.[98]

The government declined to split the law into two pieces, but made some amendments, which the ABL regarded as "fundamental," albeit inadequate as far as protecting banking secrecy was concerned. In a second letter to Karame on March 12, 1963, the ABL's president, Pierre Eddé, argued that the control mechanism outlined by the draft law was in direct conflict with the Secrecy Law of 1956. He depicted banking secrecy as a duty *imposed* on banks for the benefit of their clients rather than a privilege enjoyed by them. The Banking Secrecy Law was in the interest of the public at large, he claimed, not just the banking profession. It was a "privilege of Lebanon"—the ultimate guarantee of the nation's economic survival—and the slightest tampering with it would be catastrophic. Eddé wrote to Karame:

The [Secrecy] Law was the one that fixed the present economic organization of Lebanon and constitutes one of its main structural parts.

The effects of the Banking Secrecy Law are in fact felt beyond the frontiers of Lebanon and reach all those who trust our laws, their maintenance and stability; and, things being what they are, touching the rights of those who have trusted us is not possible nor can it be thought of. That trust has increased our economic resources and has contributed to our development and prosperity.

Therefore, the Association of Banks in Lebanon considers any attempt, even if indirect or separate, to touch the Banking Secrecy law as an attempt to change the foundation of our economic system, of our future wealth and of the well-being of our people.[99]

Eddé recognized that "some sort of control [was] necessary and useful" but stipulated that the most important provision must be to ensure that the names of people protected under the Banking Secrecy law, namely, depositors, were not mentioned at all. The ABL president also urged the government to legislate a role for the ABL in the process of implementing regulation in emulation of "a great number of countries." He suggested that the CMC and the ABL hold a series of meetings before the draft law was submitted to the cabinet for approval.[100] At the instigation of President Chehab, a series of marathon meetings between CMC and ABL officials were convened in March and April of 1963. After some back and forth, the ABL won the day.[101] Under the final agreed-upon arrangement, private banks were permitted to use numbers rather than names to organize and list client accounts. Central bank examiners were prevented from accessing banking information except through the banks' managers and via standardized forms. Central bank inspectors were denied the right to demand the names of balance-holding customers unless the balance in question was a credit one. Central bank employees were also to be sworn to secrecy regarding information on aggregate data pertaining to the banking institutions themselves, not just their clients. Employees who violated banking secrecy became subject to harsher penalties than the ones stipulated by the Secrecy Law of 1956.[102]

The ABL won another significant victory regarding the second instrument of banking regulation. It managed to eliminate provisions stipulating the obligatory classification of banks based on their credit policy. The draft law sought to categorize banks based on whether they issued short-, medium-, or long-term loans. Such a classification would have contributed to further specialization of the money market and an ability to identify and encourage the medium- and long-term lending required for economic development. During its negotiations with the CMC, the ABL argued that such a classification was unrealistic. There were no provisions in the Law of Money and Credit, ABL officials pointed out, that organized money market operations. That would have allowed banks to conduct specified types of transactions subject to classification. In response, the CMC watered down the legislation. The two categories were reduced to "specialized" and "commercial" banks. But ABL officials claimed that such categorization did not fit Lebanon's needs for growth. They demanded that the Ministry of Finance outline clearer criteria of how such classification was to take place and renewed their wholesale rejection of any form of categorization. Their objection was fully taken into account. The final draft of the Law of Money and Credit made no reference to the classification of banks.[103] A historic opportunity to provide a more conducive environment for innovational enterprise, whose absence was lamented by Sayigh, was thus missed.

The third significant instrument of direct regulation of banks by the central bank was that of cash reserve ratio requirements. The ABL did not score an absolute victory in this regard. Altering reserve requirements was seen by AUB institutionalists as a vital instrument of credit control in developing nations in the absence of a mature money market. In its final version, the Law of Money and Credit granted the central bank the authority to impose a minimum reserve ratio on private banks, not to exceed 25 percent of their demand deposits and 15 percent of their time deposits. Violators were subject to financial penalties.[104] The ABL found the ceiling too high, suggesting that ratios be set at 10 percent and 5 percent respectively. It was not the only opponent of implementing such ratios. Rafiq Naja, the minister of national economy, publicly opposed the measure, arguing that forcing banks to hold such deposits would increase interests on loans and consequently the prices of goods. But the fact that these percentiles were mere ceilings, and that banks were given a minimum of thirty days to adjust their reserves to the governor-imposed ratio, reduced the severity of the objections. Before the BDL went into operation, an ABL insider told *al-Masarif* magazine that the actual imposed ratio was unlikely to exceed 3 or 4 percent. Once it opened for business, the BDL exceeded the expectations of the ABL. No reserve requirements were imposed until 1969, when the ratio was set at a low 2.5 percent.[105]

In sum, the ABL had managed to hollow out the banking regulatory provisions of the Law of Money and Credit. Its success reflected the cumulative clout of the bankers. In a telling sign of the extent to which laissez-faire remained a governing principle of the CMC, all its members were quick to reach consensus on the preservation of Lebanon's free enterprise system. The CMC praised rather than decried the economy's heavy reliance on its services sector. It vowed to ensure that banking legislation should, as much as possible, protect rather than curtail the freedom of the banking sector. Consequently, there was little disagreement between the CMC and the ABL over the central bank's provision pertaining to monetary policy.[106]

Chehabists, however, were more assertive in imposing their own interpretation of administrative autonomy in central bank legislation than they were in preserving provisions that regulated the banking sector. The willingness of Chehabist officials to compromise more readily on questions of private banking regulation and conservative monetary policy, rather than on structures of public administration, embodied the particular characteristics of Chehabism as a style of rule and philosophy of economic development and social reform. But the battle between the ABL and the Chehabist administration was largely a quarrel among different interpretive schools of the same ideological family. Chehabist-style administra-tive autonomy did not mean a significant departure from BSL monetary and credit policy. Quite the contrary, it reproduced previous policies, but under a new, state-led managerial arrangement. Chehabism bureaucratized rather than reformed laissez-faire.

CHAPTER 4

Banque du Liban

A Façade of Economic Sovereignty

Despite the grand celebration sponsored by the president of the Republic, few in
Lebanon realized that the [commemoratory] plaque pinned at the . . . new Central
Bank, is no less important in terms of its connotations and significance than the
plaque [commemorating the evacuation of all foreign armies] fixed on the rocks
standing in a suburb of Beirut.

—Dhulfiqar Qubaysi, *al-Masarif*, April 1964

Lebanese President Fuad Chehab (in office 1958–64) once quipped that
he had not been chosen as head of state by the Lebanese people, but by
their inability to agree on any other candidate.[1] General Fuad Chehab,
commander-in-chief of the Lebanese Armed Forces, came to power after
disagreement between pro-U.S. and pro-Nasserite factions in Lebanon in
the summer of 1958 over a presidential successor to Camille Chamoun (in
office 1952–58) had escalated into civil strife. The months-long conflict left
thousands dead and injured, precipitated the first post World War II overt
U.S. military intervention in the country, and created deep sectarian and
political rifts in Lebanese society. Chehab had refused to side explicitly
with either of the warring factions, and he emerged as the compromise
candidate of the two most powerful political actors in the region at the
time, Washington and Cairo. Once in office, Chehab set about reforming
state institutions in the hope of preventing a repeat of the conflict.[2]

Despite its geopolitical and sectarian overtones, civil strife in 1958 was
equally a manifestation of socioeconomic malaise that had been building
up since the country's political independence in 1943. The unbridled policies of laissez-faire during the Khoury and Chamoun administrations had
widened the gap between rich and poor. The country's wealth became increasingly concentrated in the hands of Beirut's mercantile financial class
to the detriment of rural regions of the country. This sense of inequality
further fueled popular discontent over Chamoun's pro-U.S. policy amid

the rising tide of Arab nationalism. The conflict spilled into the streets in 1958 and took on a sectarian turn when anti-Chamoun elites sought to challenge the existing power-sharing arrangement between Christians and Muslims, but failed to effect any change in it. "No victor and no vanquished" became the watchword of the subsequent political settlement preserving the status quo.[3] Chehab recognized, however, that reforms were needed in order to preserve the status quo in the long run, and his presidency became associated with the most extensive phase of state-building in modern Lebanese history. The large imbalance in the proportional allocation of public office in favor of Christians, at least in the state bureaucracy, had to be rectified.[4] Clientalism in state institutions through which the political elite reproduced its hegemony over members of its political and social base had to be curtailed, and the country's lopsided economic development policy favoring metropolitan Beirut needed to be replaced by one of regionally balanced growth.

Chehab's state-building project was influenced by his francophile education, military training, and ideological affinity to the philosophy of humanistic economics. Chehabism was not an ideology of radical change. In its founder's own words, it was "a style of governance and a reformist pathway and the trial testing of managing a state through principles that will lead to the construction of the [Lebanese] state of independence. It is the practice of leading the ruling of Lebanon according to constant planning . . . and an advanced vision."[5] The vision was "modernization without revolution."[6] Change had to be gradual, slow, and via consensus. The two fundamental instruments of this piecemeal process were administrative reform of state structures and regionally balanced economic development. Administrative reform, Chehab reasoned, would set the stage for political reform. Building state institutions that guaranteed the basic rights of citizens would redefine the relationship between citizen and state by eliminating the need for political mediation. Meanwhile, the economic development of Lebanon's periphery would "Lebanonize" the communities of these areas facing economic marginalization. State-linked assistance would forge the loyalty of rural communities to the country rather than to their extended family, clan, or local notable.[7] Chehab's economic policies were even less radical than his political reforms. These policies were neither "diametrically opposed" to those of his two predecessors nor did their implementation seek to drastically transform the country's economic system.[8] For Chehab, social justice was not an end in itself but a bridge to national unity. What distinguished Chehabism was a heightened sense for the need to plan liberal economies through the rational expansion of the bureaucracy coupled with orderly, regionally based economic development.

Central banking stood at the crossroads of bureaucratic reform and economic development. A central bank's internal organization and governance structure tested the limits and efficacy of managerial autonomy of state institutions in a liberal economy. The institution's monetary policy, including its public lending powers and credit control instruments, directly impacted public investment and economic growth. With the BSL concession due for expiry in 1964, the Chehab administration set about drafting central banking legislation with those implications in mind. Designing the new central bank took place in the context of rapid regional transformation of national economies and central banking practices. The rise of Arab socialism in the late 1950s and early 1960s ushered in a wave of nationalization of banks and greater state control of financial markets in countries like Egypt, Syria, and Iraq. There was a flurry of legislative activity in the financial regulatory field, with newly established currency boards and central banks assuming broad and varied functions. The degree of financial control and range of central banking powers across the Arab world depended on several market and nonmarket factors. These included local politicians' developmental philosophies, the dominance of private interests, the economic orientation of the country and its dependency on foreign trade.[9] Strict control on foreign exchange were put in place in countries like Iraq, Egypt, Algeria, and Somalia. In other countries, including Tunisia, Morocco, and Libya, regulation of capital flows was less strict. Most Gulf countries, Jordan, and Lebanon retained largely free exchange markets.

Eager to assert state power, but mindful of Lebanon's free-market orientation, Chehab attempted to strike a very fine balance between state authority and private interests in the design of the future central bank. The governing structure and monetary mandate of the resulting Banque du Liban reflected his compromise-based approach. Like its predecessor the

BSL, the new central bank was recognized as the state's sole fiscal agent and the liaison with international financial institutions and foreign treasuries. It was expected to advise the government and make recommendations regarding policies affecting balance of payments, price movements, public finance, and economic growth in general. Managerial autonomy was largely secured on paper, but top appointments were open to political interference. The most hotly debated appointment was that of the former BSL official Joseph Oughourlian, recognized as the foremost Lebanese expert on central banking. Oughourlian's anticipated recruitment to head the BDL alarmed private Lebanese financial circles more because of his connection with French banking interests than because of his opposition to state-led development. Chehab eventually opted for Philip Takla, a veteran diplomat with no central banking experience, as governor, and appointed Oughourlian as deputy governor. Thanks to his past BSL experience and powerful position as the BDL's deputy governor, Oughourlian left his laissez-faire imprint on its monetary policy.

As a result, the law of money and credit issued in 1963 fell short of expectations of a more active state role in economic development. The bank's monetary mandate was even more conservative than that of its predecessor under French rule, let alone its contemporary counterparts in Arab countries with socialist leanings. At the new bank's inauguration, Lebanese state officials and media pundits celebrated the bank as a great achievement of Chehabist state-building and the final stage of attaining full independence. These officials reinforced rather than undermined laissez-faire principles. They portrayed banking regulation as the highest order of economic freedom and based such regulation on cooperation with rather than coercion of the private sector. As a result, the BDL failed to establish its authority vis-à-vis the banking sector in its first years of operation. A series of banking crises led to regulatory confusion and mounting doubt about the efficacy of BDL policies. Public opinion was divided between those who wanted a strong central bank and those who lamented the days when none had existed. The entire process exposed the fragile foundations of Chehab's state-building project and the persistence in public consciousness of the basic organizing principles of Lebanon's merchant republic, which remained embedded in state policy.

PRECARIOUS CHEHABISM: PLANNING
LIBERAL ECONOMIES

During his six-year term, Chehab tried to turn his vision into reality. In the wake of the 1958 crisis, his cabinet acquired sweeping powers for a six-month period that allowed him to circumvent the ruling political elite. In a matter of days, the cabinet issued dozens of legislative decrees aimed at restructuring public administration,[10] reorganizing the bureaucratic apparatus and creating semi-autonomous agencies like the Civil Service Council and the Central Inspection Agency, formally attached to ministries but directly accountable to the president. Their official mandate was to root out corruption and to base recruitment for public service on merit rather than political favoritism. Chehab hoped these meritocratic mechanisms would produce public servants whose loyalty was to the country, not political patrons. In underdeveloped, underserved areas like the Beqaa valley and the south and north, public works projects were launched to build roads, hospitals, schools, and irrigation and electric power networks. A national Social Security Fund and a Directorate of Social Affairs that served marginalized communities were established.[11]

Chehab's diversion of resources from metropolitan Beirut into the peripheries did not sit well with the capital's elite merchant families like the Salams and Eddés. To counter their opposition, he relied on two strategies. The first was to build selective alliances with other political figures on the national stage who benefited from his periphery-friendly approach.[12] These included the urban notable Rashid Karame in Tripoli and landowning rural *zuama* like Kamal Jumblatt in the Shouf mountains and Sabri Himadeh and his rivals, the Dandash clan, in the Hermel region. Chehab's allies also included populist movements such as Pierre Gemayel's right-wing Kataeb party.[13] Chehab's mistrust of the entire political class, however, led him to seek a parallel strategy that would empower elements within the state apparatus who were independent of ruling circles and thereby loyal directly to him. He implemented this latter strategy in selecting presidential civil aides, as well as in military intelligence and mid-level bureaucracy.[14]

In 1945, as head of the armed forces, Chehab had founded the Lebanese military's intelligence unit, which came to be called the Deuxième Bureau, and it grew in clout and reach under his presidency with loyal top officers serving as the his eyes and ears among the country's politicians.[15] Chehab's security crackdown following a failed coup against his rule in 1961 by the Socialist Syrian National Party (SSNP) gave his political enemies, including Raymond Eddé, the perfect opportunity to complain of his police state.[16] The influence of the military on state and society was not restricted to interference in political decision-making and surveillance of public life. Chehab saw the army as the "mirror image" of society at large and a model for governance.[17] Military-inspired virtues such as discreetness, rigorous planning, protocol, routine, separation of public and private, loyalty to superiors, and a systematic approach to performance were all imported into his administrative reforms. Chehab's two top French administrative consultants, Jean Lay and the priest Louis-Joseph Lebret, embodied these. They both had military backgrounds.[18] His top Lebanese aides, Elias Sarkis and Fuad Boutros, hailed from the judiciary. Both were key agents of Chehab's second element of his ruling strategy: attaching a handful of competent administrators to the presidential office These included the head of that office, Elias Sarkis, who later became governor of the BDL and then the country's president, and Fuad Boutrus.[19] The third element of Chehab's strategy was recruiting mid- and high-level civil servants with professional expertise who sympathized with his reformist agenda, like Shafiq Muharram. This social group espoused an ideology of developmental rationalism that sought to bring order to state institutions and give the government relative autonomy in the Weberian sense of the term.[20] Chehab relied on these technocrats for restructuring the administration, including the thorny issue of banking regulation and state-led economic development.

The drastic expansion of the state's role in planning economic development led to a significant increase in the magnitude of public expenditure, to the point of running a deficit, an anomaly in post-independence Lebanon. But a close examination of the composition of these expenditures across sectors and over time does not signal a qualitative difference in the attitude of Chehabism to restructuring the Lebanese economy. Public spending increased in all fields during Chehab's presidency, but the rate of growth of the overall budget in relation to Gross National Product remained roughly the same. Spurts of growth in the budget, such as those of

1961 and 1964, may have also been linked to political calculations such as election season or consolidating the legitimacy of the president after political shocks.[21] More significantly, the distribution of spending per sector (education, health, and defense) remained quite comparable to that under Chamoun and Khoury.[22] The structural composition of the laissez-faire economy was left largely intact. Trade and services continued to constitute two-thirds of it (the remainder being industry and agriculture). In effect, Chehab embraced the economic liberalism of the merchant republic and left property relations, particularly those of landownership and commercial rights, intact. Chehab's main target of state-led intervention was public works, rather than industrialization (import substitution or otherwise). He seems to have been less critical of the structural economic bias in favor of the trade and services sector even than the AUB institutionalists. He described the tertiary sector as a "golden hen" that must be safeguarded. His objection, which reflected his developmental philosophy of humanistic economics, was to keeping all Lebanon's eggs in a single basket, Beirut.[23]

HUMANISTIC ECONOMICS: CENTRAL
BANKING À LA CHEHAB

Chehab's economic philosophy was influenced by his self-professed religious piety and French education. As a devout Catholic and francophile, Chehab was drawn to *Père* Lebret's humanistic economics, which advocated comprehensive economic planning and the distribution of wealth equitably between classes and across regions.[24] Lebret, who served as head of the Institut international de formation et de recherche en vue du développement harmonisé (IRFED), preached a harmonious approach to economic development that combined broad social reform with a systematic scientific approach to fieldwork. In March 1959, Chehab invited Lebret to head a mission composed of French and Lebanese experts that would conduct a thorough survey of Lebanon's development problems and make appropriate recommendations.[25]

Chehab's laissez-faire adversaries accused the general of "Vatican socialism" and depicted the IRFED mission, as they did the military, as a state within a state.[26] Their protests notwithstanding, there was not much evidence of Chehab's "socialism" in the fields of trade and finance. Chehab did little to "reduce the dominance of the commercial sector" and even less was ultimately achieved in terms of diluting the concentration of industrial capital in Beirut.[27] Chehab was committed to deregulated exchange markets and banking secrecy, and by further shielding the banking sector from state scrutiny, the Law of Shared Account passed during his tenure in office in 1961 reinforced the Banking Secrecy Law. It allowed banks to open a single account for multiple clients. Should any of the account holders die, his or her partners are granted absolute authority to manage the account and were not obliged to provide the heirs of the deceased with any information about the account.[28] Nevertheless, Chehab's commitment to modernizing the banking sector and mitigating its exploitative character raised the ire of the freewheeling barons of Lebanese banking. Pierre Eddé and the ABL invoked the "free foundations" of Lebanon's economy to resist any meaningful regulation of the private banking sector under the relevant provisions of the Law of Money and Credit. Provisions concerned with the governing structure of the bank and its monetary policy were less controversial but were also contested among Chehabist politicians and bureaucrats, ABL-associated private bankers, and BSL-trained technocrats. All parties agreed that managerial autonomy was in principle the best guarantor against political interference, and a conservative monetary policy was the ideal path to preserve the primacy of trade and finance over other sectors of the economy. The devil, however, was in the details of which bureaucratic structures and monetary policies guaranteed such autonomy and conservatism respectively.

Managerial Autonomy

Across the Arab world up until the late 1950s, a national central bank's managerial autonomy was a matter of broad consensus among state authorities and financial consultants. As the Syrian banking expert Mohammad Tohme put it at the time, central banks had to cooperate with the state for the economic good of the country but should not become totally subservient or act as political instruments. Achieving managerial independence took different forms of central banking government across countries.[29] Tohme drew on British and French central banking practices to identify three different models of central banking authority. The first vested this authority in a body composed solely of government representatives. The second sought representation of all major interest groups with a stake in the economy. In addition to government officials, this would include debtors—not just creditors, as well as workers. The third approach added technocrats to the mix of the second.[30] All three types were to be appointed by the highest executive authority in the state, such as the president or council of ministers. Most Arab countries, including Syria, Iraq, Jordan, and Kuwait adopted the second or third strategy, or a variation of the two. Several administrative arrangements and mechanisms determined whether the balance of managerial power was ultimately tilted in favor of state executive authority, private financial interests, or technocratic actors. These included the ratio of public to private representatives on the board, as well as the process of appointing the bank's governor, his credentials, and the executive powers and immunity from dismissal he enjoyed. Government representatives often hailed from the ministries of national economy, industry, trade, and occasionally agriculture. But the central actor was the minister of finance. In addition to acting as the point of contact between the central bank and political authority, his ability to delay or veto decisions by central bank councils at the end of the day determined the extent to which managerial autonomy was secured.

In Lebanon, all members of the Council on Money and Credit (CMC) that convened in 1961 to draft the Law of Money and Credit agreed on the principle of BDL autonomy from state intervention. They disagreed, however, over the interpretation of autonomy. The question of managerial autonomy was framed in relation to the bank's ownership, governing structure, and internal organization. The ownership debate, as was the case in all other Arab countries, was swiftly settled. In recognition of its special status as a symbol of national sovereignty and guardian of economic independence, the bank was to be wholly owned by the state. But it was granted special legal status as a financially autonomous entity. The BDL was exempt from taxation and the general administrative rules and regulations governing other public institutions and private corporations. It was also granted judicial privileges in matters of debt collection, although Beirut's courts had sole jurisdiction in cases pertaining to the bank.[31] Disagreement over governing structure and internal organization were harder to untangle. These disagreements centered around three essential elements: the powers granted to the bank's governing body and its constitution, the extent of government oversight, and the role of non-state actors, such as the ABL and independent financial experts, in shaping the bank's policies and actions.

The ABL and the state-linked Economic Planning and Development Board (EPDB) stressed that the bank's governor had to hold university degrees and to have past experience in money management. The EPDB further recognized that the governor represented "the monetary power of the country," and that as such he and his deputies must exhibit high moral standards and patriotism. The EPDB and the ABL, however, were in favor of devolving power away from the post of governor and investing it in a central council. Their recommendations as to who should serve on the council reflected their divergent interests and approaches to public management. For the EPDB, the central council needed to balance the respective authorities of government, central bank administrators, and independent financial expertise. EPDB members proposed that the central council should ideally consist of the governor and his deputies, five reputable experts on money and banking, and the director-general of the Ministry of Finance acting as government representative. The latter would be capable of suspending decisions by the council for up to ten days if they were perceived as harmful to monetary policy or in violation of the bank's general directives as outlined by the cabinet. The banking association, on the other hand, pushed for eliminating government representation and replacing it with directors from within the central bank. The ABL also called for wider consultative representation of the private sector on the advisory committee.[32]

The final formula adopted by the Council on Money and Credit made the central bank subject to four interlinked authorities, the governor, the central council, the advisory committee, and the government commissariat.[33] The governor was to be appointed by the state, but was given immunity from political influence during his renewable tenure. He could not be dismissed save in specified instances of debilitating illness or grave abuse of powers. Checks were put in place to prevent any conflict of interest. The governor and his deputies were thus barred from holding any other office during or two years after the end of their central bank service. The only exception was membership in international financial organizations such as the World Bank or the IMF. As per the Bretton Woods understanding, the central bank was to serve as the institutional mediator between the national government and the international financial order. In terms of daily executive powers, the Law of Money and Credit bestowed on the governor "the widest powers in the general administration and management" of the bank including the power to appoint, supervise, and dismiss bank employees.[34]

The central council was empowered to draw up the bank's monetary, credit, and currency-issuing policies, as well as all other administrative and managerial regulations, including those outlining the governor's executive tasks and budgetary allotments. This council consisted of the governor, his three deputies, and the directors general of the Ministry of Finance and the Ministry of National Economy. The latter two, as far as the law was concerned, were not to act as government delegates. The authority of the government in terms of decision-making was restricted to a supervisory one embodied in the third administrative unit of the bank: the government commissariat, which acted as an inspecting agency that had full access to the bank's accounts, except those of third parties protected under the Banking Secrecy Law. The commissioner, who was appointed by the Minister of Finance following consultations with the central council, was explicitly barred from "intervening in any form in the caretaking [of operations] at the central bank."[35] Central council decisions had to be "immediately reported" to the commissioner, who, within two days of notification, was empowered to request the suspension of any decision he deemed was in violation of the law and the bank's bylaws, pending consultation with the minister of finance. If the matter was not resolved within five days, however, the decision automatically came into effect.[36] The final piece of the puzzle was a six-member advisory committee designed to embody the role of the private sector in the central bank's policymaking. Four of its members had to be experts in the fields of banking, commerce, industry, and agriculture respectively. They were appointed by the minister of finance based on nominations by private associations representing each of these sectors. The fifth member was chosen from the EPDB, while the sixth had to be a professor of economics of Lebanese nationality.[37]

The bank's somewhat innovative, yet cumbersome, administrative arrangement did not translate into a fundamental restructuring of its mandate as an agent of economic development. If anything, the BDL's monetary policy in relation to the question of economic development was more conservative than that of its predecessor, the BSL, and equally less so than the majority of the sister banks that were being established at the time across the Arab world.

Monetary Policy and Economic Development

Arab central banks founded after World War II mostly shared basic objectives, issuing and stabilizing currency on behalf of the state, as well as serving as the government's banker and financial consultant, but their monetary mandates and impact on economic development varied across countries, and within each country over time, as a result of the economic orientations of the governments that set them up.[38] The banks' mandates were expressed in general principles as well as specific regulations governing the bank's credit policy towards the government, like direct lending, and the private banking sector, like discount rates and reserve ration requirements. In terms of general principles, the direct relationship between monetary policy and developing the economy on a national scale was most clearly expressed in the central bank charters of countries that had adopted socialist or state-led planning in full. In Iraq, the central bank's basic goals following nationalization in 1964 were, according to its governor, Abdel Hasan Zalzalah, economic stability at the highest level of growth possible in the short run and expanding the productive base to reduce the Iraqi economy's dependency on oil revenues in the long run. As Zalzalah pointed out, nationalization of banking in Iraq had turned the central bank from a regulator of credit into a planner of economic activity as a whole.[39] In Syria, the monetary law listed the expansion of opportunities for development and increasing the gross domestic product among the central bank's main objectives.[40] By contrast, the economic development in Kuwait's market-oriented economy was referred to broadly as "economic and social progress." The central bank's role in that regard was the provision of direct credit to grow national income.[41] Similarly in Lebanon, the BDL's general mission, as stated in the 1963 Law of Money and Credit, was to "safeguard money in order to provide a foundation for permanent economic and social progress."[42] As CMC member Abdul Amir Badrud-Din pointed out in his study of the BDL, "progress" here signified a more general notion of change than "growth"; it encompassed "any kind of social improvement."[43] Such a generalization diluted rather than reinforced the BDL's commitment to economic development compared to its predecessor, the BSL. Despite the fact that the BSL was a private foreign-owned bank and its statutes were drafted in 1924 when conservative monetary policy was the norm in much of Europe and the capitalist world, its "principal objective was to promote *the economic development* [emphasis added] of Syria and Greater Lebanon."[44] Four decades later, popular support for interventionist theories of economic development was at its height. The governing mandate of the publicly owned BDL, however, invoked the vague notion of "progress" rather than "economic development." More significantly, such progress was not a direct policy objective of the BDL. The principle aim was the safeguarding of money as a *foundation* of economic and social progress.

Credit control was a major central banking mechanism for impacting economic growth. A central bank's lending policy to government either hindered or facilitated large-scale investment projects, while reserve ratio requirements for private banks and discount rates offered in the money market determined the flow of private credit across the different sectors of the economy. In heavily state-led economies like Iraq and Syria, public lending was a major engine of growth. Socialist transformation in Iraq required the control by the public sector of sources of funding and redistribution of credit. Nationalization of the entire banking sector meant that the central bank was in a better position to determine the size of credit and set its cost and its mode of use.[45] Meanwhile, government investment agencies were exempt from placing deposits at the central bank. They could determine their own agenda for development.[46] In Syria, central banking loans were capped at sixty million Syrian liras. In due course, restrictions were placed on loans for unproductive financial activity.[47] Conditions for government borrowing were much stricter in countries like Kuwait and Lebanon. In Kuwait, central bank advances to government were tied to covering deficit in revenue, capped at 10 percent of the government's budget, and subject to interest fixed after consultation with the Ministry of Finance. Loans outstanding had to be paid before the end of the same fiscal year before any further advances are granted.[48]

In Lebanon, loans to public authorities as a primary instrument of development were discouraged in the strongest language possible. Under the mandate, the BSL's public lending policy, outlined back in 1924, had explicitly stated that the extension of loans and advances to the French colonial government was a means of achieving economic development.[49] The BDL statutes set out in 1964, on the other hand, did not make such explicit links when it came to lending to the now independent government of Lebanon. State borrowing was confined to situations of "utmost necessity" and "exceptionally dangerous circumstances." Even then, it was subject to highly restrictive provisions relating to the amount and frequency of borrowing. Long-term lending, a hallmark of debt-driven economic development, was all but banned to both public and private entities.[50] While Kuwait could afford restricting government borrowing in light of its ability to draw on its oil revenues for investment, resource-poor countries like Lebanon and Syria had no such recourse. Central bank incentives for easy credit were crucial to promote long-term development projects in the agricultural and industrial sectors. This was a common practice among developing countries. Newly founded central banks in many Arab countries were allowed to discount commercial paper with longer than usual maturity if they were drawn for financing industrial development. In former North African French colonies or protectorates like Algeria, Tunisia, and Morocco, industrial paper with a maturity of up to five years could be discounted in order to encourage the growth of a negotiable securities market for financing industrial development.[51] Dwindling sums of capital surplus generated during World War II and fears of the political risk associated with foreign borrowing prompted the Syrian government to expand the central bank's powers. This allowed the bank to better direct private credit towards national industrial production and agriculture, as well as help raise private funds for government development projects.[52] Under these powers, import deposits, that is, money that importers had to place on hold for orders, were implemented to discourage luxury imports. Discount rates were set in consultation with the minister of finance.[53] The central bank was also to refrain from rediscounting consumption paper, while accepting medium-term industrial, agricultural, and commercial paper that matured at four months.[54] Estimates of guaranteed securities became more flexible to encourage industrial and agricultural loans. Two out of the three signatures required for discount rates could be replaced by a single government signature such as that of the agricultural bank.[55] At times, the government directly intervened to request that the central bank issue securities at low interest rates for financing particular projects like building oil refineries. In 1958 for instance, public debt was partly funded by asking private banks to invest at least 5 percent of their deposits in the debt in return for reducing their reserve ratio requirements by an equal amount.[56]

By contrast, the BDL's monetary tools for influencing economic development were of a much more conservative nature. They included typical instruments such as setting a bank interest rate, open-market operations, the buying and selling of gold and foreign exchange, minimum reserve ratio requirements, and advances against securities. Bank rate rules and reserve ratio requirements provided the BDL with more leverage than its BSL predecessor, but the BDL did not take advantage of either in its first years of operation. Meanwhile open-market operations and dealing in gold and foreign exchange that the BDL was empowered to conduct were subject to constraints that were virtually identical to those dictated by the BSL. The BDL's discounted paper had to have short-term maturity, thereby dismissing the possibility of financing medium- or long-term development projects. Discounted paper had to include three signatures, thereby reducing the volume of paper that could be discounted. The absence of a developed money market further reduced the influence of such operations on credit volume. Meanwhile, gold and foreign-exchange operations were mainly concerned with exchange stability and fulfilling gold-heavy note-cover requirements. The latter were quite similar to those imposed on the BSL.[57]

In short, the legal framework of the BDL provided some leverage regarding banking regulation that the BSL did not. Colonial continuity between BSL and BDL monetary policy was reinforced at the level of personnel. In

March 1963, the government agreed to transfer all staff at the BSL issue department to the BDL,[58] which, some critics complained, was the "BSL under another name." Such accusations were directed at the person of the former BSL consultant Joseph Oughourlian, who had "almost single-handedly" written the Law of Money and Credit and was subsequently appointed deputy director of the BDL.[59]

The Oughourlian Factor

Oughourlian's appointment as first deputy governor of the newly established Banque du Liban was seen by some, including the first secretary of the U.S. embassy in Beirut, Leslie Tihany, as a strong sign of continuity between the BSL and the BDL. As a longtime financial advisor to French mandatory authorities, the BSL, and the Bishara Khoury administration, Oughourlian was "by far the best equipped and trained of the new [BDL] appointees." His economic views were bound to have a significant bearing on monetary policy. These economic views, Tihany added, were decidedly "conservative" and "definitely anti-Keynesian": "[Oughourlian] abhors the current expansion of government expenditures, feeling that they might get out of hand and lead to an inflationary situation. Antagonistic to economic planning, he looks with a jaundiced eye on the work of the IRFED mission and the development bank project proposed by it. He is an ardent advocate of high gold backing for paper money and of stability in the exchange rate of the Lebanese pound."[60]

Oughourlian did play a pivotal role in shaping the conservative policy of the new central bank and in curbing Chehabist tendencies for larger government and public borrowing. But his success in doing so due to his personal authority should not be overestimated. It was as much a reflection of the broader persistence of laissez-faire currents within Chehabist circles of decision-making as it was an expression of one man's monetary philosophy. This claim is borne out by the outcome over banking regulation. While serving on the Council on Money and Credit (CMC) that drafted the Law of Money and Credit, Oughourlian had strongly opposed the demand of the banking association to shield the names of customers from central bank authorities. But the Association of Banks (ABL) view prevailed. Rashid Karame, then finance minister and head of the CMC,

voted in favor of amendments introduced by the ABL-backed member of
the CMC, Paul Klat. Karame and Klat were the only two members of the
CMC who attended the final meeting between the CMC and the ABL on
April 2, 1963, when important decisions in favor of the ABL were taken.[61]
If the Karame-Klat camp had been sufficiently opposed to Oughourlian's
conservative approach to monetary policy, it is not clear why they did not
also vote these conservative provisions down.

It was Oughourlian's antagonism to local and non-French banking
interests rather than his antipathy to state-led development that raised
alarm bells among the emerging local banking sector about his appointment. He stood for French capital embodied in the old guard of laissez-
faire, the Bishara Khoury clique. Members of this clique, like the first BDL
governor, Philip Takla, were allies of Chehab. Khoury's arch-rivals and
anti-Chehabists, including the Eddés and their local banking allies, saw
eye to eye with Oughourlian in terms of monetary policy. Their main opposition was directed at Oughourlian's attempts, while acting as a member of the CMC, to regulate the budding private sector they dominated.
By insisting on banking secrecy, the Eddé camp had largely managed to
neutralize Oughourlian's attempts to legislate for this. But they were still
weary of him retaining some influence as a guardian of rival financial
interests by way of day-to-day management of the bank. Their aversion
to him running the show was an open secret. Rumors circulating in the
summer of 1963 alleged that big bankers had voiced their objection to
Oughourlian's appointment as BDL governor for fear it would be in the
interest of his old employer the BSL, soon to become a private enterprise.
Oughourlian would "monopolize the laying out of financial planning in
the future, thereby securing the interest of French conglomerate of companies and banks to the exclusion of looking after other banks and companies," they claimed.[62]

Oughourlian had strongly coveted the position of central bank governor, but the ABL unofficially backed Paul Klat for the post, according to
U.S. diplomatic sources.[63] Based on merit, the odds of Oughourlian head-
ing the new bank were distinctly higher than Klat's or those of any other
contender. As Tihany put it, Oughourlian had "experience, education,
connections, and a forceful character." Having begun working for the fi-

nancial department of the French High Commissioner's office in Lebanon in 1928, equipped with doctoral degrees from Paris in law and finance, Oughourlian was arguably the longest-serving financial official in modern Lebanon when the BDL was founded. In 1943, he became the financial controller of the Concessionary Companies and assistant to the director general of the Ministry of Finance for currency matters, a post that enabled him to represent Lebanon for a number of years on the governing boards of both the IMF and the World Bank. He also acted as a financial advisor to President Bishara Khoury. Starting in 1952, Oughourlian became consultant to the BSL currency-issuing department, a position he continued to occupy until his appointment in 1961 as vice-chairman of the CMC. Oughourlian's professional links to state authority were buttressed by the personal ties he wove with political elites through his marriage into the Trads, a prominent Beiruti family. His wife Aurore, who was the sister-in-law of Chehab's advisor and presidential successor, Charles Helou, introduced him to the salons of French and high Lebanese society.[64]

Oughourlian was a "hard worker and very meticulous about everything that he does," with a "strong personality which usually overcomes most opposition," Tihany noted. Nonetheless, opposition to his appointment to head the central bank was "too much" to overcome,[65] and Oughourlian backed Philip Takla, Chehab's trusted foreign minister, as an alternative. Takla was not a professional banker and his appointment was not a foregone conclusion. Speculation over top appointments at the central bank reached its apogee in the late summer of 1963. The Law of Money and Credit, ratified by Chehab and published in the official gazette on August 1, stipulated that appointments to top central bank positions be made within a two-month period. A loophole in the law allowing the governor to hold another office during the transition period until the BSL concession officially expired on March 31, 1964, made Takla's appointment possible. The veteran diplomat had reportedly pinned his hopes on capping his career with the prestigious appointment of Lebanese ambassador to France, but at the persistence of Chehab, he accepted the post of governor of the BDL on the condition that Oughourlian be chosen as first deputy governor.[66] On September 7, Takla's appointment as governor was confirmed. Oughourlian's potential appointment was questioned in some circles, however, and nominations for the three deputy governorships were less certain. Candidates included the AUB economists Talha Yaffi, Elias Saba, Abdul Amir Badrud-Din, and Muhammad Atallah. But Chehab, who was on better terms with the Khoury camp than with the Eddés, seemed bent on retaining a strong francophile element at the helm of the bank's administration, and Oughourlian was confirmed as first deputy governor. Chehab's technical advisor Shafiq Muharram, a French-educated architect and public works consultant, received the second post, and the third was assigned to Badrud-din, a British-educated financial economist and AUB alumnus. Joseph Prince, former government commissioner to the BSL, retained that posting at the BDL.[67]

Takla's retention of his foreign ministry post flew in the face of the central bank's managerial autonomy as stipulated in the Law on Money and Credit, signaling Chehab's willingness to undermine his own reforms to secure political authority at a vital state institution like Banque du Liban. Moreover, Takla's preoccupation with high politics, lack of specialized knowledge of monetary and financial management, and the sympathetic ear he lent Oughourlian effectively made the latter the BDL's de facto governor and allowed him to play the key role in the transition from the Banque de Syrie et du Liban. The Law of Money and Credit was promulgated in August 1963, and the appointment of the BDL's governors was finalized in September.[68]

THE BSL-BDL TRANSITION: ECONOMIC SOVEREIGNTY AS A NATIONAL IMAGINARY

Preparations for the assumption of central banking responsibility by the BDL commenced in earnest in April 1, 1964, with the transition of duties and assets from the BSL, the organization of the BDL's administrative staff, and breaking ground on the bank's new headquarters. As stipulated by the Law of Money and Credit, the government issued decrees ordering the withdrawal of public funds from private banks, which was allowed under the BSL concession but banned under the new law, whereby all government funds had to be deposited with the BDL. The BDL's legally mandated founding capital was funded, and branches of the central bank were opened in Tripoli, Saida, and Zahle. Disputes with the BSL over a case of currency fraud, which dated back to 1952, and the amount of interest the BSL owed to the government for public deposits were resolved.[69] In the transition period, the BSL exercised its profitable right to issue bank notes to the full, ordering LL15M in new Lebanese currency from British bank-note printers towards the end of 1963, allegedly in response to market demand. Takla, operating from a makeshift office at the BSL pending the construction of the BDL's new headquarters, assured the public that this was lawful and did not require the consent of the new central bank.[70]

The BDL's newly formed central council held regular meetings to discuss internal organization and technical preparedness as well as plans for the recruitment and training of personnel. After consulting with Banque de France experts, Oughourlian proposed administrative schemes for the various departments of the BDL. The IMF offered free training to employees. The French-oriented outlook of Chehabism, however, tilted the balance in favor of seeking expert advice in francophone Europe and through the BSL rather than through Washington-based Bretton Woods institutions. During the drafting of the Law of Money and Credit, Oughourlian, who was serving at the time as deputy chair of the Council on Money and Credit (CMC), visited Europe in May 1962 to study how European central banks operated. One year later, Takla sought the close collaboration of the BSL administration and foreign experts to organize the BDL's fledgling currency-issuing department and train its personnel. In Beirut, he held a series of meetings with BSL officials to plan arrangements for sending employees of the department to train in Paris and Brussels. During an earlier two-week trip to the French capital, Takla had discussed the impact of the BSL-BDL transition on financial relations between the two countries, and the relationship of the BSL to the banking sector, with French experts. The National Bank of Belgium (NBB) agreed to train a large number of top BDL employees; meanwhile, a Banque de France mission came to Beirut to help set up the BDL's currency-issuing department.[71]

The most pressing aspect of the BSL-BDL transition was the construction of the BDL's headquarters. Monetary independence and national economic sovereignty had to be on public display in no equivocal terms. If the BDL's mission, policy, and staff training were sure signs of continuity with its predecessor, the physical space it occupied signaled a total rupture, even if the actual design remained subservient to European taste. With an eighteen-month window to design and implement a project costing LL8M, the building of the new headquarters was a testimony to President Chehab's ability to execute grand-scale projects of public works in a timely and accountable fashion.[72]

The plans for the imposing new edifice were drawn up by a Swiss firm, Addor & Julliard, in consultation with the internationally renowned architects H. Vicariot and Maurice Zuber. Execution on the ground was entrusted to a Lebanese engineer, Fayez al-Ahdab, in his capacity as head of one of Chehab's several new administrative directorates. Al-Ahdab was attached to the Ministry of Public Works and Transport's Construction Projects Execution Council. He had also served for several years as a member of the BSL's board of directors.

Construction began in the spring of 1963. The twelve-story central bank building (three of them underground) in the Sanayeh district of Beirut was lauded in the press as a marvel of modern architecture and cutting-edge technology. Reception counters used reinforced concrete and bulletproof glass. The underground vaults, where gold deposits were kept, were reportedly built to withstand earthquakes and a nuclear attack. They were fitted with "one of the largest bank doors in the world," equipped with highly advanced anti-theft electric sensors and "the most modern protection and monitoring equipment."[73] Other supplementary state-of-the-art appliances included internal wireless networks, automatic fire alarms, speedy lifts, pneumatic capsule pipelines for internal mail, and telecommunication devices. The Chehab administration made a point of employing Lebanese manpower and construction material to highlight the BDL's national character.[74] By the end of 1963, Minister of Public Works Pierre Gemayel boasted that the project would be done by the end of March 1964, in "record time."[75]

REGULATION AS ECONOMIC FREEDOM

The administration of President Fuad Chehab (in office 1958–64) delivered on its promise, and on March 31, 1964, Lebanon's long-awaited central bank, Banque du Liban, was inaugurated with state-sponsored fanfare. Dhulfiqar Qubaysi, editor in chief of the paper *al-Masarif*, declared that

the commemorative plaque unveiled at the entrance to the BDL in Beirut
on this occasion was no less significant than the plaque embedded in the
rocky banks of the Kalb River in northern Lebanon to commemorate the
1946 withdrawal of foreign armies from the country.[76] Political independence was meaningless without monetary independence, Qubaysi pointed
out. It was the creation of Banque du Liban that established "the final and
complete contours of Lebanese independence."[77]

Unlike the "masses," the ruling elite were quick to answer the celebratory call. Attendees of the gala included government ministers, heads of
diplomatic missions, top civil servants, prominent businessmen, and representatives of economic associations. Lebanon's Prime Minister Hussein
Uwayni and Foreign Minister Philip Takla, also the newly appointed central bank governor, represented President Chehab at the event and gave
speeches calling the BDL one of the "great achievements" of the Chehab
presidency. Both also praised the BSL for its cooperative relationship with
the state and constructive policies, saying that although freedom of initiative was sacrosanct, and the Banking Secrecy Law would be fully respected,
it was equally important that the laws on the organization and regulation
of the banking sector be upheld. Regulation was a guarantor of freedom,
and balancing rights with duties and economic freedom with social justice was a hallmark of Chehabism. Takla spoke of the need to organize
the fast-growing banking sector. Uwayni stressed that "the cooperation
of private banks with the central bank, in particular, and of individuals
with the state, in general" were necessary "to reconcile Lebanon's interest
in remaining a country of freedom and free initiative [in which] freedom
is coupled with social justice."[78]

The new central bank's first few years of operation would see little in
the way of monetary stability or cooperation with the banking sector. The
BDL's annual reports attempted to reflect the new configuration of Lebanon's emerging monetary space, but the making of the central bank was
far from complete, and the attainment of economic independence was far
from achieved. The BDL's ability to exert its authority over the banking
sector by coaxing rather than coercive regulation was severely strained, too,
when a growing liquidity shortage shook public confidence and reignited
the debate about the wisdom of having a central bank. The nationwide

financial crisis that erupted in 1966 exposed the structural weaknesses of the banking sector and forced a rethinking of the BDL's role and function.

THE BDL FOR BEGINNERS: COAXING
WITHOUT COERCION

Like the construction and celebration of its headquarters, the BDL's annual reports in its early years of operation tried to further consolidate the concept of an independent Lebanese economy in the national imaginary. The task proved rather elusive. In its first two years of operation, BDL officials repeatedly lamented the lack of adequate statistics necessary for painting a full picture of the economy, which were at times simply nonexistent. Statistics published were either incomplete or their object of inquiry differed from one year to the other. Each economic sector was dealt with separately, with no data produced for the gross national product, the primary statistical marker of a national economy.[79]

These reports reinforced the sanctity of laissez-faire economics celebrated by Takla and Uwayni while paying lip service to the ideals of economic development and social justice that these top officials had peddled at the ceremony. The BDL did recognize the overwhelming bias within the Lebanese private sector towards commercial rather than agricultural or industrial lending. It also acknowledged the persistence of trade balance deficits that had plagued Lebanon since its independence. But the bank's first annual report warned that it was important when addressing such imbalances "to avoid *touching* [emphasis added] the foundations of the principles of free economy and the immunity of currency and not to target invisible incomes that remain the basic factor in adjusting the Lebanese balance of trade."[80] These foundations were again cited, in addition to a "moderate" tax policy, as the main reasons behind the "satisfactory" growth and "exponential prosperity" that the Lebanese economy witnessed during the first year of the bank's operation. Other reasons of prosperity included the "free system that provided the widest of possibilities for the Lebanese to make use of their talents and characteristics" and the country's "high air quality and the beauty of nature that lasts all four seasons."[81]

BDL policy to ensure that these foundations were preserved seemed more in line with the prescriptions of the merchant republic than the declared policies of Chehabism. The bank recommended the deregulation of rent control, the rolling back of progressive tax on real estate, and the total elimination of tax on bank deposits for residents and nonresidents alike as a means of attracting foreign capital and increasing the volume of its local counterpart.[82] Laissez-faire remedies were equally invoked in the few instances when the discourse of economic development prevailed. The bank acknowledged the need for medium- and long-term credit for sustained economic development. Yet it identified the elimination of tax on bank deposits as the method of getting private companies to create the necessary medium- and long-term lending institutions. The bank's proclivity for privately driven rather than state-led initiatives was reinforced by its lending policy. BDL advances to the public sector were consistently and significantly less than those given to private institutions with little evidence that the latter were geared to development projects.[83] Even the bank's push for the regulation of the banking sector remained hardly detectable in its first year of operation.[84]

By the end of 1965, the aura of optimism surrounding the establishment of the bank had all but faded into the shadows of the collapse of three banks, a widely feared liquidity crisis, grumpy brokers at a struggling Beirut bourse, an increasingly antagonistic private banking sector, and a public increasingly skeptical of the bank's governor and his rusty Midas touch. The central bank's troubles had begun prior to its own official inauguration. In February 1964, while responsibilities were in the process of being transferred from the BSL to the BDL, the medium-sized Real Estate Bank failed to secure enough liquidity to meet demand, despite drawing on a large loan from another bank, the Commercial Bank. The transition presented serious obstacles to the summary resolution of this crisis and exposed the unstable situation precipitated by the prolonged, somewhat disorderly transfer of duties. It also illustrated the precarious balance of authority between the ABL, the BSL, and the new central bank.

Regulatory Confusion

Lacking any clear protocol of how to handle the crisis, the three institutions concerned passed the case of the troubled bank between one another like a hot potato. George Debbas, the Real Estate Bank's general manager, first approached the banking community for help before the matter took on national proportions. On February 20, he contacted the ABL and sought assistance. At an extended emergency meeting over the weekend, ABL executives devised a three-step plan.[85] The first step was to create a joint committee composed of Real Estate Bank board members and a select group of bank managers. The second was to request advances, via the committee, from the bank of issue at the time, namely, the BSL. The third was to obtain a guarantee of these advances from the Real Estate Bank's board of directors. The cycle of passing on responsibility began. Once approached by the ABL for money advances, the BSL deferred to the BDL's governor Philip Takla as the relevant authority, who in turn conferred with the BSL, given that the latter was in a better position to furnish the needed funds. Takla managed to get the BSL on board, but on condition that the ABL bankers would offer the adequate loan guarantees. The bankers expressed their willingness to take on the matter, but only if the Real Estate Bank board members unconditionally mortgaged all their possessions as a guarantee.

After a series of highly publicized meetings and announcements by public officials and private stakeholders, the parties involved failed to reach a satisfactory agreement. Both banks, the Real Estate Bank and the Commercial Bank, had to fold and declare stoppage of payment. The ABL, BSL, and BDL all wrung their hands and let the courts settle the dispute.[86] In a matter of weeks, the court came out with its verdict. On March 12, 1964, the Real Estate Bank was declared legally bankrupt for failing to abide by proper banking practices. The verdict was based on the Commercial Code given that the Law of Money and Credit was not in effect yet. The Commercial Bank got a lighter sentence. It was deemed a victim of the Real Estate Bank's irresponsible behavior and granted preventive debt settlement status.[87] The case was closed, but BDL policy and viability was seriously affected. A larger banking crisis was looming ahead.

During the Real Estate Bank crisis, Takla and Pierre Eddé, the ABL's president, dismissed it as an isolated case. Eddé assured the press that the folding of the banks had "absolutely no effect" on the general financial state of the country. Takla publicly declared that these crises can happen anywhere in the world. The low volume of discounted bills at the BSL, he pointed out, was proof that the banking sector as a whole was not facing any liquidity crisis. The Ministry of Information and Guidance also released an announcement assuring the public that this was a passing crisis and could not be compared to those of 1956 or 1958.[88] Government and ABL assurances failed to stem the tide of public speculation over the robustness of the financial sector and the ability of the new central bank to manage it efficiently and promptly. Rumors of a serious liquidity crisis persisted throughout the rest of the year, despite optimistic forecasts by the French press. Since reports indicated that there was a movement of capital out of domestic banks and into foreign ones, the crisis took on a nationalist tone. The entire financial sector became a target of public debate and criticism, including the banks, Beirut's struggling bourse, and the central bank.[89]

Signs before the Storm

Doubts over financial stability reached a crescendo during the summer months of 1964 as Chehab's term neared its end. Private banks were faced with political uncertainty, the collapse of two banks, and new—albeit inactivated—legislation granting the central bank the right to impose reserve ratio requirements, which would further strain the banks' credit capabilities. Many of these banks adopted a tight lending policy, and the money market became stagnant. Experts like Salim Hoss, who at the time had risen to become head of AUB's Business Administration Department, publicly defended the practice of reserve ratio requirements but called on the central bank to promptly announce the ratio it wished to adopt so as not to keep the banks guessing. Several members of parliament sent a formal query asking the government about the measures it was taking to resolve the financial crisis and wondering whether it was on a scale similar to that of 1958.[90]

Prominent bankers largely dismissed talk of a full-fledged crisis but acknowledged the precarious status of the sector and offered a range of solutions, which were either private-led, state-run, or a mix of the two. The former ABL vice-president Anis Bibi assured the public that Lebanese banks could withstand shocks thanks to the Banking Secrecy Law and the special national role local banks played compared to foreign ones. Domestic banks, he told the press, attracted Arab capital destined to serve "general nationalist [*qawmiyyah*] objectives," as opposed to capital deposited in foreign banks that is invested in foreign interests, let alone Israeli ones.[91] Other bankers took aim at the central bank. The veteran banker Sami Shoucair argued that calls to restrict the number of operating banks were misplaced. The problem, Shoucair explained, was not a shortage of liquidity but one of trust. Investors held off depositing their savings because they needed assurances from the central bank. Shoucair acknowledged that the BDL was a necessity but chided it for allegedly acting merely as an inspection agency. "The [central] bank is not the Ministry of Finance," he told *al-Masarif* in July 1964. "It is rather the bank of banks and the official and actual setter of economic and financial life and thereby has to act based on the principles of personal free initiative and not solely according to the protocols of administrative inspection."[92] The start-up banker George Jabbour argued that Lebanon could not tolerate a further increase in the number of banks, however, and proposed private mergers as a solution.[93] The businessman Michel Saab, who had campaigned for a central bank in 1953, called for the creation of a Lebanese deposit insurance fund as a joint public-private venture managed by the government.[94]

For their part, Beirut's money changers were more vocally critical of the central bank and demanded a larger consultative role for financial and economic associations in running it. In a public memo they submitted to the Lebanese cabinet, the brokers cautioned that "good intentions were not enough." They predicted that financial markets would remain shaky "as long as conditions at the central bank remained unchanged" and expertise was lacking. The BDL, they complained, had failed to provide them with adequate amounts of low-denomination coins and to replace "dirty" bank notes, which [did] not reflect Lebanon's "civilized" face and were understandably being turned down by tourists.[95]

In the press, the polemics for and against the BDL were framed within broader and familiar debates about planned versus laissez-faire economies. One critical editorial harkened back to the days when there was "chaos . . . that did not harm anyone," but was rather coupled with "an authentic spirit of adventure mixed with national ambition" that stood behind the country's prosperity. In response to assertions that many countries had central banks with powers like the BDL's, the editorial invoked Lebanese exceptionalism, to the point of claiming that Lebanon without a central bank had been better off financially and economically than countries with central banks that had "neither Lebanon's status nor the secret of its success nor the spirit [*nafsiyyah*] of its people. . . . We were wealthier, we were happier, our future was clearer, we used to attract the world's money, so why did we imitate them, rather than the other way around? . . . Our prosperity is the product of the independent labor of individuals, their ability to take the initiative freely and to overcome obstacles put up by the state."[96]

Other newspapers defended the BDL and turned the argument on its head. It was the absence of a central bank, one newspaper argued, that "allowed foreigners to get their hands on our country and control its economy and financial direction." Another paper asserted that the central bank was a "national institution that looks after banks and guides it along the right course and acts as a guarantor of the rights of depositors."[97] Once in office, Takla initially tried to keep out of the limelight. In the spring of 1964, he told reporters that his relationship to the press as a governor of the central bank was drastically different from what it was as foreign minister. The governor's job called for little talk and lots of work.[98] Takla admitted that there was "something unusual" going on in the money market, but suggested that it was a "temporary emergency condition" that would soon resolve itself. Lebanon's economy was "in great shape."[99]

The autumn of 1964 seemed to vindicate Takla's assessment. In the first two weeks of October, the BDL pumped LL24M into the money market.[100] Earlier in September, the election of Charles Helou as president had brought some confidence back into the money market and curbed the outflow of capital from accounts in Lebanese currency into foreign currency ones. The ABL, seemingly emboldened by the election of a right-of-center Chehabist like Helou, launched its own attack on the press, threatening to take part in legal action against publications that targeted banks, which, the ABL argued, were an attack on the "entire banking system" and "a threat to the economic safety" of Lebanon.[101] In October 1964, however, the ABL and the Press Syndicate reached an agreement to terminate both the press campaign against the banks and legal action by them so as to resolve the conflict between Lebanon's "two titans."[102] Future press reports that included criticism of banks had to be submitted to the Press Syndicate, which could solicit an obligatory response from the ABL prior to publication. Newspapers that violated these procedures would be declared legitimate targets of litigation and the Syndicate pledged not to come to their aid.[103] The bankers' stranglehold over the press was reinforced the following month when the publication of false news about banks was criminalized, with the author subject to a jail sentence of from three months to two years.[104]

Silencing the press did not bring a swift end to the crisis. In January 1965, claims by the ABL that the crisis was largely a function of press speculation were undermined by the collapse of another bank, Sogex. Unlike in the Real Estate Bank case, the central bank managed to get ten private banks to undertake the liquidation of the failing institution. But as the BDL's 1965 annual report warned, that was a one-time remedy, which could not be relied on in the long run.[105] A more sustainable solution was required. The collapse of three banks had failed to slow down the sector's expansion. In 1964, the central bank reviewed twenty-two applications to found new banks, in addition to approving the establishment of four new branches of foreign banks.[106] In 1965, four additional banks were established, bringing the number of banking institutions to eighty-six. with a total of 206 permanent branches.[107] The superabundance of banks preoccupied the BDL throughout 1965. Following a survey of the sector, the BDL explicitly asked the Lebanese cabinet, which had tightened the rules for setting up new banks in July 1965, to cease issuing any such permits except to ventures devoted to medium- and long-term lending. Even new branches had to obtain special permits. On January 5, 1966, the cabinet adopted these and other recommendations that provided incentives for banks to merge, liquidate, or turn into nonbanking businesses.[108] The measures were too little too late, however. They prevented an additional increase in the number of banks, but did not impose any new regulation on existing ones, of which there were too many. In sum, these measures did not form a coherent policy aimed at tackling the roots of the crisis. Nor did they lead to a fundamental change in the relationship between the central bank and the banking sector.

With its regulatory wings clipped and an organized banking lobby teth-
ered to its administrative arm, the BDL's calls for financial prudence had
largely fallen on deaf ears in the first two years of its operation. A couple
of banking failures and public panic over a looming liquidity crisis had
failed to jade the buoyant bankers or alter the power dynamic between
their sector and the central bank. The reappointment under President
Helou of Philip Takla as foreign minister, in addition to his being governor
of the central bank, in violation of the BDL's own statutes, only served to
weaken the BDL's authority and effectiveness.[109] It took a major storm to
shake the banking establishment. In the fall of 1966, the country's largest
bank, Intra, collapsed, and the Chehabist bureaucrats and the barons of
banking had to go back to the legislative drawing board to renegotiate
the precarious balance between cooperation and coercion they had come
up with under the Law of Money and Credit.

CHAPTER 5

Suits and Shadows

The Intra Affair

Supporting the Lebanese banks except for Intra was the lesser of two evils. It was the best of solutions and the most effective.

—Lebanon's President Charles Helou

On November 23, 1967, police in the Swiss city of Lucerne grew suspicious of a vehicle with American license plates that had been parked next to the Central Postal Office for several hours.[1] The driver, an elegant man wearing a black coat, identified himself as a Brazilian dealer in wild animal skins who had just arrived in Switzerland. Unfortunately for him, however, the Swiss police officer spoke Portuguese, and he was unable to respond in that language. He was subsequently found to be Yusif Beidas, the former head of Intra Bank, a suspect wanted by the Interpol.[2] Beidas had turned from an Arab financial guru into an international fugitive after Intra, the largest bank in Lebanon at the time, collapsed in the fall of 1966 and its founder refused to return to Beirut to face the music. A year after his arrest in Lucerne, Beidas fell ill, and he died at the age of fifty-six on November 28, 1968, a bitter and forlorn man.[3] The fate of his bank, however, was far from settled. Thanks to its size and hold on vital junctions of the Lebanese economy as well as its pioneering expansion abroad, Intra's fortunes were intimately linked to those of the Lebanese economy and the region. Its collapse threatened the entire Lebanese banking sector with bankruptcy, destabilized the Lebanese political establishment, and shook the trust of Arab and international investors in the ability of Lebanon to act as a financial entrepôt and powerhouse for the Middle East. The rise of Intra and the sequence of events that led to its crash, which are briefly outlined below, have been detailed elsewhere.[4] The causes and consequences of the bank's collapse, including the major role of Lebanon's central bank in the debacle, became the object of conspiracy theories, however, and continue to stir controversy.[5] In the wake of Intra's demise, the local press feverishly speculated over the causes of the crash. Conspiracy theories implicating the U.S. and Arab governments were floated. Some reports charged that that there was a deliberate effort to sink the bank. Other reports blamed the mismanagement of Beidas coupled with ineffective central banking policy. Speculation touched on regional and local factors. Regionally, Intra was seen as a victim of heightened tensions between the two rival Arab camps headed by Egypt's President Gamal Abdel Nasser and Saudi King Faysal Ibn Saud. Locally, the demise of Beidas was largely blamed on local financial rivals who did not wish to see a Palestinian become the country's top financier.

Archival evidence, press reports, and personal accounts of individuals involved challenge these dominant narratives that reduce the entire Intra affair to a local or global conspiracy. Local and foreign actors clearly conspired at different stages of the Intra saga and for different ends, but the collapse of Intra was equally the product of economic and political forces. Regionally, the redirection of Arab capital flows away from Beirut was prompted by deliberate U.S. hikes in interest rates. This capital migration was intertwined with Arab Cold War political rivalries between Cairo and Riyadh which in turn operated in the context of the U.S.-Soviet rivalry. Locally, the structural limitations of the newly founded central banking system of financial regulation was heightened by its high susceptibility to political interference by the barons of banking. The latter may have resented Beidas's Palestinian background, but they resented his increasing monopoly of finance a lot more. They may not have initiated the run on Intra, but they chose to let it sink in order to save their share of the sector and the laissez-faire system sustaining it. In the course of doing so, they invoked the need to protect "national" capital from foreign encroachment. But their actions further invited foreign meddling in the design and execution of structural reforms of the sector. The extent of public and private disagreements over the suitable solution was too much for their political clout and financial resources to handle. It took the activation of U.S.-backed supranational policy networks of financial consultants, diplomats, and top government officials to disentangle the competing claims to Intra's assets of stakeholders. A nonmarket solution was devised to solve what was presumably a market problem.

The Intra episode signaled the end of a bank that had been described as a "monetary miracle" whose rise was owing to much more than the Midas touch of a single man. Like his peers among the Palestinian entrepreneurs who rose to prominence in the Arab business world following their 1948 expulsion from Palestine, Beidas owed his success as much to his dynamic character as he did to a confluence of contemporary political and economic forces.[6] The ambitious and hardworking Jerusalemite gained his financial experience in Palestine at Barclays Bank and later as manager of the Arab Bank's branch in Jerusalem. Following the *nakba* ("catastrophe"—the Zionist expulsion of Palestinians from their land in 1948) and his relocation to Beirut in 1948, Beidas set up a commercial venture called International Traders in partnership with two other Palestinian entrepreneurs. They were joined by his wife's uncle Munir Abu Fadil, a prominent Lebanese politician and a former police officer in Palestine.[7] International Traders made handsome profits in the foreign-exchange market by meeting the needs of the Palestinian refugee population. It also provided transportation and money-changing services to international aid organizations such as the Red Cross and the newly created United Nations Relief and Works Agency for Palestine Refugees in the Near East (UNRWA) and signed service contracts with the U.S. giant Bechtel and other oil-refining companies that were tapping into the burgeoning Gulf oil market. By 1951, Beidas and his partners had amassed enough capital to establish their own bank. They called it Intra. In the following decade, Intra rose to become Lebanon's number one bank. Its share capital increased tenfold, from LL6.4M in 1951 to LL60M in 1962. Its banking operations topped 15 percent of Beirut's entire market, and its assets in 1965 rivaled those of the Banque du Liban.[8] Intra's influence on the Lebanese economy was not restricted to the volume of credit it controlled. Beidas pursued an aggressive policy of acquiring major stock shares in some of Lebanon's vital commercial enterprises in the sectors of air and maritime transport, tourism, media, and construction. Most of these sectors were in the hands of foreign capital thanks to concessionary privileges granted during colonial times.[9]

Faced with an increasingly saturated domestic market, Beidas set his eyes abroad. His ventures included bold buyouts of prime real estate property in New York, Geneva, and Paris, as well as the acquisition of controlling shares in France's major shipyard, the Chantier naval de La Ciotat. By 1965, a year described by Intra's board of directors as "one of the most successful," Intra's two dozen branches worldwide were spread across nine countries on four continents. The value of the bank's total declared holdings inched close to a billion Lebanese liras, its declared net profits stood at LL6.5M, and its board of directors contemplated yet another increase in share capital, up to LL120M. Three additional branches were planned for the following year.[10] But the euphoric mood prevalent among Intra officials in 1965 was deceptive. In the summer of 1966, amid rumors of cash shortages and large withdrawals, Intra began to face a liquidity problem. In the second week of October, withdrawals snowballed into a run on the bank. Close to LL51M were withdrawn between October 3 and October 14. Faced with BDL inaction and mounting withdrawals, which reached LL12M on the single day of October 14, Intra declared stoppage of payment the day after and shut its doors until further notice.[11] The Intra closure sent shockwaves across Beirut's money market and occupied front-page headlines in the press for several weeks. It triggered a political crisis that eventually brought down the government of Prime Minister Abdallah Yafi and gave rise to much speculation about the role of contemporary U.S. designs and inter-Arab rivalries in precipitating the crisis.[12]

THE ARAB CAPITAL COLD WAR

The mid-1960s saw a serious deterioration of relations between Cairo and Riyadh. Disputes erupted over the Yemen war, the larger question of pan-Arab unity, and global alliances in a Cold War setting. Nasserite forces criticized attempts by the Saudi king, Faysal Ibn Saud, to build an Islamic alliance to undermine anti-imperialist efforts, drive a wedge into Arab unity, and act as a front for pro-U.S. designs in the region. Officially, Lebanese President Charles Helou maintained a stance of neutrality in this dispute. But in the fall of 1966, Faysal grew impatient with the increasingly pro-Nasser stance of the Lebanese press and of some Lebanese government officials. So much so that it was rumored Faysal encouraged the withdrawal of Saudi and other Gulf capital from Lebanon. With Intra holding the Kuwaiti funds that constituted most of Lebanon's share of

Gulf capital, the bank bore the brunt of the attacks on the alleged scheme. Pro-Nasserite forces in Lebanon were quick to point fingers at reactionary forces. A front-page headline in Beirut's communist daily *al-Nida'* unequivocally declared: "Behind The Intra Crisis: American-Saudi Plot to Conspire against Lebanon." Unfounded press reports that Beidas had secretly loaned President Nasser LL250M to finance the Yemeni war reinforced claims of such a plot.[13]

Intra did experience heavy withdrawals of Gulf capital funds in the two months preceding its collapse. But pro-Saudi newspapers ascribed this to economic rather than political factors. *Al-Hayat* quoted "reliable" sources claiming that the crisis at Intra crisis began towards the end of August 1966, when Arab investors, lured by higher interest rates elsewhere, withdrew an estimated LL70M from the bank.[14] Intra's own consultant Paul Parker, a former U.S. Treasury representative for the Near East who had worked at Bank of America, privately told the U.S. embassy in Beirut a day before Intra's closure that large withdrawals of Kuwaiti deposits had started roughly in mid-September. That was three weeks prior to the heavy run on the bank.[15] Saudi and Kuwaiti leaders publicly denied any malicious involvement in the ordeal. On the Saudi front, Faysal reproached Lebanon for repeatedly "offending" Saudi Arabia, but dismissed charges that his regime was behind the banking crisis. Faysal called on Lebanon's government to stick to a neutral foreign policy in Arab affairs. "We did not punish Lebanon and we do not want to punish Lebanon," he added. When Kuwait's weekly *al-Siyasah* asked about Intra specifically, the king retorted: "What do we have to do with the stoppage of payment of a bank? . . . Something of this sort can happen in any country in the world when one of its financial institutions fails to abide by recognized scientific principles."[16]

Contrary to Faysal's public announcements, declassified U.S. diplomatic cables concerning the Intra crisis suggest that the Saudi regime had a hand, even if indirectly, in prompting the withdrawal of funds from Lebanon in general and Intra in particular. Some of the accounts relayed by U.S. diplomats within days of Intra's closure were second- or third-hand, hard to verify, and might have been exaggerated. These include remarks reportedly made by Faysal's son Abdullah in early October to a

U.S. official. According to Abdullah, Faysal was "extremely angry" about the Lebanese government's "unfriendly attitude" towards Saudi Arabia and "intended to take concrete action to force change," with the help of Lebanon's Patriarch Boulus Meouchi, without specifying what kind of action was planned.[17] More reliable accounts of some Saudi complicity came directly from two high-ranking Saudi officials. The first of these was Faysal's son, Prince Muhammad. At the time, Muhammad held the position of director of the Saudi Saline Water Conversion Office. On October 20, five days after the Intra closure, Muhammad told U.S. embassy officials in Jeddah that he had advised his friends to transfer their deposits out of Lebanon even before the Intra Crisis.[18] Muhammad spoke less of Intra and complained of the rise in prices in Lebanon and the alleged lack of guarantee of personal safety. The Lebanese had a tendency to profit at the expense of others, the prince scoffed, and it was time Lebanon had a more responsible government. He told U.S. officials he no longer wished to "live" there. The second official was the Saudi acting deputy foreign minister, Muhammad Ibrahim Masud. Discussing the Intra closure with U.S. officials in Jeddah, the longtime Saudi diplomat "acknowledged that Saudi withdrawals had been made and probably contributed to closure." U.S. officials, however, were not able in either case to confirm whether King Faysal gave clear instructions to withdraw the funds or simply had the foreknowledge and gave an implicit green light.[19]

Washington attempted to dissuade Riyadh from using investment funds as a way of punishing Lebanon. The U.S. administration recognized that the failure of Lebanese banks would have a serious "depressing effect on the entire Lebanese economy," which was not in the geopolitical interests of the United States and its allies in the region. The U.S. Department of State instructed its Jeddah embassy to impress upon Saudi officials the fact that "the Lebanese free enterprise system has been a living refutation of the teachings of Arab socialism. Elements in area who support Arab socialism and are hostile to U.S. and to Saudi Arabia will be greatly encouraged by any serious disruption of Lebanese economy and are already seeking to exploit Intra case in their propaganda."[20] By the end of October, Riyadh seemed keen to dispel U.S. suspicions that Saudi withdrawals were to blame or that such withdrawals were motivated by political considerations. Saudi Arabia's top financial officer, Anwar Ali, told the U.S. embassy in Jeddah that blaming Faysal was "malicious and totally unfounded." The bulk of withdrawals, he pointed out, were Kuwaiti.[21]

Kuwaiti capital deposited at Intra surpassed other Arab investments in Lebanon and consequently figured more prominently in the bank's fate. Whether made with Saudi connivance or not, the Kuwaiti withdrawals show that Intra's closure was at least partly a product of global financial politics as opposed to merely malicious political activity. Jaber al-Ahmad al-Sabah, Kuwait's crown prince and then prime minister, told the press that his government had nothing to do with the crisis. Kuwait's government had over LL200M invested in Lebanon, LL30M of which was held by Intra. Lebanon's economy, al-Sabah acknowledged, would suffer if these funds were withdrawn, but no orders to that effect had been given by the Kuwaiti government, he asserted.[22] It is possible, however, that Kuwaiti authorities were acting as proxies of or in cahoots with Saudi officials, but archival evidence of such intentions has yet to surface. More significantly, Intra's consultant Paul Parker, who had no apparent interest in exonerating Kuwait's government, privately attributed early withdrawals of Kuwaiti sums to high interest rates in Europe. According to Abdullah al-Ghanim, then vice-president of Kuwait's Chamber of Commerce, Beidas and Parker had made a discreet visit to Kuwait three weeks before the crash in an unsuccessful attempt to halt large-scale Kuwaiti withdrawals and solicit short-term loans from that country's government.[23]

In fact, the migration of Arab capital from Lebanese and regional banks to Western ones predated the Intra collapse by many months. Beirut's banking sector was highly dependent on Arab capital, the inflow of which was sustained throughout the 1950s and early 1960s by Lebanon's lack of capital controls and banking secrecy practices. By the mid-1960s, however, Beirut's quasi-monopolistic role as an entrepôt between Gulf oil economies and Western financial centers was eroding. A credit crunch accompanied by instability in foreign-exchange rates and a rush to gold hit money markets worldwide.[24] Petrodollars became a highly sought-after commodity and a financial cold war for Arab capital took place. European and American banks attempted to bypass Beirut, while other Arab capitals played catch up. By early 1966, U.S. and European financiers and bankers, including Chase Manhattan's David Rockefeller, were personally flocking to the Middle East to secure funds from Gulf sheikhs and rulers by offering record high interest rates.[25] Competition for surplus Arab capital was not restricted to initiatives by private agents of European and American capital. In the Arab world, the governments of Iraq and Egypt took proactive measures to facilitate foreign Arab investments in their countries. In February 1966, the governments of Egypt and Kuwait signed a joint declaration of "full economic cooperation" to encourage Kuwaiti capital investments in Egypt. Under the deal, Kuwaiti national banks would offer government-guaranteed credit facilities in the amount of fifteen million Kuwaiti dinars to Egypt's central bank.[26] Two months later, Iraq's government adopted new liberalizing measures to attract Arab capital. Bids to prevent the westward migration of Arab capital were also made by the private Arab banking sector outside Lebanon. In Jordan, the Arab Bank revealed its plan in June of the same year to establish an investment company that would "keep Arab monies for the Arabs."[27]

With capital flowing through new channels both globally and regionally, Beirut was losing its privileged position and became highly vulnerable to capital flight. Little was done by the Lebanese banking establishment or the government to adapt to the new reality. Proponents of laissez-faire like Joseph Mughayzil peddled the broken record that the Banking Secrecy Law was the key to ensuring Lebanon's role as "the coffer of the Arabs." The secrecy law was suddenly framed in relation to Arab rather than Lebanese culture. Guarding secrets, Mughayzil argued, was a longtime Arab trait.[28] The lack of capital controls is a two-way street, however. Under the right conditions, capital exits a market as quickly as it entered. In 1966, such conditions had materialized, and Beirut's money market was hit hard. In February alone, the holdings of Lebanese banks dropped by LL224M, or 18 percent. The following month, they decreased by an almost equal amount (LL209M, or 20 percent). Liquidity, including Intra's, remained low throughout the summer.[29] The inability of the banking sector to curb this outflow exposed the precarious regulatory foundations of Lebanon's money market, and Intra became its scapegoat.

SINKING INTRA, SAVING THE SECTOR

Yusif Beidas was well aware of the impact of the global financial crisis on liquidity levels in Lebanon. In his open letter to the Lebanese people, published a couple of weeks after Intra's closure, Beidas claimed that as early as eight months prior to his bank's collapse, he had feared that the world credit crisis and rising interest rates were bound to affect Beirut, and that he had expressed his concerns to the competent authorities in Lebanon. Despite these worries, Beidas maintained that as late as September 1966, when he left for New York to attend annual meetings of the World Bank, he had been confident that Intra enjoyed adequate levels of liquidity to weather the international crisis. What he had not anticipated, he wrote, was that Intra would have to face an additional "domestically provoked crisis aimed at controlling companies and utilities vital to our country and abetted by individuals with personal goals or private ends." Beidas thus assigned major blame for the ultimate downfall of his financial empire to local political rather than global economic forces. He framed the crisis as the result of a conspiracy over the control of national capital and resources, coupled with the failure of the central banking authority to act according to national interest. Citing his worry that exposing these individuals and their machinations might endanger the recovery of the bank, Beidas contended himself with reproaching the BDL for failing to come to the aid of Intra. Meanwhile, he thanked President Helou for his efforts to reach an agreeable compromise to resolve the crisis.[30]

Conspiracy and Counterconspiracy

In private, however, Beidas placed the Helou administration at the center of the alleged conspiracy to destroy his bank. At issue were the proceedings of a fateful meeting between the two men on August 23, 1966. Beidas and Helou provided contradictory accounts as to what transpired during their encounter. Beidas relayed a detailed account of the meeting to Najib Alamuddin, the chairman of Middle East Airlines, a member of Intra's board of directors. According to this version, Helou had summoned Beidas to argue that Intra, rather than foreign companies, should invest in development projects that would contribute to Lebanon's prosperity. Beidas purportedly objected that Intra had already "overinvested" in Lebanon and did not wish to tie up more capital in the country, given its plans for expansion abroad. Helou, Beidas contended, suggested that Beidas place valuable Intra assets invested in Lebanese companies at the BDL as collateral in return for a BDL loan of about LL150M, which would then be used for local development projects. "Go and see [BDL Deputy Governor] Joseph Oughourlian," Helou reportedly told Beidas. When Beidas discussed the president's directive with Oughourlian at the World Bank meeting in New York in September, Oughourlian allegedly burst out at Beidas: "You are not Lebanese, and Lebanon does not want your control of its economy." Shortly afterwards, rumors spread that Intra was asking the BDL for help in the face of a serious liquidity crisis, which sparked off the run on the bank.[31]

In his memoirs, published three decades later, Helou claimed that it was Beidas who had requested the August meeting and volunteered to place his "vast resources" in the service of Lebanon's national economy and of development projects. Beidas allegedly offered to do so contingent on the BDL supplying Intra with the necessary funds in return for depositing stocks at the BDL as collateral. Helou allegedly told Beidas that such a request was not within the president's jurisdiction, since "the governorship of Banque du Liban, under Lebanese law and international norms, enjoys autonomy in its dealings with banks." When, upon the insistence of Beidas, Helou allegedly inquired about the possibility of such a measure, the president was told by the BDL's governors that they recently decided to cut down on making loans in return for stock collateral in order to hedge against a weaker Lebanese pound. Helou also claimed in his memoirs that in mid-September 1966, his presidential chief of staff, Elias Sarkis, had informed him that a special emissary had been sent by Beidas to request immediate, discreet assistance from the government and the central bank. Two weeks later at the World Bank meetings, Beidas reportedly approached Oughourlian and requested that the BDL provide financial assistance to Intra in return for the services by it to the Lebanese economy. In response, Oughourlian had allegedly cited the strict rules under which the BDL operated, but expressed his willingness to consult with the BDL's governorship regarding steps that could be taken to help Intra.[32]

Helou had given a different account in December 1966, when he told
U.S. Ambassador Dwight J. Porter that Beidas himself had suggested that
Intra might help finance government-approved projects by making its portfolio available to the BDL, and that as president he had been "delighted"
to hear this (which hardly squared with his having lectured Beidas on the
central bank's autonomy, as he claimed in his memoirs). Shortly afterwards,
however, he told Porter, a "suspicious cable" from Beidas requesting "urgent financial assistance" had made him realize that Beidas's talk of doing
something for the country had been no more than a "deceitful tale."[33]

One scenario that departs from both accounts posits that the infamous
Beidas-Helou meeting was a plot devised by the Chehabists and Beidas.
The latter's brother-in-law and confidant Yusif Salameh, who was general
manager of Intra's New York branch at the time of its collapse, alleged in
his memoirs that Beidas had told him of a secret deal he had struck with
the presidential hopeful Elias Sarkis, Helou's chief of staff, that would
both secure Chehabist rule well after the end of Helou's term and give
Intra unprecedented political and financial control over Lebanon. The
BDL was supposed to provide Intra with a low-interest loan of LL100M,
which would be put to work in the market at a higher interest rate and
the profits used to finance Sarkis's presidential campaign. Beidas would
have to gain the approval of Helou for this, however, so the Beidas-Helou
meeting was arranged. Helou, it was hoped, would then get his brother-
in-law Oughourlian, the BDL's deputy governor, to approve the loan.[34]

If such a financially reckless plot did exist, why did the deal fall through,
given that both parties, Beidas and the Chehabist establishment, were in
on it and stood to benefit? Two reasonable alternative hypotheses present
themselves. The first is that Sarkis set Beidas up in order to precipitate a
run on Intra. It is not clear why Beidas would have so gullibly fallen into
such a trap, however, given the amount of ill-will he later said was harbored
by the Lebanese ruling elite towards his enterprise. Moreover, if Beidas
felt no shortage of liquidity, he could have easily financed Sarkis's political campaign without resorting to such a roundabout way. News of Intra
obtaining a big loan from the BDL was bound to leak out and possibly
spark a run on the bank, the way it eventually did, given the international
liquidity crisis at the time. The second, more probable hypothesis is that

Beidas, or an intermediary like Edward Baroudy, Beidas's and Sarkis's go-between, concocted the scheme in order to secure badly needed liquidity from the BDL for Intra without sounding alarm bells, with gaining political clout merely a welcome windfall.[35]

BDL Connivance and ABL Complicity

While this second hypothesis absolves the Helou administration of hatching a malicious plot to destroy Intra, it does not exonerate it from aiding and abetting its downfall. If Intra was facing a serious liquidity shortage and sought assistance from the government and the BDL, as Helou maintained, both parties, that is, the government and the BDL, exacerbated rather than alleviated the crisis. Amid public fears of Intra's collapse, the Helou cabinet abstained from issuing public assurances to calm the financial market and was accused of fueling speculation by leaking news of Intra's troubles. The BDL's actions, meanwhile, resembled those of a loan shark rather than a bank of banks. When Intra's acting chair Najib Salha approached Oughourlian on October 6 for urgent liquidity relief, the latter imposed strict terms under which the BDL was willing to supply liquid funds. Under the deal concluded on the same day, the BDL was given the sole right to evaluate stocks mortgaged by Intra as collateral for a BDL line of credit that did not exceed LL15M, with an interest rate of 7 percent. The rate was subject to adjustment at the sole discretion of the Central Bank. The BDL also failed to execute these measures in a discreet manner to avoid a further market scare. According to Salha, collateral bonds were to be brought into the BDL at an early hour of the day and through a back entrance. On the assigned day however, the BDL's doors were not open until regular hours and trucks carrying the bonds were asked to unload them into the bank's main hallway, causing a sensational stir among BDL employees and spreading news of an imminent Intra collapse.[36]

Within ten days of the deal, the BDL line of credit was exhausted and additional checks drawn on the BDL began to bounce. On Friday, October 14, angry crowds of depositors gathered at Intra's Beirut branch, and police were called in. Intra's board of directors made a last-ditch attempt to save the bank. Intra's consultant Rafiq Naja, a former minister of the economy, personally reached out to President Helou for help. In a meeting with Helou attended by Oughourlian, Sarkis, and Prime Minister Abdallah Yafi, Naja recommended that the government issue a statement to calm markets and loan Intra an additional LL50M in return for collectible guarantees. Sensing the gravity of the situation, Helou called in a council of ministers' emergency meeting that lasted from Friday afternoon until the early morning hours of Saturday. Intra's Salha, along with Naja, was present at different intervals of the meeting. Despite pleas by Intra officials, the government decided against extending any further assistance. Salha and Naja returned empty-handed to meet with Intra's board of directors. Shortly afterwards, Intra declared stoppage of payment.[37]

The Helou cabinet found itself in a worse quandary as the run began to spread to other banks. The Association of Banks in Lebanon (ABL) called an extraordinary general membership meeting. Government officials feared a total collapse of the banking sector, which would inevitably lead to a crumbling of Lebanon's entire finance-dependent economy, and they scrambled to take concrete action. On Sunday, Helou convened a permanent session of the council of ministers with the participation of the ABL's president, Pierre Eddé. The hands-off approach that left Intra to the mercy of market forces was replaced by heavy-handed state intervention at the request of the banking barons of laissez-faire. The ABL threatened that banks would go on "strike" starting Monday morning in protest if the government did not step in and the BDL failed to provide adequate cash to banks in return for collateral. Acting on the ABL's "recommendations," as Helou put it in his memoirs, the government imposed a three-day bank "holiday" starting the next day, and the BDL promised that when they reopened for business the following Thursday, it would supply the necessary liquidity to all the banks—except for Intra.[38]

Helou justified the decision to treat Intra separately by citing the actions of its management and distinguishing its legal and financial status from that of other banks. While trust in other banks was shaken, Helou argued, it had not been entirely lost, since these banks had not stopped payment. Intra's doing so had created a crisis of trust. If the government extended its guarantee of payment to Intra, the latter's debtors were certain to demand full repayment. Intra's branches and obligations spread across the world, the president warned, and this would mean paying hundreds of millions of Lebanese liras. The uncertainty as to how much liquidity was needed was another reason stated by Helou for excluding Intra from the scheme. During the emergency cabinet meeting on the evening of Friday, October 14, Intra's acting chairman, Najib Salha, had refused to sign and certify the bank's balance sheet and was unable to provide a rough estimate of how much cash was needed. The absence of Intra's founder, Beidas, and the apparent ignorance of Intra's most senior officials of the financial status of the bank convinced Helou that extending aid to Intra exposed the Lebanese pound to worldwide speculation and rewarded those responsible.[39]

Social Capital versus National Identity

Critics of the government's decision to exclude Intra from its aid package saw the measure as further proof of a conspiracy. Beidas's Palestinian origin was identified as the major source of this discrimination. The Lebanese establishment, the argument went, resented the fact that a Palestinian had managed to become the most powerful financial figure in the country. Lebanese Zionists, in cahoots with foreign ones, were purportedly in on the plot.[40] There may be some truth to these sentiments. But associating Beidas solely with Palestinian national identity misrepresents Beidas's own identification with Palestine. It also fails to capture the class and transnational dynamics of Beidas's project and the confessional framework within which the Lebanese elites operated at the time. The primary loyalty of Beidas was to profit, not Palestine. His contribution to the political project of liberating Palestine did little to threaten the political project of international Zionism or right-wing elements in the Lebanese establishment. Like other members of the Palestinian higher bourgeoisie, such as Hasib Sabbagh, Beidas was on good terms with powerful international Zionists in the world of finance, such as David Rockefeller.[41] Beidas was also in contact with the U.S. embassy as early as 1958 and provided it with updates on foreign-exchange transactions in Beirut's money market.[42] As his business grew abroad, Beidas struck international financial deals that seemed to benefit different, and at times opposing, political agendas. When Washington and Paris were at odds over global currency regulations, Intra financed the import of U.S. wheat into Lebanon, while investing in French capital projects that earned him accolades from the French government. According to letters Beidas sent from his exile in Switzerland to the Lebanese leader Kamal Jumblatt, the Intra founder had proposed a global monetary scheme to create an alternative currency to the U.S. dollar, dubbed the petro-dinar, to buy and sell oil. Beidas told Jumblatt that the proposal had been enthusiastically received by France's President Charles de Gaulle and Egypt's Gamal Abdel Nasser. Beidas cited the scheme as a reason behind a global conspiracy to destroy his bank. Another controversial scheme Beidas allegedly tried to facilitate was the financing of large gold purchases outside the established channels of international trade, and the establishment of a gold refinery in Beirut with French blessing.[43]

In terms of capital shares, Intra was largely a Lebanese, rather than a Palestinian enterprise. Close to 80 percent of its shareholders were Lebanese, while most of the rest were Gulf Arabs. Beidas himself was half Lebanese and married to a Lebanese. He was at pains to assert his Lebanese identity before and after the crisis.[44] In the context of Lebanon's confessional political system, his Christian religious background was just as relevant as his Palestinian origin in the eyes of Lebanese ruling elites, if not more so, and some of his fiercest opponents, like Abdallah Yafi and Saeb Salam, publicly identified with Arab nationalism and the Palestinian cause.[45]

What set Beidas apart from Lebanon's wealthy and powerful was his weak association with the country's ruling-class families, whether those of the landed or commercial bourgeoisie. His influence had been largely owing to his wealth, and he had begun to overshadow the very powerful elites he paid off, who envied his success, resented his purported nouveau riche manners, and feared his encroachment on their economic privileges.[46] Beidas bought off political patronage by granting powerful figures posts in the management of his banking business, attending to their borrowing needs, or giving them a personal stake in his success by enticing them into buying stocks in his ventures. But he had no social base of his own to fall back on in order to guard his financial interests when the market failed to do so and his beneficiaries turned against him. The competitive Beidas also failed to join the "banking fraternity" at the core of Lebanon's powerful mercantile-financial class, which might have stood up for him. He only grudgingly agreed to register Intra as an ABL member and antagonized the association's powerful president, Pierre Eddé.[47]

As Helou speculated, Beidas and Intra officials might have bet on the government's realization that Intra was too big to fail. Refusing to aid Intra was tantamount to putting the entire Lebanese economy at risk. The ruling clique surrounding Helou bet instead on being able to weather a national crisis in return for eliminating an adversary. To that end, they sought full state intervention, via the powerful instrument of central banking, which flew in the face of their much-touted adherence to laissez-faire. ABL machinations, which led to Helou declaring a bank holiday and the BDL acting as guarantor of bank deposits, ensured that the banking sector, aside from Intra, escaped immediate harm. They succeeded in preventing a massive flight of capital on the day when the banks reopened. Resolving the Intra crisis to the satisfaction of all stakeholders was a much more complicated process. It turned into a highly politicized and transnational affair that triggered debates over national capital protection and showed how financially subservient Lebanon was to U.S. and Gulf Arab influence.

REFLOATING INTRA, RELEGATING SOVEREIGNTY

Refloating Intra was a messy affair. The Lebanese government's decision to exclude the bank from its aid package, along with several complicating factors, stood in the way of an orderly and consensus-based resolution of the matter. Locally, the size of Intra's business and its control of major Lebanese corporations, such as the national airline, MEA, meant that saving Intra's assets was a matter of national interest. Self-identified socialists like Kamal Jumblatt, with whom Beidas had serious ideological disagreements, insisted on supporting the banking system and on bailing out Intra or nationalizing it as a means of seizing or keeping control of these vital assets.[48] The crisis had also coincided with, and further fueled, a swell of strikes and other union-based protest activities that threatened to paralyze the entire economy and destabilize the country.[49] Globally, the international character of the bank's creditors created a slew of legal claims and counterclaims over its overseas assets. Some of these top clients were formally or informally tied to foreign governments, namely, those of the United States, Kuwait, and Qatar. This politicized the process even further. To add to the quandary of those involved, there was no precedent in Lebanon of a bank collapse of this magnitude and the Law of Money and Credit was silent on the question of bankruptcy. In the absence of an experienced central bank and a fully sovereign national government immune to external influence, the task of untying all the financial, legal, and political knots was fraught with uncertainty and subject to dispute by a host of public and private forces acting within a supranational setting.

Outward Dependency and Nonmarket Solutions

The lack of a single authority, whether national or international, willing to or capable of dictating the final outcome of the crisis resulted in the development of the case along three different yet interdependent tracks. The first track was composed of private initiatives, namely, those of Intra officials, to seek market solutions such as finding a buyer that would bail the bank out. Given its exclusion from governmental financial assistance, Intra had to secure funds to stay in business or face the prospect of forced liquidation. The bank's top brass, led by its new chairman, Najib Salha, scurried around to solicit support from a spectrum of potential benefactors. A second parallel track lay within the Lebanese court system. Two days after closing its doors, Intra was either persuaded or pressured into filing for bankruptcy protection through debt settlement.[50] Beirut's commercial court became the stage for the financial trial of the century. The third track unraveled in the power corridors of the Lebanese government. Intra's fate was too intimately linked to the fate of the country's economy, foreign relations, and domestic stability for the Helou administration to let the courts become its sole arbiter. The government stepped in with its own series of legislative and diplomatic actions.

On the first track seeking privately raised bailouts, early initiatives included a stillborn scheme to use $200M worth of Batista-era Cuban pesos held by an American-French-Arab group to refloat the bank.[51] More serious efforts were exerted by Intra's post-crisis chairman. As soon as Intra was excluded from liquidity guarantees by the Lebanese government, Najib Salha's first instinct was to turn to the U.S. government for assistance. On Monday October 17, the first day of the bank "holiday," Salha contacted the U.S. embassy in Beirut and played the Cold War card. He spoke of an

offer of assistance from the USSR, "which would be painful for him to accept," and hoped that American banks such as Chase Manhattan would
step in to buy 50 percent or more Intra stock.[52] The following day, Middle
East Airline (MEA) President Najib Alamuddin, who was also a member
of Intra's board of directors, "confirmed" to U.S. embassy officials that
a Soviet offer of $200M to refloat the bank had been made. Alamuddin,
however, assured the embassy that in return for providing liquidity, he
would "go a long way" to support a deal under which the U.S. business
tycoon Daniel Ludwig, in association with Chase Manhattan Bank, would
buy out a controlling share of Intra, and consequently of MEA. A sale to
Ludwig, Alamuddin lamented, would be akin to a deal with the "devil,"
but it would save Intra and the Lebanese economy, and would be strictly
preferable to dealing with the "communist devil."[53]

Pleas by Intra officials for immediate U.S. assistance bore little fruit.
Instead of rushing to the aid of Intra, American banks like Chase Manhattan refused to release Intra funds they held in New York. Meanwhile,
the U.S. government lobbied its Lebanese counterpart to secure preferred
payments that Intra owed to the U.S. Commodity Credit Corporation
(CCC), an agency "created to stabilize, support, and protect farm income
and prices." Washington pushed for suspending Lebanon's banking secrecy
law in order to identify the bank's ability to repay.[54] Rebuffed by Washington, Salha turned to Kuwaiti capital for a lifeline.[55] Earlier, the Kuwaiti
government had turned down a Lebanese government offer proposing a
joint purchase of Intra in return for tax breaks and bad debt guarantees.[56]
Salha's private initiative made more progress. Throughout November, Intra
emissaries including Salha, Ali Arab, and Rafiq Naja shuttled between
Beirut and Kuwait in a bid to strike a deal with the Kuwaiti government
to refloat the bank.[57] Salha recognized the vital role of Lebanese government backing for his efforts. In late November, as news of an imminent
deal emerged, he sought and secured a support letter from Helou. Given
the amount of Kuwaiti capital invested in Intra both as deposits and stocks
(estimated at LL150M), Kuwait's Prime Minister Jaber al-Sabah seemed
keen to work out some arrangement with Salha. But given Intra's shaky
financial position, Sabah had difficulty persuading private Kuwaiti banks
and businesses to chip in,[58] and he turned to American banks, calling on

Chase Manhattan to be part of the Kuwaiti buyout with a 10 percent contribution. In the last week of November, several meetings were held between top Kuwaiti, Intra, and Chase Manhattan officials but no final agreement was reached.[59] In lieu of a buyout, Sabah opted for a commercially conservative, state-mediated interim solution. In return for collateral stock, a quasi-government agency, the Kuwait Foreign Trading Contracting and Investment (KFTCI), would lend Intra LL50M, while the Sabah family's government holdings at Intra (LL30M) would be frozen for a few years. A letter of understanding to that effect was signed between KFTCI and Intra on December 1, but politics stood in the way, and Intra failed to obtain the release of its collateral from the BDL. A month later, KFTCI withdrew the offer.[60] The most serious offer to resolve the crisis thus succumbed to bad diplomacy and BDL intransigence.[61]

Prospects of an Intra-brokered settlement were fading fast as things developed on the second, legal track. Court proceedings began in earnest the day Intra filed for debt settlement. Two committees of certified experts appointed to look into the case concluded that the guarantees offered by Intra were insufficient to meet its obligations. Intra was insolvent, with a deficit of LL43M.[62] The question of Intra's solvency was not, however, laid to rest by the court's findings. Since many Intra assets were outside Lebanon, and given the speculative nature of property valuation before the conclusion of a sale, the hasty estimates produced by the court committee were disputed by Intra officials and Arab depositors. Price Waterhouse, then auditor of the World Bank, was tasked with conducting a parallel independent valuation to assuage the fears of foreign investors and further validate the court decision. The Lebanese government dismissed the auditing firm, however, after the British journalist Patrick Seale reported in the *Observer* on November 5, 1966, that its senior partner, Eric McMillan, had told him that Intra was probably solvent. The dismissal further fueled claims of government connivance to bring down Intra. On December 23, another internationally renowned British auditing firm, Cooper Brothers, was commissioned by the Lebanese government to conduct yet another valuation.[63] But the court did not wait for its report. On January 4, the presiding judge, Abdel Basit Ghandour, declared Intra officially bankrupt.

The court decision threatened to derail concurrent efforts by the Helou administration to take full control of the refloating process through a special piece of legislation. When the bankruptcy verdict was issued, parliament was in the midst of debating bill 2/67, which prohibited bank bankruptcy. This came to be known as "Intra's law." After its passage, banks deemed unable to pay their debts immediately came under the management of a committee appointed by the commercial court at the request of the BDL. Within six months, the committee, composed of representatives of creditors and shareholders, as well as state officials and independent experts, was expected to determine whether the bank was salvageable and should refloated or whether it had to be liquidated. In order to overrule Ghandour's decision and evade a forced liquidation of Intra, the final version of the bill, which was passed on January 16, 1967, was made to apply retroactively as far back as October 1, 1966.[64] Like every other aspect of the Intra crisis, the formation, mandate, and workings of the management committee was mired in controversy.[65] The committee failed to submit an official report within the six-month period assigned by law, and Intra would have faced liquidation had not the government intervened at the last minute on August 5 to amend the law and allow for the creation of yet another committee that would carry on the task of the first for an additional two months. The second committee, made up entirely of bureaucrats and experts, was chaired, ex officio, by the BDL's governor. The committee's powers were expanded to include those of an extraordinary general assembly, and it was commissioned to "find solutions that safeguard the interests of rights holders promptly in the best way."[66] The Helou administration thus managed to remove the issue from the courts' jurisdiction and place it in central bank hands.

Intra's law was the culmination of a series of legislative and diplomatic steps charted by the government on a track parallel to that of the commercial court proceedings. This included the so-called LL50M law. To preempt any mobilization of small depositors by Intra stakeholders upset by the exclusion, the government authorized payment of up to LL50M to depositors holding accounts of LL15,000 or less, giving priority to account holders with LL5,000 or less. In return for paying off small depositors, the law granted the Lebanese government all the rights and privileges of the depositors that were to be reimbursed.[67] In other words, the LL50M was not a loan by the BDL to Intra to pay off creditors, but rather a nonconsensual, legally imposed transfer of creditors' rights from private to public hands. As a result, the Lebanese government became a major stakeholder in Intra. Upon the formation of the second committee in August 1967, the Helou administration had also become the ultimate arbiter of the bank's fate. Since the three other leading creditors were Kuwait, Qatar, and the U.S. government, represented by the CCC, refloating Intra became an almost entirely intergovernmental affair.

Roger Tamraz and Supranational Policy Networks

The hierarchy of power relations between the governments involved in refloating Intra and the financial circles attached to each proved a greater determinant than the logic of market forces as regards which refloating bid made the cut. Based on the amount of credit owed by Intra to each government and on the nationality of the bank involved, the governments of Kuwait (the largest creditor) and Lebanon (the national government) should have held the most sway. Both, however, displayed deference to U.S. opinion and interests. The influence of Washington largely did not take the form of direct political pressure. It was rather due to the superior bargaining position of the U.S. government, thanks to what may be termed supranational policy networks that had developed in the region as an important instrument of U.S. hegemony. These policy networks were arranged like concentrated loci or nodes of knowledge accumulation and power dissemination, with the U.S. embassy in the center and the majority of public and private actors involved linked to it through direct channels of communication.

These networks were of two types. The first type was composed of the extensive networks of local informants and interlocutors developed by U.S. embassies which penetrated deeply into the state bureaucracy, business circles, and research community of Lebanon and to a lesser extent Kuwait. The fact that the U.S. government was a major stakeholder with a direct interest in the outcome did not deter many of these informants—who included Lebanon's emissary to Kuwait, Talha Yaffi; the director general of the Lebanese Ministry of Finance, Khalil Salem; and the appointed head of the Intra management committee, Shawkat Munla—from directly sharing information with Washington that prejudiced the negotiation process in favor of the CCC.[68] In one instance, information of an imminent deal between Intra's branch in Beirut and its sister bank in Geneva passed on to the Americans led to direct action by Chase Manhattan to its benefit and the detriment of Intra. The leaker of the Geneva-linked information was Roger Tamraz, the point man of the New York financial consulting company Kidder Peabody, which made one of three major offers to refloat Intra and eventually won the bid. Tamraz represented the second, transient type of policy network at play. These networks formed during the crisis thanks to the intimate coordination of U.S. foreign policy between the U.S. government and powerful agents of American financial capital, namely, banks and investment firms. The prestige of U.S. financial expertise and the clout of U.S. financial institutions in global money markets further empowered these networks in the eyes of regional governments and private actors.

Members of this second type of networks such as Tamraz, Paul Parker, and Eugene Black had an advantage over other competing European actors. Tamraz was "discreetly" introduced into the high circles of power in Kuwait by the U.S. government to represent private U.S. interests, after which U.S. government officials would have less direct involvement, preventing the "erroneous impression [that the U.S. government] has role to play re [the] future of Intra." Kuwaiti high officials, on the other hand, were keen to learn from Tamraz, who was formally acting in a private capacity, whether his proposal had U.S. government approval.[69] Kuwait also lent an ear to the U.S. financier and foreign policy consultant Eugene Black. Back in November, before the court-appointed management committee was set up, Kuwaiti Prime Minister Jaber al-Sabah had withheld his approval of Salha's offer pending further consultation with Black, whose role as a representative of U.S. government and private business interests was augmented more than Tamraz's by his "independent," institutionally secured position as consultant to the Kuwaitis. Black was s former president of the World Bank and a Chase Manhattan board member. He simultaneously sat on the Kuwait Investment Advisory Board, to which the Kuwaiti Prime Minister turned for advice.[70] The loyalties of Intra's acting manager, Paul Parker, were even further divided among three stakeholders. Parker, who had been recruited by Beidas from Bank of America shortly before the collapse to put Intra's house in order, had served as Near East representative for the U.S. Treasury. Despite the conflict of interest involved, Parker regularly updated the U.S. embassy in Beirut on Intra's condition and refloating efforts.[71]

Parker's financial reputation also enabled him to draw in, and later dismiss, one of the major offers to buy out Intra by Fides, a subsidiary of Credit Suisse. The offer was made through Beirut-based Banque de l'économie arabe (BEA), which hired Parker as a consultant. By the end of June 1967, a preliminary agreement had been reached under which the BEA would take over Intra loans, effectively becoming a reconstituted Intra bank.[72] In the first week of August, a contract was dawn up, but eleventh-hour disagreements with the Lebanese government placed the deal on hold.[73] The Credit Suisse offer remained on the table and was discussed by U.S. and French officials as late as September 20. The odds, nonetheless, had ceased to be in Credit Suisse's favor.[74]

The Credit Suisse deal had already been on shaky ground after the U.S. embassy raised suspicions over the financial integrity of the BEA.[75] This prompted Parker to sever his ties with the BEA and help bring Kidder Peabody back into the picture by working more closely with Tamraz towards an alternative offer. Rather than the traditional buyout under which the new owner assumes the debt obligations of the defunct bank, Kidder Peabody proposed a reorganization of Intra through the conversion of large creditors into shareholders of a newly constituted holding company and a spin-off bank with a modest share capital. As such, Intra's liabilities would be "neutralized" by converting them into shares. By subordinating Intra's original shareholders to large creditors like Kuwaiti capital and CCC, Tamraz reasoned that his offer would gain the support of powerful political elements. It did.[76]

By late September, Tamraz had hammered out the details of the agreement with Lebanese finance officials and economists. He also got BDL support. Yet he later tried to prevent the Lebanese government from becoming a shareholder by suggesting that the money owed to the BDL be converted to long-term debt rather than shares. Shortly afterwards, Tamraz gained the consent of the three other large creditors, namely, the

Kuwaiti and Qatari governments and the CCC. On October 11, a protocol was signed between the court-appointed management committee and
representatives of the four major creditors (Kuwait, Lebanon, CCC, and
Qatar). The protocol outlined the terms under which the new holding
company and bank were constituted.[77] The liquidation of Intra had been
averted, but the bank was not saved and its global investment outreach
was eliminated. In effect, it was turned into an international consortium
called the Financial Investment Company. The signed protocol transferred
the titles, rights and interests of the former shareholders to creditors and
depositors. Meanwhile, the original shares were declared void as a result
of Intra's reported insolvency. Creditors and depositors had been made
whole entirely at the expense of Intra's original shareholders.[78]

The Kidder Peabody settlement was as controversial as every other development in the Intra crisis. Different stakeholders made different assess-
ments of the fairness and profitability of the deal. Detractors condemned
the reorganization as outright confiscation of profitable investments. In
the words of Najib Alamuddin, converting creditors into shareholders by
the force of law was "a masterpiece of legal hocus-pocus."[79] Intra stakeholders in France, including some of the bank's employees, were among
the most vociferous opponents of the deal and placed it in the context
of rivalry between French and U.S. financial interests. They launched a
press campaign that criticized the French finance minister, Michel Debré,
for failing to "lift one finger" to ensure that a French rather than a U.S.
banking group was awarded refloating rights. Intra's role, they argued,
had been to draw Kuwaiti funds away from "dollar-sterling tutelage."[80]

In contrast to Intra sympathizers in France and Lebanon, Washington
and Kidder Peabody were in a celebratory mood. Tamraz, who earned high
fees for refloating and later managing the restructured company, saw the
scheme as one step towards introducing Kidder Peabody into the Middle
Eastern money market as a pioneer of modern underwriting techniques.[81]
Meanwhile, the U.S. government, which sought to discredit French objections and "alert" Sarkis, who by then had been appointed BDL governor,
of the "swindlers" behind the French group, became a major shareholder
of the new holding company through CCC shares. The protocol even
upheld CCC's priority rights against Intra's assets in the United States.[82]

U.S. embassy officials viewed the deal as a significant step towards more constructive American-Arab relations. The United States was "at long last" seen as "a force for economic development and order in the Middle East."[83] Pronouncements about changing anti-American sentiments across the Arab world in the wake of a bank refloating deal were wishful diplomatic thinking. As far as the Intra debacle was concerned, however, these officials rightly pointed out that the "financial stake of the [U.S. government] has been protected in a highly satisfactory manner." The same could not be said of the financial interests of Lebanon's financial oligarchs opposed to monetary regulation. Restoring long-term trust in the country's banking sector required sweeping reforms of central bank functions that had been anathema to Beirut's barons of banking but that became necessary for their very survival in the wake of the Intra affair. State-sponsored financial regulation became laissez-faire's last refuge.

CHAPTER 6

Financial Regime Change
The Last Refuge of Laissez-faire

There is not a single official at the central bank who has studied the science of banking.
—Dhulfiqar Qubaysi, editor-in-chief of *al-Masarif*

Kidder Peabody settled the Intra affair,[1] but did not address the two deeper and intertwined roots of the broader banking crisis. Unsound private banking practices, including unaccountable, highly concentrated management structures, risky credit policy, and the lack of specialization in long- versus short-term lending, were the first of these. Inadequate banking regulation, both at the level of legislation and enforcement, which would have put a lid on these unsound practices, was the second. Both shortcomings were debated during the Intra affair. Critics of Intra's founder focused on unsound banking practices, namely, Beidas's maverick managing style and the investment of short-term deposits in illiquid assets with long-term returns. Critics of the government, on the other hand, blamed Intra's collapse on the lack of proper regulation and central bank inaction. In reality, there was enough blame to go around. Managerial incompetence and regulatory deficiencies fed into each other. Amid demands for a major overhaul of central banking practices, Band-Aid solutions were no longer possible. In the year following Intra's collapse, the Helou administration introduced several major pieces of banking legislation. In addition to Intra's law outlining a clear process for handling troubled banks, the new provisions created three sector-specific institutions: the National Deposits Insurance Scheme (NDIC), the Higher Banking Commission (HBC), and the Banking Control Commission (BCC). Together, these laws and institutions constituted a new regulatory regime governing the entire sector.

The administrative structure and financial function of this new regulatory regime were the culmination of public debates and bargains among Lebanese and foreign state officials, domestic banks, and their foreign counterparts.

154

The rivalry between the latter two had grown into outright antagonism in the wake of the Intra crisis. Socialists and Arab nationalist forces in Lebanon had railed against the domination and machinations of foreign, especially European and U.S., banks. But it took a crisis of the caliber of Intra for the laissez-faire-loving banking community to join the bandwagon. The fall of Intra prompted a major flow of capital out of local and into international banks. Local bankers, including the prominent, U.S.-friendly Pierre Eddé and Sami Shoucair, became increasingly bitter at the sight of branches of foreign banks weathering the Intra crisis unscathed while Lebanese banks teetered towards an uncertain future. When informal ABL attempts to get foreign banks to agree to a national insurance scheme failed, Lebanese bankers closed ranks with the government to force foreign bank compliance by law. Financial experts backed the scheme. AUB institutionalists like Salim Hoss and Talha Yaffi impressed upon public opinion and financial elites the usefulness of a deposit insurance scheme. Yaffi proposed a draft law to the Association of Banks, while Hoss outlined the benefits of adopting the U.S. model in the press.[2] Hoss also actively took part in consultations at the Ministry of Finance. He recommended the creation of the HBC and the BCC and was eventually appointed president of the latter.[3] Together, these two institutional bodies were charged with restructuring the banking sector and monitoring its operations.

In the short run, these reforms bestowed considerable powers on the state that undermined the fundamentals of laissez-faire. Thanks to Intra's law, the state became the mandatory adjudicator of last resort for all bank bankruptcies. Meanwhile, the HBC and BCC were granted extraordinary power to oversee the liquidation, takeover, and merging of banks in line with state-stipulated rules. In the long run, however, the restructuring process developed the legal framework and bureaucratic practices of banking regulation in order better to resist future shocks. Laissez-faire was given a new lease on life with a revamped central bank—under the new rule of financial experts—standing guard at the market's gates. By 1975, when civil war broke out, central banking had been transformed from an object of domestic doubt and international criticism in the wake of Intra's collapse into an indispensable bureaucratic instrument of banker power and prestige.

BLAMING BANQUE DU LIBAN

There is little doubt that Beidas adopted a risk-taking approach to managing Intra and increasingly monopolized decision-making in the few years prior to the bank's collapse.[4] The court handling the Intra case found evidence of this. Beidas's bad banking practices included advances to executive board members beyond prescribed quotas, the generation of illusory profits, and the divestment of capital into fake real estate companies, as well as maintaining low liquidity levels because of large investments in real estate.[5] There is equally incriminating evidence, however, of the failings of the central bank. According to the Intra official Hanna Asfour, the court did not find any evidence of correspondence between the BDL and Intra in which the former urged the latter to get its house in order.[6] More significantly, the 1963 Law of Money of Credit had granted banks five long years to comply with new financial regulations. Technically, Intra in 1966 had at least two more years before it became liable for violating the law.[7] Intra's liquidity shortage and potential insolvency were also partly a result of lax central banking regulation. Thanks to lobbying by private banks, the Law of Money and Credit itself did not enforce reserve ratio requirements that Intra would have had to abide by. Attempts by the drafting committee of the Law of Money and Credit to classify banks based on short- versus long-term credit policy were equally scuttled. Such measures would have curtailed Intra's investment of short-term deposits in long-term projects and thereby secured high liquidity and ensured quick solvency. Even the BDL's most avid enthusiasts decried its dereliction of duty. The veteran journalist Dhulfiqar Qubaysi, editor of *al-Masarif,* who had celebrated the launching of the BDL in 1964 as the final step towards Lebanon's full independence, put the onus of Intra's failure squarely on the central bank. On the day Intra closed its doors, he had harsh words for the BDL's policy and lack of scientific expertise:

Lebanon is one big bank. Its largest branch [Intra] stopped payment. Who is responsible? Is it the government [*al-dawlah*]? No. The government does not understand the science of banking. . . . Who else but the central bank? Since its founding, the central bank has been content to act as an observer. . . . The central bank did not act prior, during, or after the Intra incident, and it will not act. Many wonder why. Is it waiting for the right moment? The answer is no. The central bank does not know how to act. It does not know what to do. The answer is simple: lack of expertise. We say it bluntly to the Lebanese, and we take full responsibility for doing so. There is not a single official at the central bank who has studied the science of banking.[8]

Qubaysi's distinction between the government and the central bank does not hold up to scrutiny. Since the founding of the BDL in 1964, central banking had remained largely dominated by a tense alliance between the big bankers and the Chehabists. The BDL lacked autonomy vis-à-vis the government as well as the banking lobby. The Chehabist foreign minister Philip Takla was appointed governor in clear violation of the Law of Money and Credit. The bank's top technocrat, Joseph Oughourlian, had immediately deferred to the government when the Intra faced the threat of closure. The government in turn did not act before consulting the Association of Banks (ABL). At the time, government and ABL officials jointly decided to provide immediate financial relief and monetary guarantees to banks other than Intra, following a three-day bank "holiday." These measures, administered by the BDL, were meant to restore trust in the money market to avoid large-scale capital flight. But as was the case with the signing of the Franco-Lebanese monetary agreement two decades earlier, the Lebanese ruling elite did not have confidence in their own ability to self-manage monetary crises without external help. President Helou and Governor Takla sought the assistance of foreign governments. They immediately appealed to Lebanon's former colonial ruler, France, and the world's superpower, the United States.

International Criticism

Paris and Washington responded in a lukewarm manner to Helou's pleas. Despite Lebanese press reports of France coming to Lebanon's aid, confidential diplomatic records indicate that the French government and the Bank of France had chosen to stay aloof from what they saw as a domestic financial quagmire. They referred Lebanese officials to international financial institutions. According to Bernard Clappier, then deputy governor of the Bank of France, French authorities deemed the Bank of International Settlement (BIS) more capable of providing a "disinterested, international cover" for assistance and, if need be, of recruiting a "consortium of central banks to associate themselves with the operations." The BIS responded with enthusiasm to French requests and dispatched its top managers to Beirut. The Lebanese government continued to demand technical assistance from the Bank of France, however, in order to uncover the causes of the crisis and offer recommendations for recovery. Since technocratic advice did not involve financial cost, the Bank of France ultimately obliged. The move was largely a symbolic show of support aimed at restoring confidence in the Lebanese lira in international financial circles.[9]

Washington was likewise reluctant to extend any direct financial assistance. Instead, the U.S. Department of State vigorously pursued the recovery of the money Intra owed the CCC. Washington decided against "persuading American banks to purchase shares in IntraBank [sic] or otherwise extend funds to meet current crisis." Like Paris, Washington had also preferred international to bilateral mechanisms of aid. While the former approached the Basel-based BIS, the latter sought IMF intervention. Few days into the crisis, the IMF was willing to provide expert advice, should the Lebanese government seek any, but none had been sought until then.[10] Several weeks later, Helou reportedly concurred with John Gunter, chief of the Middle East Department at the IMF, that given Lebanon's very small IMF quota ($6.57M), there was "very little" the Fund could do to help resolve the banking crisis in Lebanon.[11]

With little international material support came a lot of policy advice. Ian Michie, VP for Near Eastern Affairs at Chase Manhattan Bank, urged the BDL's acting governor, Joseph Oughourlian, to include Intra among the blanket liquidity guarantees extended to other banks *before* the audit results of Intra came out and *regardless* of such results. Only then would foreign confidence in the banking system be restored and capital flight held in check.[12] The IMF's Gunter, meanwhile, lamented that there were few people at the BDL with central banking backgrounds. Oughourlian, Gunter added, did understand central banking, but his bad relationship with the commercial bankers posed a serious obstacle to effective operations, since a successful central banker needed to have the commercial bankers on board. Takla, Gunter thought, would do the trick.[13]

The BDL's handling of Intra's foreign branches was also an object of criticism. Jordan's central bank governor, Khalil Salem, described the Lebanese government's reluctance to speedily transfer funds abroad to save Intra's foreign branches as too "legalistic." Under the new Intra's law, any such transfers had to be approved by the court-appointed management committee. The U.S. ambassador in Beirut, Dwight Porter, saw the opposition to such transfers of members of Karame's government like Raymond Eddé as "parochial," noting their "curious unwillingness to grasp the idea that [transferring funds abroad] is not 'paying off foreigners' . . . but rather to preserve assets essential to refloating the bank for the benefit of all, including the Lebanese."[14]

Local Impunity

The BDL's two top officials, Oughourlian and Takla, were largely impervious to the barrage of criticism hurled at them. Oughourlian reportedly reacted "blandly" to Michie's recommendation that the BDL's guarantee of liquidity be extended to Intra. When Oughourlian updated the U.S. embassy on the status of commercial banks ten days after the crisis, he sounded bitter, not remorseful. He told U.S. officials that had he agreed to extend further funds to Intra, which he argued was well beyond what existing banking laws permitted, he would have landed in jail.[15] Likewise, Takla was not at all critical of his role or of the BDL's overall economic policy and performance. On October 31, two weeks after Intra stopped payment, Takla assured his U.S. embassy interlocutors that Lebanon's economic policy worked well, *except* for Intra. The latter, Takla surmised, might have been too big and overextended worldwide for a small country like Lebanon. Takla conceptualized the problem as one of having to "catch the thieves" and those seeking to create instability. As for the BDL's performance, what Qubaysi saw as central bank "inaction," Takla described as a "policy of flexibility" necessary for the period of transition from an entirely laissez-faire regime to one of limited supervision and controls. In this regard, Takla conceded that BDL reform would have to take place, but in a way that would not affect any change in the principles of "free exchange, free trade, and free enterprise."

Takla pondered the possibility of amending banking legislation, but conceived of central banking reform as largely limited to boosting the technical competence of its personnel to detect dishonest banking practices. Takla did not question his own financial competence. He evidently told Gunter that he wanted to remain at the helm of the BDL. Rather than quit his financial post and remain in his diplomatic one, Takla did the reverse. On November 28, he resigned as foreign minister in order to devote his attention to central banking reform.[16] The reforms that ensued were well beyond what Takla might have envisioned, or was capable of implementing.

A NEW REGULATORY REGIME

Pressure for state intervention to fix and regulate the banking sector beyond the minor modifications suggested by Takla continued to mount throughout the months following Intra's collapse. Qubaysi's lamentation of the lack of "scientific" expertise at the BDL turned into a clarion call for reform. As was the case in the formative period of the founding of the BDL, financial experts and technocrats resurfaced as authoritative advocates of reform. Calls for the introduction of expertise into the central bank served to consolidate the authority of the technocrats. AUB institutionalists, especially third-generation members like Elias Saba , Talha Yaffi, and Salim Hoss, were at the forefront of these efforts.[17] The ABL was equally keen to play a formative part to ensure that the vested interests of its members were not significantly compromised by any new legislation. Throughout 1967, over a dozen pieces of banking legislation (both parliamentary laws and presidential decrees) were enacted.[18]

Three of these laws, and their amendments, constituted the pillars of the new regulatory regime that governed the banking sector and the constantly evolving institutional relationship between private banks and central banking authority. Bill 22/67, which was passed on April 24, for the first time decreed the classification of banks based on their credit policy. Banks were categorized as either commercial or specialized in medium- and long-term lending. Banks engaged in mid- and long-term lending had to have a minimum share capital of LL15M, fivefold that of commercial banks. They were barred from accepting time deposits that matured in less than two years but were given seven-year tax breaks and the authority to issue debt certificates that did not conform to commercial bank guidelines. Despite such incentives to encourage the creation of such banks and several future amendments, the new 1967 law failed to end the dominance of commercial banking in Lebanon.[19] The other two laws, Intra's law and Bill 28/67, were more successful in putting breaks on the haphazard proliferation of banks and setting a safety network for future crises. The ABL had successfully resisted such measures when the Law of Money and Credit was drafted.

Intra's Law

In the short run, Intra's law (Bill 2/67) was created to prevent the outright liquidation of Intra and allow the Helou administration to gain control of the bank's assets. In the long run, the law institutionalized the procedures by which the state, through its central bank and the judiciary, was empowered to take immediate control of any bank that was obliged to stop payment. Specific criteria under which a bank was deemed to have stopped payment, with retroactive force to apply to Intra's case, were put in place. These included the bank itself declaring stoppage, failing to pay a debt it owed to the BDL on its due date, drawing a check on the BDL without sufficient consideration, or not providing adequate consideration to cover a debit that had arisen out of clearing operations. Once any of these criteria were met, the central bank would initiate an automatic process of state takeover. A management committee, composed of state-appointed members and those representing creditors and shareholders of the bank, would assume the full powers of the bank's general assembly and the board of directors. The committee was given six months to file a report to the court recommending that the bank resume its operations or undergo liquidation. Failure to submit a report automatically led to liquidation under a newly constituted liquidation committee.[20]

When the first management committee appointed to handle the Intra case failed to produce such a report, the Helou administration intervened again to avoid liquidation. It amended Intra's law on August 5, 1967 (Decree 44). Under the amended legislation, if the first committee failed to file its report on time, the council of ministers was authorized to form a second management committee, which would be granted two additional months to deliberate and issue its verdict. Both committees typified the Chehabist approach of public-private partnership in the administration of regulatory bodies. The amendment altered the nature of state intervention. The change in the committee's makeup shifted decision-making to government officials. While creditors and shareholders were in the majority vote on the first committee, the second committee that would take over after six months was exclusively composed of officials with legal and financial backgrounds. In addition, the first committee's chair had to be a creditor, while that of the second was, ex officio, the central bank governor. Lastly, the second committee was appointed by the sitting government, not the commercial court. In effect, thanks to the outcome of the Intra case, the central bank and the state bureaucracy became the mandatory adjudicators of last resort for all bank bankruptcies.[21]

Intra's law regulated the very last stage of a banking crisis—a bank's collapse—rather than its roots. To address crises in a more fundamental, long-term manner, the Helou administration drafted an omnibus bill on banking that became the cornerstone of banking "reform" for decades to come. Bill 28/67, which was passed by the Chamber of Deputies on May 5, 1967, created three new institutional bodies. Together with the central bank, these institutions formed a labyrinthine integrated bureaucratic apparatus that insured, monitored, and regulated banking. The first of these bodies was the National Deposit Insurance Corporation (NDIC), aimed at guaranteeing private deposits in Lebanon against loss. The scheme inserted a wedge between local and foreign banks, prompting the state to intervene on behalf of the former.[22]

International Capital and National Insurance

By early 1967, in the wake of the Intra affair, opposition to foreign banks in Lebanese financial circles had turned into a press campaign with nationalistic undertones. The influential ABL member Sami Shoucair, who had been a U.S. embassy snitch in the heyday of the merchant republic, attacked foreign banks for their unfair advantage in the market, given their virtually unlimited ability to draw on liquid funds from abroad. Their foreign headquarters, he protested, were acting as a banker's bank and escaped any regulation. Shoucair's press campaign was carried out in the pages of *Le Commerce du Levant*. The campaign took on an institutional dimension when the ABL, itself a champion of laissez-faire, pushed for the regulation of "foreign" banks through private channels. A few days after Intra's closure, Eddé urged the U.S. embassy to address "the negative attitude" adopted by U.S. correspondent banks that Eddé claimed were delaying transactions at Lebanese banks. Meanwhile, the American member of the ABL's board of directors relayed similar sentiments to branch managers and representatives of U.S. banks in Beirut.[23] Eddé himself sought a "gentleman's agreement" with branches of foreign banks that would regulate their operations. Shoucair suggested a series of measures as part of the "gentleman's agreement" including the requirement that foreign branches publish their balance sheets, refrain from paying interest rates on deposits not invested in Lebanon, and possibly turn down deposits from Lebanese.[24] Beirut-based managers of non-Lebanese banks brushed the ABL demands aside. American bankers deferred to U.S. law, and a British bank manager told Eddé that foreign bank deposits in Lebanon were a favor to the country, and that his Gulf clients' money could be moved directly abroad "without ever touching Beirut." Short of state regulation, the British banker added, there would be no compliance with ABL requests.[25]

U.S. officials surmised that the British banker had bet that no such state regulation would be imposed.[26] The bet was misplaced. Towards the end of February, branches of foreign banks found themselves pitted against the BDL and its governor, Philip Takla. The stickiest issue was getting foreign banks to contribute financially to an insurance fund to cover failing banks. Local small banks were particularly vulnerable to failure as money advanced by the BDL was quickly finding its way into larger banks through client transfers of their savings from small to larger and more secure banks.[27] Initially, Takla envisioned a voluntary insurance scheme with private banks (both domestic and foreign) contributing 60 percent and the remainder financed by the central bank. Based on U.S. embassy reports, the degree of resistance to such a scheme varied among foreign banks. Among "foreign-foreign" banks, that is, U.S. and European ones, Anglo-Saxon branches exhibited the fiercest opposition, while Italian and French ones were less antagonistic, despite reservations. "Foreign-Arab" banks, including the large Arab Bank, however, were sympathetic to Takla's proposal.[28] Unable to bring foreign banks on board in a consensual manner, the BDL sought legislation to enforce such a scheme and create the National Deposit Insurance Corporation (NDIC).

One of the immediate aims of the NDIC was to pay off depositors of banks that were slated for closure by central banking authorities. These banks were assigned for liquidation by the two newly created institutions, the Banking Control Commission (BCC) and the Higher Banking Commission (HBC). Foreign bankers protested to Takla at having to make contributions before the first premium was assessed, and when the losses were known in advance. They described the scheme as "no insurance." Takla retorted that the U.S. Federal Deposit Insurance Corporation (FDIC) had been set up under identical conditions during the Great Depression.[29] Takla's prompt invocation of U.S. banking regulations was no coincidence. Less than two weeks after Intra collapsed, the Lebanese government and the BDL asked the U.S. embassy for details of how the FDIC operated in order to draft comparable Lebanese laws for banking insurance.[30]

While the insurance mechanism and financial function of the NDIC were inspired by U.S. banking regulation practices, its administrative organization was fine-tuned to reflect the power relations that existed at the time between Lebanon's barons of banking and the Chehabists. Thanks to ABL lobbying, the state agreed to provide an annual contribution that equaled the total contributions of the banking sector, even though it was assigned a minority of seats on the NDIC's board of directors. In other words, instead of the state penalizing high-risk banking behavior, it became a public co-guarantor of private loss. Furthermore, small local banks and the national currency were given preferential treatment. A temporary article in the NDIC law had provided for blanket insurance against loss for all deposits, regardless of their value or denomination, to assuage fears still simmering in the immediate aftermath of the Intra crisis. Starting in 1969, however, only Lebanese deposits, and up to fifteen thousand LL per depositor per bank, were insured, while annual premiums were levied on all deposits regardless of their denomination.[31] A mixed public-private administrative structure was also adopted in the makeup of the two other bodies created by Law 28/67 that were dedicated to the monitoring and regulation of banks. The BCC and the HBC were co-managed by representatives or appointees of the central bank, the Ministry of Finance, and the ABL. They were in turn linked administratively to the NDIC through chairing committee members who served on more than one board.[32] A new level of bureaucratic skill and technocratic knowledge became necessary for both the state and the private banking sector to run this new regulatory regime and adapt to it.

Banker Bureaucrat, Banker Technocrat

The creation of commissions whose members were sworn to banking secrecy did not introduce innovative mechanisms to banking practices in Lebanon the way the NDIC did. The commissions gave advice on or enforced existing laws. The control commission was tasked with monitoring banks and ensuring the proper implementation of the Law of Money and Credit, which stipulated the creation of a "control department" that, like the control commission, was to be answerable directly to the governor.[33] But such a department was not set up. The newly formed control commission also acted as a consulting body recommending best practices to banks and filing updated reports on their financial standing to the higher banking commission, which had the authority to take disciplinary action against the banks, but within the penal provisions already prescribed by the Law of Money and Credit.[34]

Preserving the status quo required a further expansion and complication of the system of checks and balances that kept the whole thing running. The new institutions (NDIC, BCC, HBC) were all structurally tied to, but at an arm's length from, the BDL. The overly legalistic dimension of these new structures meant that managing the system, from the state side, and coopting or abiding by it, from the private banking side, required highly sophisticated legal expertise and specialized knowledge of the science of banking. The banker-bureaucrat capable of deciphering the plethora of regulations and the banker-technocrat capable of designing macro financial policy became indispensable actors in Lebanon's economic and financial life. In order to develop the banking sector's human capital, the ABL partnered with Beirut's Université Saint-Joseph to set up an institute for banking studies. A few years later, a collective agreement—the first of its kind in Lebanon—was signed between the ABL and the sector's employees after a series of strikes.[35] At the state level, Elias Sarkis and Salim Hoss, who became respectively BDL governor and head of the Banking Control Commission in the middle of 1967, embodied the new type highly skilled regulator. Sarkis, a seasoned judge and top administrative bureaucrat, had served as presidential advisor to Chehab and Helou. His administrative skills stood in contrast to the itinerant diplomat Takla, long accused by the banking community of incompetence in financial matters. Hoss was a highly educated economist and an expert in central banking reform. The banking community had long resisted his ideas and those of his fellow AUB institutionalists during the conflict over setting up the central bank. The calamity of Intra left little room for further intransigence.

Sarkis and Hoss first met at the swearing-in ceremony for the newly appointed members of the BCC on June 5, 1967. Sarkis was in attendance as presidential chief of staff, not yet having been appointed BDL governor, and Hoss was being sworn in as BCC head. President Helou, as Hoss recalled many years later, entered the room with a sullen face and conducted the affair in a hasty manner. Before he departed, the seemingly troubled president advised the new appointees to take care when evaluating banks rather than clamp down on them. The banks, Helou told his audience, would be facing yet another crisis and would have to operate under sensitive conditions.[36] Earlier that day, the Arab-Israeli Six-Day War had broken out. Lebanon did not officially participate in the war, but immediately felt its financial repercussions. On the first day of hostilities, banks experienced a rush of money withdrawals. With the Intra debacle still fresh in memory, the Helou administration promptly shut down Lebanon's banks for three days, later extended until June 12, six days after the end of the war. The government took advantage of extraordinary powers granted to it by parliament and decreed limits on personal withdrawals, while allowing bank transfers for commercial transactions. These measures were lifted on June 24. No major capital flight was recorded.[37]

With another emergency crisis averted, the new cadre of central banking experts could redirect their attention to the long-term structural problems they had been entrusted with fixing. In the ensuing two years of their appointment, Sarkis and Hoss set to work. Ratio reserve requirements, long resisted by the banking community, were introduced, albeit at a modest rate of 5 percent. The HBC and BCC were given extraordinary, albeit temporary, powers to clean up the banking sector by taking over banks that were deemed financially unviable.[38] Ten banks were liquidated by the state, and five others opted for self-liquidation. All were Lebanese-owned. A five-year moratorium on issuing new bank licenses was put in place, later extended for another five. These measures consolidated and streamlined the local banking sector after two decades of unfettered expansion. Thanks to a hike in world oil prices, a new surge of Gulf capital flows soon ushered in another "golden age" for Lebanese banking, which was cut short by a brutal civil war.[39]

TWILIGHT CAPITAL

In the 1970s, the Arab banking sector witnessed unprecedented consolidation and expansion amid an increased differentiation of Arab economies into oil-rich economies with excess capital surplus on one hand and oil-poor economies facing mounting public debts on the other. Banking policies did not fall neatly in line with a country's classification as an oil or non-oil economy. Ideology was a more decisive factor. Socialist-leaning countries like oil-rich Iraq and Algeria, as well as oil-poor South Yemen, further centralized their financial systems. Iraq's banking sector was entirely taken over by the state, and oil-poor countries like Syria and Egypt cut down on banking legislation, with Egypt adopting an "open door policy" that saw the liberalization of its economy. These regulatory transformations coincided with a net outflow of capital from Gulf countries into regional and international markets. Thanks to skyrocketing oil prices in the wake of the Arab-Israeli war of 1973, Gulf states experienced the largest capital surpluses. Much of this money was absorbed by international money markets like those of the United States and Japan.[40] The rest was invested in developmental projects across the Arab world or found its way into the coffers of private banks sprouting across the region. Gulf states created a number of trans-Arab development funds in the form of government agencies with some private-sector participation, such as the separate Kuwait and Abu Dhabi Funds for Arab Economic Development. Intergovernmental ventures like the Arab Investment Company, the Arab Bank for Economic Development in Africa, and the Islamic Development bank were also set up. Together, these funds constituted the institutional bedrock of an emerging financial Arab market that Lebanese bankers were eager to capitalize on.[41]

Capital Overflow

In Beirut, there was no shortage of hot capital inflow. Between 1970 and 1974, total banking sector deposits grew a staggering 240 percent, with a monthly inflow estimated at an average of LL120M.[42] The influx was more than Beirut's money market could handle. Bankers turned to the state to invest their excess liquidity. An ABL delegation visited President Sulieman Franjieh and expressed the sector's willingness to finance state-led developmental projects by buying treasury bonds. Franjieh told his visitors that the state was not ready to go beyond its means to invest in projects that it did not consider a priority at the moment. Banks sought relief in foreign markets, capitalizing on the Lebanese lira's reputation for stability. Some banks bought up debt bonds in emerging markets like Algeria and India, and the World Bank issued bonds dominated in Lebanese liras. The French automaker Renault issued long-term bonds in Lebanese liras, too, at the initiative of Lebanon's Bank Audi.[43] Lebanese monetary authorities tried to discourage such practices so as to prevent the emergence of an international market for Lebanese liras and the speculative activity that might ensue.[44] As a result, large sums stagnated in Lebanese banks, further heating up of the local financial market. Mounting inflationary pressure prompted the BDL to introduce cooling down measures like raising discount rates and issuing ceilings on credit. The Law of Money and Credit had also empowered the BDL to cap interest on deposits to discourage further savings and to punish banks who violated its instructions. A decree to that effect was issued, but without an enforcement mechanism. Banks resisted state-imposed interest rates. ABL attempts at self-regulation through mutual agreement between banks were equally unsuccessful.[45]

By 1972, the ABL was pushing to amend the Law of Money and Credit in order to expand the scope of banking operations and strengthen the ABL's consultancy status vis-à-vis the state. The following year, amendments were introduced in accordance with ABL recommendations. The BDL became a lender of first rather than last resort. Banks were permitted to draw annual and renewable loans from the BDL in return for depositing commercial paper, as long as these loans were invested in agriculture, industry, public works, or the financing of Lebanese exports. In addition, government bonds were deemed countable towards reserve ratio requirements. This meant that banks could invest their excess liquidity in treasury bills and then deposit these bills with the central bank to meet their reserve ratio requirements. This money maneuver would free more liquid assets for private lending. Ceilings on credit were eased, and caps and restrictions on borrowing by top bank officials were loosened. Finally, the amended law explicitly required the BDL to consult with the ABL regarding regulations governing the relationship of private banks with its depositors and agents. The logic of unfettered laissez-faire had seeped back into the system. It was tempered by calls to invest excess capital in the secondary and tertiary sectors resembling those that had accompanied deregulatory efforts in the 1950s. But concrete efforts to set up investment banks for this purpose suffered from shortcomings similar to those of ventures initiated in the 1950s. In the 1970s, the flagship project, the National Bank for Industrial and Touristic Development, was billed as an attempt to achieve the priorities of the national economy. It remained marginal, however, and did not exclude the services sector, namely, tourism, from benefiting. Such an exclusion would have ensured that loans were solely directed to more productive sectors. Private bankers were also hesitant to finance the bank until after obtaining a say in its management and securing the appointment of the ABL-trusted expert and BCC head Salim Hoss at the new bank's helm.[46]

Beirut's Money Market Bubble

The drive to liberalize the money market was a lot more assertive than the shy attempts to invest in developmental projects. As late as 1974, the banking community continued to have high hopes that Beirut would regain its status as a regional financial hub. Financiers were eager to fulfill their big dream of a free banking zone. By then the country's most prominent financial expert, Salim Hoss elaborated ways to promote Beirut as an international money market. During a seminar organized by the ABL, he told his audience that despite a palpable shift towards industrialization between 1967 and 1973, Lebanon's services sector would reassert itself, with banking and finance holding the "greatest promise." This did not mean, however, that Lebanon would become the leading regional financial market.[47] Several Arab countries, top among them Kuwait, had already started developing theirs, which were likely to continue to grow internationally. Meanwhile, Hoss cautioned, the Lebanese money market remained highly underdeveloped. Financial instruments like commercial bills, certificates of deposits, and treasury bills were either virtually nonexistent or traded in rudimentary form.[48] This left little room for open market operations by the BDL or private actors that could further deepen the market. The Beirut Stock Exchange (BSE), Hoss lamented, seemed "to have defied all efforts to develop it since its establishment in 1920," with a mere forty-three stocks traded. The biggest obstacle to developing the BSE, he pointed out, was the absence of medium- and large-scale corporations, something Hoss attributed to progressive corporate tax rather than the lopsided growth of the commercial sector at the expense of large-scale investment.[49]

Hoss was equally if not more keenly aware of the challenge posed to developing Lebanon's local banking and money market by the "veritable invasion" of the region by international banks.[50] With vast resources at their disposal, international banks outcompeted their local counterparts by expanding their operations in Beirut to attract Gulf capital. Unable to set up shop anew due to the ban on establishing new banks, these foreign banks bought existing licensing at exorbitant prices and expanded their holdings.[51] A restructuring of bank ownership took place. By 1970, foreign-designated banks came to control 77 percent of all deposits, either directly or through newly bought shares in local banks. Ownership became highly concentrated, with no more than ten banks holding more than 50 percent of deposits.[52]

Hoss tried to balance the need for sophisticated, large-scale foreign banking services to cope with high capital flows with the wish to shield the local market from being swallowed up. He suggested the creation of a free-banking zone inspired by what he saw as innovative practices in Singapore. License restrictions would not apply in this zone, but new licenses would be subjected to "stringent and rigorous" conditions akin to those imposed in Singapore. A "new breed of banks" along the lines of offshore banks in the island state would be set up, which would ex-clusively specialize in foreign business and refrain from dealing with resi-dents. Hoss thought such a zone would also lure in smaller local banks. To avoid foreign-designated banks getting an unfair advantage, they would be expected to bail out their branches and affiliates in the case of a crisis.[53] Plans for a free banking zone did not materialize until 1977. But a series of prior market developments and nonmarket initiatives raised hopes of turning the vision of Beirut as an international financial center into a reality. For its part, in collaboration with the Arab League, the ABL set up the Union of Arab Banks, with Beirut as its headquarters.[54] Private joint ventures between local and international banks, includ-ing Belgian, French, and Japanese banks, also bore fruit. Banks became bigger and more powerful, with their total budgets ballooning into 110 percent of the country's GDP.[55]

Despite these promising transformations, ambitions to revive Beirut's celebrated role as an entrepôt of international capital markets were hard to reconcile with the financial facts. The size of the Lebanese banking sector was large compared to the country's total economy, but remained modest compared to other financial centers. The Lebanese money market was barely a tenth the size of Switzerland's, a country held up by Lebanese bankers as the banking model. Whatever its potential, any such transna-tional role by Lebanese banks was quickly shattered by the outbreak of the civil war in 1975, the front lines of which ran right through Beirut's commercial and financial center.[56] For many ordinary Lebanese, Beirut's banking district symbolized the inequality hiding behind the elite façade of prosperity. Some banks were plundered, others destroyed by shelling. Banks moved their headquarters out of the downtown, and ABL meetings were suspended. A year later, Sarkis and Hoss tried to come to the rescue again, this time as president and prime minister of the republic. As the 1976 presidential election drew near, the fighting factions found a poten-tial compromise in the moderate Sarkis, who had earned his accolades as a civil servant.[57] Following his election to the presidency, he called on his former partner in banking reform, Hoss, to join him as prime minister and appointed a prominent banker, Farid Roufayel, as minister of finance. The new technocrat-studded cabinet took advantage of the cessation of fighting in 1977 and issued a series of decrees aimed at "guaranteeing the safety of the banking sector" and creating a conducive environment for reconstruction. However, Israel invaded the south of the country in 1978, and local fighting resumed. Sarkis, Hoss and their team of technocrats became largely irrelevant amid the swell of armed militias and foreign armies that fought on and off over Lebanon for the next twelve years.

Capital Conflict

The civil war presented a new host of conflicts, challenges, and opportunities to banker power. The war economy stood for everything that laissez-faire proponents publicly denounced: unstable, inflationary prices, large budget deficits, and a negative balance of payments. Banker power, however, was not always on the losing end of this disruption. Private banks were accused of currency speculation that fueled battles and filled coffers. As the BDL's governor Riad Salameh later put it, "Battles during the civil war used to take place in the exchange market."[58] Competing networks of financial interests vied for control of global financial flows entering Lebanon. In Najib Hourani's words, the war was a "conflict of capitalists," inasmuch as men like the Saudi billionaire Rafic Hariri and Kidder Peabody's Roger Tamraz became monetary warlords, so to speak, by financing warring factions.[59]

As the war progressed, the BDL faced the double task of resisting the encroachments of central authority, now under the influence of militia leaders, and restraining an increasingly fragile yet freewheeling banking sector. The managerial autonomy designed into the BDL's administrative structure under Chehab proved essential in fulfilling the first task of resisting government abuse of BDL powers. The ABL also worked under difficult logistical conditions but retained its institutional resilience and access to decision-making circles. The relationship of the BDL to the ABL and the private banks became shaky at several junctures. Several rounds of bargaining and negotiation took place throughout the 1980s between the two sides. The gradual erosion of currency stability produced the worst fallout.[60] In the second half of the 1980s, the continual devaluation of the Lebanese pound led to a dollarization of the Lebanese economy that persists to this day. Financial collapse in 1988 was accompanied with a crisis of political legitimacy when the two major warring camps were unable to settle on a presidential successor to Amin Gemayal and decided to form their own government. The bank became a target of constant political pressure, which at times turned into outright military attack.[61] Each government sought to deprive its adversary of the financial services that the BDL offered, which included the disbursing government employees' salaries and the subsidization of essential commodities like fuel oil. The BDL was caught between two rival governments ruling a war-torn country.

Sovereign Debt, Sovereign Banks

Sometimes the state might call on the central bank for assistance, but today the central bank has become a substitute for the state.

—Riad Salameh, governor of Lebanon's central bank, 2015

Acting as the country's de facto "economic government," resisting pressure from both sides in the Lebanese civil war to dictate his policy priorities, Edmond Naim, the BDL's governor, camped inside the central bank's headquarters and earned himself the sobriquet "the banker in the bunker." The BDL had become "the only government authority standing between Lebanon and insolvency," Ihsan Hijazi reported in the *New York Times.*[1]

By the end of the civil war, Lebanon had become internationally synonymous with a failed state and endemic sectarian violence. State institutions including the military, the judiciary, the presidency, parliament, and public education were seen as weak, corrupt, partisan, or powerless. By contrast, the central bank remained largely resilient in the face of war, significantly autonomous from government intervention, and relatively immune to sectarian manipulation. It kept the very idea of a viable, stable, independent Lebanon alive in the national imagination. Lebanon's private banking sector, which kept growing in size amid a flailing economy, continued to occupy a secondary but similarly respected place in the national imagination. This idealizing narrative gained additional currency after the country plunged into another period of political turmoil following the assassination of Prime Minister Rafic Hariri in 2005.

Hariri, a Lebanese construction mogul who had made his fortune in Saudi Arabia following the oil glut in the 1970s, dominated Lebanese politics throughout the postwar period. In line with prevailing global trends at the time, he embraced neoliberal policies unreservedly.[2] His privatization drives, real estate construction in downtown Beirut, and unproductive public works projects drained the treasury and enriched private stakeholders. Major economic consequences included growing rentierization, a surge in

real estate prices, further migration of skilled labor, exacerbated class inequality as a result of a lax tax policy, the creation of new forms of capital
ownership in the form of holding companies, a growing trade deficit, and
major recapitalization of the banking sector.[3] Most significantly, Hariri
relied on public debt rather than taxation to fund his reconstruction project and finance public expenditure. Lebanon became a chronically debtor
nation. Sovereign debt shot to over 120 percent of GDP, from U.S.$3.3
billion in 1993 to U.S.$70 billion in 2015.[4] Banker power was reshaped
by this restructuring. Around half of Lebanon's public debt was held by
local banks. The intimate links between the bankers and the state were
institutionally sealed.

Lebanese banks were able to secure a steady high level of profit via sovereign lending thanks to generous interest rates and financial engineering
policies set by the BDL. Throughout Hariri's era, the BDL remained a key
decision-maker in managing the debt, the currency, and the money market.
To that end, Hariri recruited Riad Salameh from Merrill Lynch to become
governor in 1993. Salameh, forty-two at the time, has become Lebanon's
longest-serving central bank governor. After more than twenty-two years
at the helm, he is one of the nation's best-known public figures. Salameh
distinguished himself in the wake of the 2006 Israeli war on Lebanon and
the 2008 global financial crisis. During the 2006 war, his appeal to U.S.
ambassador in Lebanon, Jeffery Feltman, facilitated the safe transfer of
much needed cash via helicopter from nearby Cyprus. Feltman, as Salameh
divulged a decade later, had chosen to reside temporarily at the central
bank to prevent the Israelis from bombing it.[5] Two years later, in the run-
up to the 2008 financial crisis, contrary to International Monetary Fund
(IMF) advice, Salameh introduced financial measures, including a ban
on derivative trading and subprime mortgages that not only shielded the
Lebanese banking sector from the repercussions of the crisis, but secured
billions of dollars of new deposits. The BDL's foreign-exchange reserves
jumped from U.S.$3.3 billion in 2008 to U.S.$30 billion in 2016.[6]

As their influence grew, the BDL and the ABL sought to further impress themselves on the Lebanese collective imagination. In 2009, the
ABL published a glossy *Golden Jubilee Book, 1959–2009* to celebrate its
fiftieth anniversary, and when the BDL turned fifty in 2014, passengers

on Lebanon's Middle East Airlines were treated to a special screening of a documentary titled *Governor by Order of the Lira,* whose narrator, the prominent news anchor George Ghanem, hailed the BDL as a pillar of national independence and economic prosperity. The BDL also commissioned the country's leading newspaper, *al-Safir,* to publish a commemorative volume, which came out in 2015. In his introductory remarks to this book, *al-Safir*'s editor in chief, Talal Salman, described the sense of awe that he experienced whenever he entered the bank and extolled its "grave national mission" of safeguarding the national currency and defending the public purse against adventurist politicians. Salameh was, in Salman's words, the "golden guarantee" of that stability.[7] Prominent Lebanese private bankers, who constituted the vast majority of contributors to this commemorative volume, heaped further praise on the central bank and its governor.

The BDL and ABL both have much to cheer about. The cooperative relationship between them that took shape in the mid twentieth century laid the groundwork for an ever-growing financial oligarchy that has survived financial crises, economic downturns, political turmoil, foreign occupations, and a prolonged civil war (1975–90). By 2015, with a struggling local economy and a dwindling middle class, private bank holdings had grown to almost four times Lebanon's GDP. Thanks to financial engineering by the BDL, the bankers continued to finance the state and make handsome profits in return.[8] Local Lebanese banks held more than 50 percent of the country's ballooning sovereign debt. Their share is uncommon in the annals of the sovereign debt of developing nations, often held hostage to foreign lenders.[9] For centuries, sovereign debt, particularly by foreign creditors, was—and has remained—a means of undermining financial independence and inviting foreign interference. The mechanisms involved ranged from "colonizing by lending" during imperialist times to the "conditionality" of twentieth-century international financial institutions.[10] In the case of Lebanon, the government's ultraconservative monetary policy in thepost–World War II period espoused balanced budgets and eschewed state borrowing even for economic development. This made it less susceptible to financial conditioning by IFIs, but it did not imply a guarantee of independence from foreign influence and local manipulation.

Foreign influence in the design of Lebanon's financial regulatory regime ranged from IMF missions in the 1950s that pushed for banking regulation to the shaping of public debate and mid-level public policy through the intellectual contributions of the AUB institutionalists, to direct U.S. and other government interference in the resolution of banking crises such as the Intra affair. This "soft" form of intervention was a result of the political orientation of Lebanese ruling elites. By and large, the Lebanese financial class and their allies in government saw their interests as aligned with those of the Western capitalist camp and neoliberalism. In the post–World War II period, I focus on in this book, Lebanon's economic policy was more anti-communist and anti-socialist than the United States could have hoped for in an Arab world teeming with nationalist and socialist political currents. As a result, the interests of Lebanon's top bankers were often aligned with those of international capital. Petrodollars lay at the heart of the bankers' prosperity, and a dirigiste economy was never on their agenda. When a divergence of interests did occur between local and international bankers, as was the case during the 1966 Intra crisis, the former tried painstakingly to balance their parochial interests with the exigencies of global forces. They expediently sought state intervention to prevent foreign banking from totally taking over their enclave in the domestic money market.

Half a century later, the institutional overlap between the banks and the state is stronger than ever. Major shareholders in eighteen out of the top thirty banks are linked to political elites, and an estimated 43 percent of the entire sector's assets are held by individuals closely tied to politicians.[11] Sovereign lending, sustained by central banking engineering policies, serves as the glue binding the fate of the bankers to that of the state and vice versa. The Lebanese banking sector is not only the largest in the Middle East and North Africa region but one of the largest in the world as a share of GDP.[12] It constitutes 97 percent of the country's financial sector, and more than half of its aggregate assets are in the form of government securities and deposits at the BDL.[13]

Without a strong and diversified economy to guarantee a stable financial system, the BDL and the bankers have continued to trumpet price stability as the golden calf of sound monetary policy. In their view, the cornerstone of this stability has been the pegging of the Lebanese lira to the U.S. dollar. Contributors to the commemorative volume celebrating the BDL's fiftieth anniversary extolled this fixed exchange rate as a "guarantee of the national economy."[14] The only dissenting voice among the contributors was that of Elias Saba. The former AUB institutionalist, who also served as minister of finance in the early 1970s, criticized the peg as a forfeiture by the BDL of an important monetary mechanism of adjustment to economic development.[15] Saba recalled the now forgotten battle over founding the central bank half a century earlier, in which he participated as an expert. It was, as he put it, "an uneven arm-wrestle" between two groups. The first were a minority, including himself, who wished to grant the BDL broad jurisdiction to act as a modern central bank. The opposing camp, the majority, simply wanted to accommodate the prevalent "trend" of setting up a central bank, but deprive it of effective authority. The second group won. Saba reminded his readers that the disagreement was fundamentally ideological. It was rooted in the economic philosophy espoused by each side. He was, and remains, a Keynesian, while Lebanese decision-makers were, and still are, adherents of laissez-faire.[16]

More recently, IMF officials have also expressed concerns regarding the overall stability of Lebanon's financial system. While central bank policies have in their view helped maintain confidence, several macroeconomic and financial vulnerabilities have accumulated over time. Top among them is the financing of the ballooning public debt, which in light of sluggish economic growth requires a constant inflow of nonresident deposits and remittances. Unofficial background notes by the IMF have been more candid in expressing alarm at the increased risks to sovereign solvency, deposit rollover, and currency instability. According to such notes obtained by Beirut's daily *al-Akhbar*, these risks are a consequence of large public debt, persistent dependency on short-term deposit inflows, and high dollarization.[17] Despite the fact that these risks reflect deep structural problems in Lebanon's political economy that have persisted since independence, the IMF's recommendations draw on the standard neoliberal formula of austerity. In their official report, IMF experts focused on fiscal adjustment, including measures like tax increases on fuel and restructuring of pension plans, rather than central banking reform, to fix these financial problems.[18] But as the story of the Lebanon's financial foundations shows, focusing on fiscal policy may be misleading. Lebanon's uneven economic structure—which is largely shaped by central banking regulation and the private mercantile-financial interests it serves—is what lies at the root of renewed vulnerability to financial risk. Taking full account of these foundations, not as a one-time event in the past, but as an ongoing process of constructing state-embedded regulatory regimes, would be a major step towards a strong, stable economic future neither subject to the dictates of international financial institutions nor subordinate to private banker power.

Notes

Introduction

1. The BIO was first reconstituted as the Banque de Syrie, then as the Banque de Syrie et Grand Liban, and finally as the Banque de Syrie et du Liban (BSL).

2. Pauly, *Who Elected the Bankers?* attributes the call for central banks to be independent and free of political interference to the 1933 London Economic Conference (p. 63). See also Yaffi, "Monetary and Banking System of Lebanon," 174.

3. Plumptre, *Central Banking in the British Dominions*, 14.

4. Owen, *State, Power, and Politics*, 5–6.

5. Sen, *Central Banking in Undeveloped Money Markets*, 5, 6.

6. For a list of central banks established between 1920 and 1954, see Yaffi, "Monetary and Banking System of Lebanon," 185–87.

7. Mitchell's *Colonizing Egypt* was one of the earliest anglophone studies of Arab state formation in the late and post-Ottoman context, and his *Rule of Experts* examines the "economy" in particular as a site of producing the nation in the Middle East, in which respect see also Owen, "Middle Eastern National Economy" and Seikaly's exploration of dynamic class constructions in mandate Palestine in her *Men of Capital*. On the making of national identity, see Massad, *Colonial Effects*. Thompson, *Colonial Citizens*, considers the production of state and citizen from the perspective of gender. On authoritarian political economy, see Bassam Haddad's *Business Networks in Syria*. Finance is much less studied. Davis, *Challenging Colonialism*, examines the rise and collapse of Bank Misr in Egypt, but does not extend to the postcolonial period; see also Izz al-Arab, *European Control*. More recently, Adam Hanieh has opened new horizons of understanding financialization and money market formation in the contemporary Arab world; see his *Money, Markets, and Monarchies*.

8. Oughourlian, *Histoire de la monnaie libanaise*, 28.

9. Unless otherwise stated, the term "bankers" throughout this book refers to bank owners and first-tier executives rather than bank employees.

10. Nasr and Dubar, *al-Tabaqat al-Ijtimaiyyah fi Lubnan*, 134.

11. Achi and Ayache, *Tarikh al-Masarif fi Lubnan*, 166.

12. Gates, *Merchant Republic of Lebanon*.

13. See Sayigh, *Entrepreneurs of Lebanon*; Khalaf, *Lebanon's Predicament*; Makdisi, *Lessons of Lebanon*.

14. Gaspard, *Political Economy of Lebanon*; Gates, *Merchant Republic of Lebanon*.

15. See also Abu-Rish, "Conflict and Institution Building in Lebanon"; Pauly,

Who Elected the Bankers?; Cassis, *Crises and Opportunities;* Calomiris and Haber, *Fragile by Design.*

16. Eddé made these remarks to *Le Commerce du Levant* on August 6, 1955; see Achi and Ayache, *Tarikh al-Masarif fi Lubnan,* 163.

17. Association of Banks in Lebanon, "Annual Report 1960," 12.

18. See Hakim, *Origins of the Lebanese National Idea.*

19. Chiha, *Propos d'économie libanaise,* 10. On Chiha's geographic determinism, see Traboulsi, *Ṣilat Bi-La Wasl.*

20. See El-Khazen, *Communal Pact of National Identities.*

21. See Citino, *Envisioning the Arab Future.*

22. On Chiha's Lebanese trading mythology, see Olsaretti and Hartman, "'First Boat and the First Oar,'" 37–65.

23. Amel, *Muqaddimat Nazariyah,* 291.

24. In Middle East studies, the most cited case of economic nationalism in a colonial setting is that of the Bank Misr. See Franck, "Economic Nationalism in the Middle East," 429; Beinin and Lockman, *Workers on the Nile;* Vitalis, *When Capitalists Collide.*

25. One of the few studies on economic nationalism that emphasize the role of state-linked financial institutions is Izz al-Arab, *European Control.*

26. U.S. Department of State to Jeddah, telegram 69262, October 19, 1966; FN 6 LEB; 1963–66 Subject Numeric File; RG 59; National Archives Building [henceforth cited as NAB], Washington, DC.

Chapter 1

1. Chapter epigraph: Khaled al-'Azm, *Mudhakkirat Khalid al-'Azm,* 92.

2. Autheman, *Banque impériale ottomane,* v, xi.

3. See Birdal, *Political Economy of Ottoman Public Debt.*

4. Clay, *Gold for the Sultan,* 14–15. In April 1851, in a dispatch to the British foreign secretary, Lord Palmerston, Ambassador Stratford Canning expressed his frustration at Ottoman attitudes to foreign capital, suggesting that a national bank was needed. There were only two Turks who knew the least thing about European banking, Colonel Rose lamented in 1852; another British envoy, Lord Ponsonby, said that Grand Vizier Reşid Pasha "did not understand the business, and forgot it, and lost the paper."

5. The first of these privileges—printing bank notes—was exclusive, but the BIO's charter did not explicitly grant it a monopoly of the other functions, including lending to the government. One of the effects of the BIO's charter was to streamline borrowing by the state, which could now be done only through the Ministry of Finance. Issuing bank notes was seen as the BIO's most lucrative privilege, although public trust in the currency was low, especially after the empire's 1875 bankruptcy. See Clay, *Gold for the Sultan,* 74–75.

6. The government called on money changers in Istanbul's Galata district for immediate relief. During the second financial term of 1873, short-term advances

to the state treasury continued to grow beyond 1.7 million Ottoman lira, and the international financial crisis in which the Turkish government found itself embroiled brought the role of the BIO back to the forefront; see Autheman, *Banque impériale ottomane*, 42.

7. For debt service estimates at the time of crisis, see Birdal, *Political Economy of Ottoman Public Debt*, 6.

8. For a social history of Lebanese women workers' struggle against French monopoly over tobacco production, see Abisaab, *Militant Women of a Fragile Nation*. On the role of the BIO in financing transport infrastructure, the port company and the railway company, see Hanssen, *Fin de Siècle Beirut*, 89, 96.

9. In 1905, the BIO's Beirut branch was relocated to an imposing building on the first quay of the city's port; see ibid., 254.

10. At the turn of the century, decision-making increasingly became the prerogative of the French committee. The London committee was largely populated by bankers of lesser caliber. The French co-founders of the BIO, on the other hand, included the most prestigious and wealthy elements of France's *haute-banque* consortia, including Crédit Mobilier, Hottinguer, and Fould; see Clay, *Gold for the Sultan*, 78–83. For a comprehensive list of committee members and bank directors, see Autheman, *Banque impériale ottomane*, app. 1, 271–73.

11. The Ottoman government requested a loan from the BIO shortly before it entered the war and to expand the bank's lending capacity raised the cap on note issue 100 percent. When the BIO refused to oblige, the Ottomans resorted to their war allies, Germany and Austria-Hungary, for financial assistance. Loans granted by the latter had to be deposited with the Reichsbank and the Austro-Hungarian bank. They could not be withdrawn by Istanbul but could be used as guarantee for government paper money issue; see Himadeh, *Monetary and Banking System of Syria*, 35–36.

12. El-Saleh, "Une évaluation," 385–86.

13. As Philip Khoury points out, mandate rule was transitory by definition, premised on the idea of eventual independence; see Khoury, *Syria and the French Mandate*.

14. Peter Frank details the ways in which this problematic partition led Damascene industrialists to orient their production towards a Syrian "national" market and promote protectionist policies, while calling for enhanced access to Palestinian and Iraqi markets; see Frank, "Dismemberment of Empire," 430–31.

15. Quwwatli was dubbed the apricot king (*malik al-mishmish*); see Philip S. Khoury, *Syria and the French Mandate*, 281–82.

16. Philip S. Khoury, "Syrian Independence Movement," 25–36, 31.

17. El-Saleh, "Une évaluation," 390–392.

18. Zeifer, "Les élites techniques."

19. On the French and British competing models, see Longuenesse, "Système éducatif et modèle professionnel." Saba was one of the promoters of the concept of the "ideal economic subject" in an Arab intellectual and cultural renaissance; see Seikaly, *Men of Capital*, 23.

20. On the various monetary and currency systems in the post-Ottoman Arab world, see Sayyid Ali, *al-Tatawwur al-Tarikhi*.

21. Decree no. 11, promulgated on November 1, 1918, listed the different currencies acceptable for the purpose of military payments. A supplementary decree, no. 31, on November 24, made Egyptian paper money legal tender; anyone refusing to accept it was liable to imprisonment for up to six months. For the full text of decrees 11 and 31, see Oughourlian, *Histoire de la monnaie libanaise*, 18–19, 23.

22. A financial crisis beset France in March 1919 when British war credit was terminated, since German reparations were far from collectable. De Caix's comments were addressed to the Permanent Mandates Commission in 1926. He was the accredited representative of the French government at the time; see Himadeh, *Monetary and Banking System of Syria*, 61–63.

23. The Syrian lira became the "official money" in the "west zone" of allied-controlled territory through a unilateral decree (no. 129) issued on March 31, 1920, by the newly appointed French high commissioner General Henri Gouraud; see ibid., app. 1, 317–18.

24. Ibid., 61–63.

25. Philip S. Khoury, *Syria and the French Mandate*, 40.

26. Other demands in Gouraud's ultimatum included unconditional recognition of the French mandate, a reduction in the size of the Syrian army, the abolition of conscription, punishment for those who attacked French detachments, and French military control of Aleppo and the Rayaq-Aleppo railway; see Hourani, *Syria and Lebanon*, 54. The Syrian lira was declared official money in the east zone on August 9, 1920, by decree no. 302. Two years later, on June 28, 1922, decree no. 1459 proclaimed the Syrian territories under French rule to be a single monetary and customs unit; see Oughourlian, *Histoire de la monnaie libanaise*, 28.

27. Armed members of the Armenian Revolutionary Federation, or Dashnaktsutiun, stormed the BIO's premises in Istanbul on August 26, 1896, to protest Ottoman policies towards Armenians; see Balakian, *Burning Tigris*, 103–15.

28. Clay, *Gold for the Sultan*, 74.

29. At a general meeting at 7 rue Meyerbeer in Paris on January 2, 1919, the shareholders of the newly established Banque de Syrie declared a starting share capital of 10M francs. This was raised to 20M francs the following year and to 25M on December 13, 1921, after the BIO transferred assets valued at 5.5M francs, including its Beirut, Tripoli, Saida, Zahle, Aleppo, Alexandretta, Damascus, Hama, and Homs branches, to the Banque de Syrie; see Oughourlian, *Histoire de la monnaie libanaise*, 62–63. Headquartered in Paris, and with an office in Marseilles, the Banque de Syrie had opened additional branches in Deir-e-Zor, Latakia, Idlib, Tartous, and Soueida by 1935; see Himadeh, *Monetary and Banking System of Syria*, 138.

30. On May 23, 1921, a year before France was officially granted mandatory power in Syria, and two years before the mandate came into effect, the French finance minister acknowledged receipt of confirmation by the Banque de Syrie that

its parent bank, the BIO, had completely transferred its assets in Syrian territories in which "France exerts its mandate" to the Banque de Syrie; see Oughourlian, *Histoire de la monnaie libanaise*, 63–65.

31. Since the Treaty of Sèvres, which was signed on August 10, 1920 and partitioned the Turkish mainland among allied forces, was never ratified by the Turkish government, the Banque de Syrie's citation of it as a legal justification in order to formalize its new privileges in Syria was questionable, Oughourlian points out. In its appeal to the French Finance Ministry, the bank also recommended keeping the franc as the base currency of circulation. For all correspondence references, see ibid., 64.

32. Soubhy Barakat, president of the Federation of Syrian States, Colonel Toufic Bey el Atrache, representing the state of Jabal Druze, and Privat-Antoine Aubouard, the French governor of Greater Lebanon, signed the 1924 Banque de Syria et du Grand Liban accord, assisted by Secretary-General Auguste Adib Pasha. Local governments demanded that Syrians participate in ownership and management of the bank and exercise a supervisory role. In response, the bank made a noncontrolling 16 percent of shares (eight thousand shares out of fifty-one thousand) available for purchase on the local market, but only half of these were bought, according to French high commissioner Robert de Caix,. Four members, two from the Syrian Federation and two from Greater Lebanon, were added to the ten-member board of directors. An eight-member committee of local shareholders was also formed, but its function was consultative not executive, largely confined to advice regarding credit extension queries. The managing general director, a Frenchman, delegated the day-to-day carrying out of business to his assistant, usually a local; see Himadeh, *Monetary and Banking System of Syria*, 69–72, 139, 319.

33. All banking and credit institutions, as well as public and private administrations and commercial businesses, had to set prices and draft contracts in Syrian liras. Offenders were subject to imprisonment or fines. In addition to decrees 11, 31, 129, 302, and 1459 discussed so far, decrees 653 and 956 of September 28, 1926, and April 11, 1927, established the Lebano-Syrian gold piaster as a money of account. But the high commissioner annulled those with decree no. 2094, which required that "all budgets, taxes, fees, contracts, and in general all public finances and prices of all private establishments under public control, beginning September 1, 1928, must be established in Syrian paper money"; see Himadeh, *Monetary and Banking System of Syria*, 96.

34. For transitional provisions to settle older debts in Egyptian currency, see articles 8 and 9 of decree 129, ibid., app. 1, 318.

35. For details concerning the unpopularity of the franc exchange standard among the local population, see ibid., 84–87.

36. The more a city like Beirut adopted Syrian paper money, the more it was affected by currency fluctuations. On the preference for Turkish gold money and the existence of a dual currency regime, see ibid., 102–12. al-'Azm confirms Hima-

NOTES

deh's assertion that Turkish gold coin remained the primary medium of exchange, at least until 1928; see al-'Azm, *Mudhakkirat Khalid al-'Azm*, 2: 80.

37. Rogan, *Frontiers of the State in the Late Ottoman Empire*, 18.

38. Ibid., 102–3.

39. French financial groups that set up shop in the empire outside of Istanbul included Société générale, which set up the Crédit générale ottomane in 1869 with a share capital of 50 million francs. The mother bank also later bought Salonica Bank, established in 1888 by the Rothschild Group. Earlier, in 1875, Crédit lyonnais opened two branches in Beirut and Jerusalem and in addition to commercial business relating to silk exports to Lyon, took part in financing public debt through the issuing of diversified loans. German capital was a latecomer to this bank rush, setting up the Deutsche-Palestina Bank in 1889 and Deutsche-Orient Bank in 1906; see Achi and Ayache, *Tarikh al-Masarif fi Lubnan*, 37–40.

40. On the rise of the silk industry in the nineteenth century and its role in linking Mount Lebanon to French capital, see Chevallier, *Mujtama' Jabal Lubnan*. On the founding of local money houses, see ibid., 51–53.

41. "Bursat Bayrut," *al-Masarif*, December 1963, 46.

42. U.S. embassy Beirut to Department of State, May 9, 1952, FN 883a.131/5-952; Central Decimal File 1950–54; RG 59; NAB.

43. Under the 1924 convention, the bank retained a monopoly on issuing bank notes and acquired two additional powers: holding deposits of public funds and floating public loans by third parties. It also became the government's lender of first resort. The government put its gendarmerie in the bank's service gratis, adding to its aura of being a state bank. In return for these privileges, the Lebanese and Syrian governments were granted a share of the profits earned from issuing bank notes and were offered a free advance of relatively small value redeemable at the time of expiry of the convention. The bank would also safe-keep public securities and transfer public funds without charge. For the full text of the 1924 convention detailing the duties and privileges of the BSGL, see ibid., app. 2, 319–29.

44. For a list of dates and names of various missions and studies, see ibid., 153n43.

45. See the full text of the 1924 convention detailing the duties and privileges of the BSL, ibid., app. 2.

46. Between 1925 and 1932, the BSL's net annual earnings as a percentage of paid-up capital ranged from 17.3 to 26.5 percent (2.6 and 3.7 million francs); see ibid., 161, table 29. In 1932, BSGL deposited funds invested in French government securities or other foreign obligations guaranteed by the Bank of France amounted to about half of the BSGL's deposit liability; see ibid., 163. Asfour pointed out the harm precipitated by the constant currency fluctuations. As a result of pegging the lira to the franc, the building up of exchange reserves was mainly aimed at providing for the population's need for currency for transaction and liquidity purposes, rather than for the import of capital goods; see Asfour, *Syria: Development and Monetary Policy*, 52.

47. Achi and Ayache, *Tarikh al-Masarif fi Lubnan*, 83.

48. For a list of BSL branches established during the mandate period, see Himadeh, *Monetary and Banking System of Syria*, 165.

49. In 1914, France was already the largest single investor in Syria with 200M francs concentrated in public utilities, transportation infrastructure such as railways, and tobacco and silk production. In the interwar period alone, an additional billion francs were invested in the region. The bulk of this investment went to financing foreign trade with France; see Philip S. Khoury, *Syria and the French Mandate*, 49–50, which argues that France's financial policy in the Levant was designed to serve two long-term goals: "perpetuate her political domination . . . and, whenever possible, to promote her economic interests there" (ibid., 85). on the eve of World War I, France was the Ottoman empire's leading creditor; see Himadeh, *Monetary and Banking System of Syria*, 40.

50. The Banque française de Syrie (est. 1919), believed wholly owned by Société générale, was a commercial bank with branches in Beirut, Aleppo, Damascus, and Tripoli and capital of 10M francs (25 percent paid up). Crédit foncier d'Algérie et de Tunisie was a much larger corporation with a head office in Algiers and central one in Paris. In 1932, the bank boasted 132 branches worldwide. They included four in Syria, with the first one opened in Beirut in 1921. The bank conducted all sorts of financial business, ranging from commercial to large-scale mortgage and investment banking. The Compagnie algérienne was a major bank that expanded its business into Syria later than the other two (1931) by opening a branch in Beirut. It dealt with both commercial and investment operations. Non-French banks included the Banco di Roma, which opened three branches in 1919, at Beirut, Damascus, and Aleppo. The Anglo-Palestine bank, the bank of the Zionist movement, shut up shop in 1933. Himadeh laments the difficulty of evaluating the extent of business of these banks in the Levant, because at the time, their annual statements were consolidated, with no specification of the Levant share; see Himadeh, *Monetary and Banking System of Syria*, 165–68.

51. For more on the organization, administration, and operations of state agricultural banks, see ibid., 233–39.

52. Large-scale projects financed by Crédit foncier d'Algérie et de Tunisie included Eléctricité d'Alep and Société des grands hotels du Levant as well as the co-founding of the Compagnie libano-syrienne des tabacs, which succeeded the Régie des tabacs. The Syrian government attempted to establish an industrial bank dedicated to economic development, issued a decree to this end in 1929, and sought the approval of the High Commissariat, but six years later the project was yet to bear fruit; see Himadeh, *Monetary and Banking System of Syria*, 129–30. On the finance methods of national industries, see ibid., 202–4. On the share capital and founding history of Banque Misr-Syrie-Liban, see Achi and Ayache, *Tarikh al-Masarif fi Lubnan*, 111.

53. One of the main bankruptcies that triggered calls for regulating the banking professions was that of Kiryakos and Zuheir that took place on March 10,

1932. For details, see Achi and Ayache, *Tarikh al-Masarif fi Lubnan*, 117–19. For more on the activities and areas of specialization of foreign versus so-called native banks, see Himadeh, *Monetary and Banking System of Syria*, 131–34, and on why local discount houses, moneylenders, and banking operators survived amid fierce foreign competition, ibid., 186–89.

54. On the emergence of mass politics in this period, see Thompson, "Colonial Welfare State in Syria and Lebanon," 62.

55. The Common Interests Department, formed in 1928, fell under the direct control of the French high commissioner. A transfer to local governments did eventually take place on January 4, 1944. A new Syro-Lebanese administrative body was established to take over. The Higher Council for the Common Interests (HCCI) embodied the promise of institutional cooperation of the two countries in the age of independence. Such high hopes evaporated as the HCCI turned into the primary instrument of discord and ultimate economic separation; see Chaitani, *Post-Colonial Syria*, 18–21.

56. Frangieh's defense of the 1937 treaty was detailed in a report prepared for its ratification in parliament and published by the mouthpiece of Lebanon's constitutionalist bloc, *Le Jour*, no 3 (July 1937). Frangieh' s fellow constitutionalist Habib Abi Shahla considered the report a "wonder among the wonders of the science of money and law"; see Frangieh and Frangieh, *Hamid Frangieh*, 119–25.

57. The agreement was ratified on June 2, 1937. For more details on its provision, see ibid. The concession's extension was slated to begin starting from the date of expiry of the 1924 concession, i.e., April 1, 1939. Syrian renewal triggered the resignation of the Quwwatli government as rumors spread that Jamil Mardam, who had negotiated the deal in Paris, had agreed to secret clauses; see Philip S. Khoury, *Syria and the French Mandate*, 489, 568, 572.

58. On the failure to reach an agreement with the Syrian government and the unilateral decision by France to renew the concession, as well as regarding monetary measures taken by French authorities following the outbreak of World War II, see Achi, *al-Nizam al-Naqdi fi Suriya*, 8, 9, 27. These measures included bans or restrictions on contracting financial obligations in gold or any derivatives (such as gold currencies or jewelry). As late as March 1943, General Catroux forbade banks, financial corporations, and any other legal persons from issuing loans backed by bullion or gold-made material; see Achi and Ayache, *Tarikh al-Masarif fi Lubnan*, 81. On the Vichy theft of gold reserves, see Chaitani, *Post-Colonial Syria*, 95. The office des changes was nominally handed over to local government under the 1944 accord; see Gates, *Merchant Republic of Lebanon*, 42–43.

59. On the role of MESC in the reshaping of state-market relations in Syria and Lebanon and the institutional impact they had on local governance, see Heydemann, "War, Keynesianism, and Colonialism."

60. Khalid al-'Azm, then Syrian minister of finance, said he came up with this compromise settlement while attending a banquet held by Foreign Minister Jamil Mardam in honor of General Catroux the day before the latter's departure for

Algeria, where the Anglo-French monetary accord was signed; see al-'Azm, *Mudhakkirat Khalid al-'Azm*, 2: 85–87.

61. Translated excerpts from the French memos (March and December 1946) abrogating the sterling accords of 1944 can be found in Frangieh and Frangieh, *Hamid Frangieh*, 278–80. The agreement with the BSL would see the transfer of close to 16.6 million francs to the bank as a final measure of revaluating the bank's holdings in francs that had lost value after the latter's depreciation. The BSL deal was ratified by the French national assembly on August 23, 1947.

62. The money paper supply more than quadrupled in one year, surging from around 30 million liras in 1939 to 142 million in 1940; ibid., 279.

63. The Lebanese government lamented the disorder brought by France's action to the economy at large and the state's budget in specific in a memo it sent to the U.S. delegation in Beirut in early 1947. In response, the U.S. State Department opined that France was only "morally" obliged to fulfill its commitment of currency coverage and linked any backing of Lebanon's position to the latter's accession to the IMF. Similar appeals by Lebanese officials for foreign support were made to the British government, but conversations with British and U.S. officials convinced the Lebanese that London had no interest in the Paris negotiations; see ibid., 284–86. For the claim by Frangieh that Egypt and Saudi Arabic had also turned down requests for currency coverage, see Gates, *Merchant Republic of Lebanon*, 97.

64. President Bishara Khoury's administration invited van Zeeland to Beirut for consultation in April 1947, and while in Lebanon, he received a similar invitation to Damascus. On his advice, see Khoury, *Haqaiq Lubnaniyyah*, 86. Van Zeeland was also invited to meet with the Lebanese delegation in Paris during the negotiations (see Frangieh and Frangieh, *Hamid Frangieh*, 286, 287, 304, 305). Returning to Beirut in April 1948, he reportedly told Joseph Oughourlian, a delegation member and presidential economic consultant, that the treaty was "really bad" (see Oughourlian, *Histoire de la monnaie libanaise*, 117–22). "I don't know what makes [Lebanon's laissez-faire economy] work, but it's doing very well and I won't advise you to touch it," he allegedly said, however (Gates, *Merchant Republic of Lebanon*, xv).

65. The Paris negotiations kicked off at 5:30 pm on Wednesday, October 1, 1947 at the Quay d'Orsay (salon de l'Horloge) with the presence of France's deputy prime minister and acting minister of foreign affairs, M. Teitgan, and the attendance of the three delegations of France, Syria, and Lebanon, headed by Armand Gazal, Khalid al-'Azm, and Hamid Frangieh respectively. Joseph Oughourlian was a member of the Lebanese delegation. See Oughourlian, *Histoire de la monnaie libanaise*, 110–15.

66. The French assessed Troupes spéciales expenses at 184 million liras, which would have reduced the total debt owing to Lebanon and Syria by 40 percent (the total being estimated at 420 million liras). Another sticky point was the cost of French military gear left behind in Lebanon, which France valued at 7 million liras, while counterestimates sent to Frangieh from Beirut did not exceed half a

million. In his dispatches to Beirut, Frangieh expressed his frustration at the tardiness of the Lebanese government in providing him with detailed and "reliable" counterestimates, some of which varied drastically from those of the French; see Frangieh and Frangieh, *Hamid Frangieh*, 290–96.

67. When Khoury cabled Frangieh to say that a Syro-Lebanese summit was planned and asked Busson to return to Beirut, Frangieh cabled back seeking further details and describing Busson's presence in Paris as "necessary"; ibid., 298. When Busson was in Beirut, Khoury delegated the hammering out of draft agreements with Damascus to Busson while the president was on a trip to Iraq in late November 1947. He brought Busson—and Michel Chiha—along for meetings held with Syrian officials at the Bekaa valley town of Chtaura for consultation, and when the French franc collapsed on January 24, 1948, Khoury spent the "entire night" with Busson considering all the options available to avoid a subsequent collapse of the Lebanese lira; see Khoury, *Haqaʿiq Lubnaniyyah*, 3: 87–90.

68. According to the Lebanese periodical *Le Commerce du Levant*, al-ʿAzm attended a meeting of the BSL's consultative committee on credit policy in 1940; see Achi and Ayache, *Tarikh al-Masarif fi Lubnan*, 85–87.

69. For details on exchanges between al-ʿAzm and Busson in relation to the 1944 accord and five years later pertaining to the Zaim decree and the renewal of the BSL concession, see al-ʿAzm, *Mudhakkirat Khalid al-ʿAzm*, 2: 86–95.

70. Chaitani, *Post-Colonial Syria*, 101–3.

71. Lebanon's Maronite Patriarch Antoine Arida issued a memorandum objecting to the HCCI as a body whose legislative powers allegedly infringed on the sovereignty and independence of Lebanon. To assuage his concerns, a bill was sent by Lebanese President Bishara Khoury to parliament to remove any such "vagueness," and Riad Solh paid a cordial visit to the patriarchate's seat in Bkirki; see ibid., 21–22.

72. On attempts by Lebanese nationalist circles to underplay the impact of monetary separation on the customs union, see ibid., 103.

73. Two financial experts, the Syrian Husni Sawwaf and the Lebanese George Hakim, were entrusted with devising measures to reduce the growing gap in the Syro-Lebanese exchange rate. A joint report was issued on September 1949 in which achieving parity between the two currencies was deemed in the interest of both countries. A Syrian recommendation to create a currency stabilization fund was supplanted by one entrusting the BSL with the task while Syria's call for declaring both currencies legal tender in both countries was deemed unrealistic by Hakim. For details on the recommendations of the two experts and subsequent correspondence between Beirut and Syria, see al-ʿAzm, *Mudhakkirat Khalid al-ʿAzm*, 2: 105–6.

74. Ibid., 2: 92.

75. As fate would have it, Sami Hinnawi's countercoup against Husni Zaim took place on August 14, 1949, the same day the latter's legislative decree renewing the BSL concession was slated for publication in the official gazette, which was the

final step needed to turn the decree into law. al-'Azm's government formed under Hinnawi halted the publication in its tracks. A legal argument over whether the decree had gone into effect ensued between Busson and the French government, on the one hand, and al-'Azm, on the other. The Hinnawi coup invested legislative powers in the executive council headed by al-'Azm that it established. The latter pounced on the opportunity and passed the needed legislation. For more details on the unraveling of Busson's scheme with Zaim, see ibid., 2: 95–96.

76. Achi, *al-Nizam al-Naqdi fi Suriya*, 110, 111.

77. For more details on the mechanisms of gradually divesting the BSL of its monetary functions, see al-'Azm, *Mudhakkirat Khalid al-'Azm*, 2: 109–15.

78. The central bank was created by government decree 87 on March 28, 1953. For more details and Shishakli's comment, see Achi, *al-Nizam al-Naqdi fi Suriya*, 256–59.

79. Christian d'Halloy, French chargé d'affaires in Damascus, to French Ministry of Foreign Affairs in Africa and the Levant, SL/5/332, CAN.

80. On Syria's measures to support its currency and develop its economy, see al-'Azm, *Mudhakkirat Khalid al-'Azm*, 2: 100–103; on the Syrian stance on economic sovereignty, see ibid., 28, 86, 91; on Syrian confidence in the Lebanese economy's ability to weather the transition to full financial independence, see Chaitani, *Post-Colonial Syria*, 100; and on Lebanon's ruling clique's approach, see Khoury, *Haqaiq Lubnaniyyah*, 3: 83, 88, and Frangieh and Frangieh, *Hamid Frangieh*, 282.

Chapter 2

1. On the influence of SERIAC, see Gates, *Merchant Republic of Lebanon*, 93.

2. Chapter epigraph: Chiha, *Propos d'économie libanaise*, 10.

3. Gates, *Merchant Republic of Lebanon*, 7. On Chehabism as the only developmental phase and its brevity and failure, see Gaspard, *Political Economy of Lebanon, 1948–2002*, 62, and Shehadi, *Idea of Lebanon*.

4. See Kingston, "Ambassador," 30–50; on the growing political and economic influence of the United States in the merchant republic era, see Gendzier, *Notes from the Minefield*.

5. Chiha, *Propos d'économie libanaise*, 10.

6. U.S. embassy officials in Beirut were not able to confirm the cause of resignation, but speculated that the BSL board in Paris was critical of Busson's alleged backroom deals at the bank in favor of his local allies. Busson was replaced by Émile Oudet; see Beirut embassy to U.S. Secretary of State, telegram 758, June 14, 1951; FN 883a.14/6-1451; Central Decimal File 1950–54; RG 59; NAB.

7. Rosenberg, *Financial Missionaries*, 15. Willis served as the first president of the Philippines National Bank, which was set up in 1916 by American business interests with the collusion of Filipino landed elites under U.S. government supervision; see Nagano, *State and Finance in the Philippines, 1898–1941*, illustrations, 66–69.

8. Rosenberg, *Financial Missionaries*, 53.

9. Schuker, "Money Doctors between the Wars," 67.

10. Flandreau, "Crises and Punishment," 26.

11. For a definition of embedded liberalism, see Helleiner, "Southern Side," 249. On U.S. geostrategic motivations, see ibid., 256.

12. For list of FRB missions, see ibid., 251.

13. Ibid., 255–59.

14. IMF officials pointed out that "no balance of payments figures are available for Lebanon. The only official information on the subject is a passage in the Annual Report of the Banque de Syrie et du Liban"; see IMF, secretary to Executive Board, August 28, 1950, IMF/SM/50/521; EBD Collection; Ref. 287697.

15. IMF, secretary to Executive Board, memorandum on monetary systems by the Fund's research department, August, 29, 1946, IMF/RD/46/16; EBD Collection; Ref. 273410.

16. IMF, report titled "Balance of Payments of Syria and Lebanon," July 29, 1947, IMF/RD/47/334; EBD Collection; Ref. 271573. See also IMF, secretary to Executive Board, survey of the economy of Syria and Lebanon, March 12, 1948, IMF/RD/48/554; EBD Collection; Ref. 294769.

17. Portions were to be calculated on the basis of population ratios or national income ratios of the two countries, with the former leading to a lower quota than the latter; see IMF, "Analysis of Quota for Lebanon," August 8, 1946, IMF/RD/46/6. The Fund struck an informal understanding with Lebanon (and Syria) that the two countries would not draw on it "for the time being" once their currencies' par values were accepted; see IMF, secretary to Executive Board, March 12, 1948, IMF/RD/48/554; EBD Collection; Ref. 294769.

18. Lebanese government gold purchases amounted to an estimated $US15M bought in local market and an additional $US3M from the U.S. Federal Reserve bank; see IMF, secretary to Executive Board, May 8, 1950, suppl. 1, IMF/SM/50/472; EBD Collection; Ref. 288575.

19. U.S. officials sent a detailed report on French control of banking in Lebanon, including that of Busson via the BSL; see Beirut embassy to U.S. Department of State, dispatch 669, June 13, 1951; FN 883a.14/6–1351; Central Decimal files 1950–54; RG 59; NAB.

20. The BSL was regarded as banker's bank, but was clearly no substitute for a central bank proper; see IMF, secretary to Executive Board, October 30, 1953, IMF/SM/53/87; EBD Collection; Ref. 281063.

21. The Lebanese government, like many other governments at the time, invoked the transitional period clause (Article XIV of IMF statutes) to delay exchange-rate reform. The Fund doubted the applicability of the article in the case of Lebanon but abstained from deeming such invocation unreasonable; see IMF, Executive Board minutes, October 15, 1952, IMF/EBM/52/60; EBD Collection; Ref. 282945.

22. IMF, secretary to Executive Board, March 29, 1951, IMF/SM/51/574; EBD Collection; Ref. 286457. See also ibid., suppl. 1 (Ref. 286455) and suppl. 2 (Ref. 286453).

23. IMF representatives at the consultation meeting in Mexico suggested that technical experts be sent to Lebanon to help deal with the issue of exchange rates and balance of payments, but their Lebanese counterparts did not wish for such a mission and said the problem would be discussed with the Lebanese authorities upon their return; see IMF, secretary to Executive Board, October 1, 1952, IMF/SM/52/66; EBD Collection; Ref. 283011. Lebanon did not seek the IMF's approval when it set exchange-rate policy in 1948; see IMF, secretary to Executive Board, December 10, 1948, IMF/EBD/48/386, suppl. 1; EBD Collection; Ref. 293019. It did so four years later, however, when it sought to liberalize it; see IMF, secretary to Executive Board, March 11, 1952, IMF/SM/52/15; EBD Collection; Ref. 284143.

24. For full text of the Keesing report, see IMF, acting secretary to Executive Board, May 13, 1955, IMF/SM/55/33. It was estimated that the mission would last from three to four months; idem, October 21, 1954, IMF/EBD/54/132; EBD Collection; Ref. 279243.

25. Oughourlian's disdain for foreign experts with whom he disagreed was not restricted to Keesing. Commenting on the level of experts serving on the IRFED mission during the Chehab era, Oughourlian marveled that IRFED's financial advisor had confessed to him at the time that he was a firefighter; see Oughourlian, *Histoire de la monnaie libanaise,* 177. The excerpt quoted above was part of an article published by Oughourlian on November 1, 1955 in the mouthpiece of Chihism, *Le Jour;* see ibid., 171. I have translated the original French text into English.

26. This and all future quotations in the remainder of this section of Oughourlian's commentary on the Keesing report are from Oughourlian, *Histoire de la monnaie libanaise,* 171–75.

27. Hall, *Political Power of Economic Ideas,* 7.

28. The term was coined by another famed Lebanese economist and technocrat, Georges Corm; see Corm, "al-Itqtisad fi Muhadarat al-Nadwah al-Lubnaniyyah," 577.

29. Participants in these studies included graduating and postgraduate students of economics and commerce of the class of 1932–33; see Himadeh, *Economic Organization of Syria,* vii. Among Himadeh's eager students and admirers of at the time was Yusif Sayigh, a business administration student who would become one of the principal second-generation members of the AUB group. In his autobiography, Sayigh describes Himadeh as an upright, hard-to-please instructor and an avid researcher who tried to instill that work ethic into his students; see Sayigh, *Yusif Sayigh,* 152. On the role of Henry Parker Willis, see the autograph dedication to him by Himadeh in a copy of the latter's *Monetary and Banking System of Syria* at the University of Toronto's Robarts Library.

30. Hakim taught courses on commercial law and the history of economic ideologies, including one on Marx, and shared books on political economy with Sayigh outside the classroom. These included the work of the post-Keynesian Joan Robinson whose theories of imperfect markets posed a serious challenge to classical economics. For Sayigh's account on Hakim, see ibid., 144, 152, 174.

31. The daily *Bayrut al-Masaʿ* solicited Himadeh's opinion on the best way to support the lira following the 1948 monetary treaty with France and published his view; see Menassa, *Plan de reconstruction,* 258.

32. For "notre ami" reference, see ibid., 92.

33. Himadeh delivered his Cénacle libanais lecture on January 6, 1947; see Himadeh, "Mushkilaatunah al-Iqtisadiyyah," 101–11.

34. Hakim delivered his Cénacle libanais lecture on January 5, 1953; see Hakim, "Tanzim al-Inma al-Iqtisadi," 227–33.

35. Although he expressed misgivings about the Lebanese government, Khalid al-ʿAzm looked favorably upon the report produced by the two-member committee of Hakim (representing the Lebanese side) and Husni Sawwaf representing the Syrian side; see al-ʿAzm, *Mudhakkirat Khalid al-ʿAzm,* 2: 105. Sawwaf was a colleague of Hakim's at AUB, which suggests that the influence of AUB economists shaped Syro-Lebanese economic relations on both sides of the border; see Sayigh, *Yusif Sayigh,* 152.

36. Hakim served as minister of finance, economy, and agriculture in the government of Khalid Shihab from September 30, 1952, till April 30, 1953, and as minister of national economy and foreign affairs in the government headed by Saeb Salam from April 30, 1953, till August 16, 1954. During his first appointment, his fellow minister Musa Mubarak resigned, reportedly due to Hakim's support for economic union with Syria; see Majid, *Tarikh al-Hukumat al-Lubnaniyyah,* 93,96.

37. In 1952, Hakim and Oughourlian were respectively replaced by Andre Tueni and Farid Solh; see IMF, secretary to Executive Board, September 1, 1949, IMF/EBD/49/509; EBD Collection; Ref. 290789, and idem, April 29, 1952, IMF/EBD/52/79; EBD Collection; Ref. 283915.

38. Badre was both mentor and colleague to Sayigh. Upon the encouragement of Badre and his mentorship, Sayigh had returned to academia in the early 1950s to teach at the AUB and later pursued a PhD in economics in the United States; see Sayigh, *Yusif Sayigh,* 296–97.

39. Klat served alongside Badre on Lebanon's Economic Planning and Development Board for several years in the 1950s–60s and wrote at least one detailed paper for the IMF, titled "Report on Economic and Financial Conditions in Syria and Lebanon" (December 15, 1949). Follow-up reports do not bear the names of their authors and some of them may have also been written by him; see IMF, secretary to Executive Board, January 30, 1950, IMF/SM/50/425; EBD Collection; Ref. 289625. Based on the biographies attached to their contributions to *MEEP* that I looked at, Klat and Badre served on the EPDB at least from 1956 to 1962 and 1955 to 1956 respectively.

40. "Memorandum on the Establishment of a Statistical and Research Institute," December 23, 1952; Folder 05500044, FA732A, R0805, Grant PA 52–174, FF Records, RAC.

41. Badre and Himadeh clashed over which department at AUB should house the institute. Himadeh argued that it should be affiliated to both, his home de-

partment of Business Administration and Badre's of Economics. Badre, however, lobbied to house it exclusively at the Economics Department and eventually got his way. Both took Sayigh on campus walks and tried to sway him to support their respective proposals but Sayigh was neutral, lest he upset either; Sayigh, *Yusif Sayigh*, 294–99. This rivalry might explain the total absence of any contribution by Himadeh to *MEEP*.

42. "Request and Authorization for Program Action," March 2, 1955; FN B-469, FA723A, R0794, Grant PA55–48, FF Records, RAC.

43. On ERI's role in the management and provision of services to ISEC, see "Support for the International Research Center," December 22, 1954; FA723A, R0794, Grant PA55–27, FF Records, RAC. Courses in the International Statistics Education Center began in November of 1954; see Porter, "Statistical Services in the Middle East," 103–4.

44. Albert Badre, foreword to the first issue of *Middle East Economic Papers*, v.

45. I deduced the outreach of these networks based on a systematic examination of *MEEP* contributions between 1954 and 1964.

46. Badre co-authored a major study of the Middle East labor market in the oil sector; see Badre and Siksek, *Manpower and Oil in Arab Countries*.

47. Sayigh's proposed conference aimed to streamline economic terminology in Arabic and address what he saw as the inadequacy of economics textbooks; see "Seminar for Teachers of Economics from Arab Countries," June 13, 1958; FN C-582; FA732A, R0796, Grant PA58–241, FF Records, RAC.

48. Earlier local attempts, including a major one by Menassa's SLEP, where Badre had worked as a rapporteur, had failed to produce convincing or authoritative results; see Menassa, *Plan de reconstruction*, 2, Arabic insert. Badre's stint as rapporteur at SLEP's Research Council had exposed him to diverse views of economists, businessmen, financiers, and government officials on the thorny subject of "invisibles"; see Badre, "Economic Development of Lebanon," 95. An IMF research department study aimed at determining Lebanon's quota cited a national income figure for the year 1940 (U.S.$100M), but does not source it; see IMF, "Analysis of Quota for Lebanon," August 8, 1946, IMF/RD/46/6; EBD Collection; Ref. 273457.

49. Corm, "al-Itqtisad fi Muhadarat al-Nadwah al-Lubnaniyyah," 577.

50. Badre's series spanned the years 1950 to 1958; the series generated by the Economic Division of the U.S. embassy in Beirut surveyed the years 1954 to 1957. On the impact of Badre's study, see Beirut embassy to U.S. Department of State, dispatch 502, March 31, 1952; FN 883a.10/3–3152; 1950–54 Central Decimal File; RG59; NAB. U.S. embassy numbers are quoted by Benjamin Higgin's authoritative study "Financing Lebanese Development: A Report on Fiscal Policy" issued in 1960 in Beirut; see Hoss, "Roles of Central Banking in Lebanon," 7–9.

51. Gaspard, *Political Economy of Lebanon, 1948–2002*, 242.

52. Other members of this generation include Edmund Asfour, George Medawar, and Yahya Mahmasani (a student of Paul Klat's). The latter two's doctoral disser-

tations were dedicated to the question of Lebanon's monetary policy and central banking reform respectively; see Medawar, "Monetary Policy in Lebanon," and Mahmasani, "Central Bank for Lebanon." Hoss worked as Tapline accountant from 1952 until 1954 and as a correspondent for Beirut's Chamber of Commerce from 1954 till 1955; see Hoss, "Roles of Central Banking in Lebanon," 140.

53. American institutionalism has itself suffered from historiographical neglect and intellectual dismissal as a marginal current and passing phase of economic thought. Recent revisionist history resituated the movement as part of mainstream economic thought that left its mark on economic praxis and policy; see Rutherford, *Institutionalist Movement*.

54. On the defining features of the institutionalist movement, see ibid., 8–9.

55. According to Meyer, "Economic Thought," 66–68, nineteenth-century German nationalism, classical British economics, and the mercantilism of Louis XIV were all influential in the Middle East of the 1920s, but institutionalism was the dominant school of thought.

56. On Himadeh as a student of Wesley Mitchell's, see Meyer, "Economic Thought," 68. See also Shehadi, *Idea of Lebanon*, 22.

57. AUB reformists used a similar strategy to their American counterparts in relation to influencing policy. ERI's mandate and activities in some ways resembled those of the U.S. National Bureau of Economic Research (NBER), which was led by Mitchell. A notable difference was the link each had to the state. ERI was a private academic venture, whereas NBER was part and parcel of the state apparatus. On NBER, see Rutherford, *Institutionalist Movement*, 257–88.

58. Sayigh's preparation for his MA in 1950 under Badre supervision included studying Keynesianism. He had not previously heard of Keynes. See Sayigh, *Yusif Sayigh*, 294. On the type of Keynesianism adopted by the institutionalists, see Badre, "Economic Development of Lebanon."

59. The major tenets of AUB's developmental institutionalists summarized in the text here are based on my survey of their writings in *MEEP* and their lectures at the Cénacle libanais. Chiha's views on the economy are best summarized in his collected essays on the subject, *Propos d'économie libanaise*.

60. Yusif Sayigh, "The Place of Agriculture in Economic Development," *Land Economics,* November 1959, folder 33, box 2, series 833, RG 1.2, RF, RAC.

61. The key according to Menassa was finding the right formula to preserve liberty and private initiative while preventing the "grave errors of an unscrupulous and individualistic capitalism" (Menassa, *Plan de reconstruction*, 60).

62. The refrain of Lebanon as a refuge for minorities was one of Chiha's tropes for the country (crossroads of three continents, juxtaposition of sea and mountains, outward-looking) based on geographic determinism. For a critical reading of Chiha's ideology and tropes, see Traboulsi, *Silat bi-la Wasl.*

63. See Corm, "al-Itqtisad fi Muhadarat al-Nadwah al-Lubnaniyyah," 278.

64. Badre mused that van Zeeland's mythical "deep secret" of the Lebanese economy became so powerful that it entered Lebanese popular tradition through

its caricatural commemoration by the folklore artist Omar Z'inni; see Badre, "Nahwa Afaaq Iqtisadiyyah Jadidah," 370.

65. Ibid., 373–74.

66. Ibid., 91, 99–106.

67. On Menassa's praise of the franc exchange standard, see ibid., 253. On France's role as "super-state" and the divergence of Syrian and Lebanese interests, see ibid., 72. On intra-SLEP disagreement regarding monetary policy, see ibid., 259.

68. On deeming the IMF framework in the interest of Lebanon, see Menassa, *Plan de reconstruction*, 256. On details of plan to solicit U.S. dollars, see ibid., 264–65. The pro-American, right-wing ideologue Charles Malik also sought U.S. economic patronage after Lebanon's weaning from Mother France; see Traboulsi, *Silat bi-la Wasl*, 246.

69. On the immediate and long-term monetary challenges, see Menassa, *Plan de reconstruction*, 78–79. On best measures to remedy monetary challenge, see ibid., 265–66.

70. On proposed composition of the currency board and need to preserve BSL arrangement, see Menassa, *Plan de reconstruction*, 261–62.

71. See Yaffi, "Monetary and Banking System of Lebanon"; Hoss, "Roles of Central Banking in Lebanon"; Mahmasani, "Central Bank for Lebanon"; and Medawar, "Monetary Policy in Lebanon."

72. Himadeh framed the need for a single central banking authority in relation to the quest for currency stability, price controls, and, to a lesser extent, "economic progress"; see Himadeh, *Monetary and Banking System of Syria*, 276–77.

73. Plumptre, *Central Banking in the British Dominions*, and Sen, *Central Banking in Undeveloped Money Markets*, were the two main works cited by third-generation AUB scholars. Hoss was also influenced by Milton Friedman's writings on "positive economics" but did not always agree with his prognosis regarding money market management; see Hoss, "Roles of Central Banking in Lebanon," 82, 105, 118, 120.

74. On the universality of central bank objectives but specificity of its institutional organization and operational strategies; see Sen, *Central Banking in Undeveloped Money Markets*, 8–9.

75. Money markets in the British Dominions reached a certain level of maturity thanks to World War I and its financial exigencies. They thus stood halfway between fully developed markets of imperialist centers like London and New York and global south ones. On the role of World War I in developing money markets in the British Dominions, see Plumptre, *Central Banking in the British Dominions*, 9–12.

76. On cash reserve requirements and variation as the most effective tools of central banking in underdeveloped markets, see Sen, *Central Banking in Undeveloped Money Markets*, 143. On characteristics and operations in a developed money market, see Plumptre, *Central Banking in the British Dominions*, 4–5. On the importance and requirement of banks supplying information, the

"raw material of control," see Sen, *Central Banking in Undeveloped Money Markets,* 200–201.

77. Yaffi proposed the establishment of a supervision and examination department that could demand and periodically monitor data independently of the central bank if need be. He also recommended the appointment of an auditor and the establishment of a department of research that would produce a monthly bulletin with analysis of the status of the banking sector; see Yaffi, "Monetary and Banking System of Lebanon," 240–41.

78. On Himadeh's critique of BSL, see Himadeh, *Monetary and Banking System of Syria,* 310.

79. On the BSL's failure to act as central bank during Korean War, see Yaffi, "Monetary and Banking System of Lebanon," 134. On the BSL's passive role in credit control, government pressure on it to act during the Suez crisis and local disturbances of 1958, and its lack of legal mandate and authority, see Hoss, "Roles of Central Banking in Lebanon," 62–63, 110.

80. Yaffi was able to obtain BSL statistics from the Ministry of Finance in his capacity as a member of the EPDB; see Yaffi, "Monetary and Banking System of Lebanon," 119–34. Hoss reported that BSL had six times more public deposits than private ones by end of 1958 and 1959; see Hoss, "Roles of Central Banking in Lebanon," 89. On the declining proportion of private deposits and increasing government ones, see Mahmasani, "Central Bank for Lebanon," 62–63.

81. On the FRB and Bank of France as models, see Himadeh, *Monetary and Banking System of Syria,* 277–78. On the BSL as the most suitable body to be turned into central bank, see ibid., 310. On board composition and government authority, see ibid., 312.

82. On the four options of transition, see Yaffi, "Monetary and Banking System of Lebanon," 208–10. On the endorsement of EPDB for the fourth option and the share capital deemed adequate, see ibid., 214–15, 225.

83. See Mahmasani, "Central Bank for Lebanon," 73, 89, 103.

84. Yaffi, "Monetary and Banking System of Lebanon," 226–27, proposed that the minister of finance should be the honorary chairman of the Council of Money and Credit, with the central bank governor serving as chairman in his absence, and that its members should include two recognized experts, in the fields of commercial banking and industry and commerce respectively; a fourth, monetary expert from the EPDB; a university professor of economics; and the director general of the Ministry of Finance. Mahmasani adopted Yaffi's proposal and stressed the need for separate and independent management by experts; see Mahmasani, "Central Bank for Lebanon," 107–8,110.

85. On Himadeh's aversion to revolution, see Himadeh, "Mushkilaatunah al-Iqtisadiyyah," 104. On Badre's praise of imperialism, see Badre, "Economic Development of Lebanon," 2–3.

86. Yaffi, "Monetary and Banking System of Lebanon," 215, 225; Mahmasani, "Central Bank for Lebanon," 108.

87. Yaffi, "Monetary and Banking System of Lebanon," 138.

Chapter 3

1. Chapter epigraph: Pierre Eddé quoted in Qubaysi, "Qissat al-Bunuk fi Lubnan," *al-Masarif*, July 1963, 54.

2. Philip Hitti to Henry A. Byroade, assistant secretary of state, U.S. Department of State, December 15, 1953; FN 883a.14/12–1553; 1950–54 Central Decimal File; RG 59; NAB.

3. French and Arabic versions of the petition had been published on June 24, 1953 in four of Lebanon's major newspapers: *al-Nahar*, *L'Orient*, *al-Hayat*, and the *Beirut Gazette*. The signatories were: Kamal Jumblat's Socialist Progressive Party (SPP); Pierre Gemayel's Kataeb and its adversaries al-Najadah and the Syrian Socialist Nationalist Party (SSNP); the two Armenian parties, Henchak and Ramgavar; the General Arab Feminist Union; the Lebanese National Party; the National Youth Party; the National Representative Party; the Fruit Growers Association of Tripoli; and the Union of Agriculturalists of Saida. A copy of the petition was enclosed with Hitti's letter to Byroade (ibid.). For a list of the signatories, see Michel Saab, American Inter-Asian Trading Co. Inc., to Henry A. Byroade, U.S. assistant secretary of state, July 1, 1953; FN 883a.14/7–153; 1950–54 Central Decimal File; RG 59; NAB.

4. *Bayt al-mal* is the term used to refer to the treasury in Islamic tradition. Its use by the petitioners to promote the concept of a central bank in a manner that would resonate with large swathes of the population may have been deliberate, which is why I have decided to transliterate it. Saab's translation of the statement in his letter to Byroade omits the *bayt al-mal* reference and speaks of a central *reserve* [emphasis added] bank; see Saab to Byroade, July 1, 1953; FN 883a.14/7–153; 1950–54 Central Decimal File; RG 59; NAB. My translation is from the original Arabic text as found in newspaper clippings sent with Hitti's letter to Byroade cited in n. 2 above.

5. The Syrian Central Bank was established by law on March 28, 1953, by decree 87; see Achi, *al-Nizam al-Naqdi fi Suriya*, 8.

6. The title suggested for the commercial bank was the Lebanon-America Bank Ltd. The capital was to be split 50–50 between residents in Lebanon and others; see letter from Commercial Secretariat, Beirut Legation, Beirut to Foreign Office London, December, 6, 1950, FO 371/82285/ E L1115/2, United Kingdom National Archives (TNA).

7. For Menassa's argument, see chapter 2.

8. Sayigh, *Entrepreneurs of Lebanon*. For details of this study, see ibid., 46–47.

9. Ibid., 43–44.

10. Ibid., 118.

11. These claims seem to run contrary to the study's own findings that entrepreneurship of the Schumpeterian type was rare.

12. Sayigh's "social fragmentation" is presumably a reference to sectarianism, though Sayigh does not use that term.

13. The sociopolitical constraints preventing reform and facilitating a culture of corruption in the public sector are also factored in as reasons for seeking economic "freedom" and shielding the private sector from government planning; see Sayigh, *Entrepreneurs of Lebanon*, 3–5.

14. Ibid., 125.

15. Ibid., 137.

16. Ibid., 6–11.

17. See, e.g., al-Azhari, *Numan al-Azhari*, 100, and Achi and Ayache, *Tarikh al-Masarif fi Lubnan*.

18. Beirut embassy to U.S. Department of State, dispatch 160, September 8, 1958; FN 883.14/9–858; 1955–59 Central Decimal File; RG 59; NAB.

19. Beirut embassy to U.S. Department of State, dispatch 465, February 9, 1954; FN 883a.14/2–954; 1950–54 Central Decimal File; RG 59; NAB.

20. The idea behind the bank was first broached to Lebanese President Bishara Khoury by three of its founders: Khoury's minister of finance, Hussein Uwayni; the leading Lebanese industrialist and head of Lebanon's Economic Councils, Boutros Khoury; and the Brazilian businessman George Maalouf. The trio envisioned a financial institution that would develop business links between Lebanon and its expat community in Brazil. The president gave his blessing. Maalouf, who was also Philip Takla's father-in-law, managed to get the Lebanese-Brazilian cotton-weaving industry mogul Nagib Jafet, on board. On the origins of BLOM, see al-Azhari, *Nu'man al-Azhari*, 78–79. AUB's Jafet library is named after Nagib's father, Nami Jafet. The family's original Arabic name was Yafith. On history of Jafet family and their success in building a cotton-weaving industrial empire, see www.aub.edu.lb/ulibraries/about/Pages/namijafet.aspx.

21. According to longtime BLOM manager Numan al-Azhari, meetings of the bank's board of directors were jolly occasions. Uwayni, Khoury, and Takla would often talk politics, crack jokes, and then sign minutes without reading them. See *Nu'man al-Azhari*, 80–83.

22. As the chairman and deputy chairman of BLOM's board of directors, Uwayni and Boutros Khoury were the Lebanese face of the bank. Other shareholders included Uwayni's longtime Saudi business partner Ibrahim Shakir and the former Saudi minister of finance Surur al-Sabban. For a list of Uwayni's businesses and partnerships, see Gehchan, *Hussein 'Uwayni*, 561–62. 'Uwayni's first encounter with Abd al-Aziz Ibn Saud took place when he was sent as an emissary by the Lebanese American writer Amin Rihani to mediate between Ibn Saud and his Hijazi rival, Ali Ibn Hussein. On Uwayni's mission to Ibn Saud, see ibid., 25–34. On Uwayni's role as an agent of Saudi capital and a political representative, see ibid., 73–91. On the overall early penetration of Saudi influence into Lebanon, see Traboulsi, "Saudi Expansion."

23. Crédit foncier d'Algérie et de Tunisie (CFAT) held 10 percent of BLOM's shares; see al-Azhari, *N'uman al-Azhari*, 40.

24. The bank's founders included Mohamed Ben Saud al-Saud, a member of the Saudi royal family, and the influential Lebanese politician Najib Salha, who served on the board of several top banks, including al-Ahli and Intra Bank; see Beirut embassy to U.S. Department of State, dispatch 518, March 3, 1959; FN 883a.14/3–359; 1955–59 Central Decimal File; RG 59; NAB.

25. Pharaon was president of the Compagnie immobilière libanaise, a port operator, which would have benefited greatly from the development of marine infrastructure; see Beirut embassy to U.S. Department of State, dispatch 322, FN 883a.14/12–1262; 1960–63 Central Decimal File; RG 59; NAB.

26. Zanaty had managed to bring several rich Lebanese expatriates in the United States, Cuba, and the UAR on board and was sounding the idea out to delegates at the convention; see Beirut embassy to U.S. Department of State, dispatch 130, August 26, 1959; FN 883A.14/8–2659; 1955–59 Central Decimal File; RG 59; NAB.

27. Gendzier, *Notes from the Minefield*, 88.

28. See Sayigh, *Entrepreneurs of Lebanon*, 6–11.

29. For details on the Pharaon-Khoury scheme and conversation, as well as correspondence with the U.S. ambassador in Beirut, including remarks cited, see Beirut embassy to U.S. Department of State, dispatch 566, March 31, 1959; FN 883a.14/3–3159, and dispatch 633, April 29, 1959; FN 883a.14/4–2959; 1955–59 Central Decimal File; RG 59; NAB.

30. Saab to Byroade, July 1, 1953, FN 883A.14/7–153; 1950–54 Central Decimal File; RG 59; NAB. The prominent Arab businessman and Lebanese politician Émile Bustani, who died in a plane crash in 1963, was a major advocate for an Arab Development Bank; see Beirut embassy to U.S. Department of State, dispatch 566, March 31, 1959; FN 883.14/3–3159; 1955–59 Central Decimal File; RG 59; NAB.

31. Beirut embassy to U.S. Department of State, "Report on Mr. Harold Johnson's Activities in Lebanon," enclosure no.1 in dispatch 250, November 12, 1953; FN 883a.14/11–1253; 1950–54 Central Decimal File; RG 59; NAB.

32. The Federal Bank of Lebanon (al-Bank al-Lubnani al-Muttahid) was incorporated under decree 236 on October 25, 1951. It commenced its operations in Beirut on October 31, 1952, with the professed objective of funding industrial enterprises with real estate as collateral. Its authorized capital was LL7M, with majority of shares held by the chairman of its board of director, Michel Saab. The bank's financial correspondents in the United States were at the time believed to be National City Bank of New York and the Guaranty Trust Company of New York; see Beirut embassy to U.S. Department of State, dispatch 399, January 16, 1953; FN 883A.14/1–1653; 1950–54 Central Decimal File; RG 59; NAB. By 1958, the bank had opened a branch in Baghdad; see Achi and Ayache, *Tarikh al-Masarif fi Lubnan*, 169.

33. Founders of the BNFCI included Najib Salha, a prominent capitalist and

politician who later became embroiled in the Intra Bank affair; Désiré A. Kettaneh, a member of the firm F.A. Kettaneh; the banker Michel Doumit, one of Lebanon's top gold brokers; the former Lebanese deputy minister and wealthy lumber importer George Karam; and Jean Fattal, a Lebanese of Syrian origin and partner in the Syro-Lebanese firm Khalil Fattal & Fils; see from Beirut embassy to U.S. Department of State, dispatch 54, July 26, 1953; FN 883A.14/7–2853; 1950–54 Central Decimal File; RG 59; NAB.

34. The BSL acknowledged its support for the BNFCI but denied a direct interest. The BSL's general manager, Émile Gudot, however, served as one of the directors of the Banque de Paris et de Pays-Bas, which had bought shares in the new BNFCI; see ibid.

35. Johnson's mission, which commenced on August 7 was a follow-up to an exploratory visit to Beirut in February of that year by the IBRD's special representative in Turkey, Pieter Lieftinck. Unless otherwise stated, all the information in this section on the BCAIF project in relation to the Johnson mission is from Beirut embassy to U.S. Department of State, dispatch 250, November 12, 1953; FN 883a.14/11–1253; 1950–54 Central Decimal File; RG 59; NAB.

36. On Michel and Joseph Saab's role in getting private banks on board, see ibid., with its enclosure no. 3, "Further Information on Mr. Johnson's Activities in Lebanon." The other banks were the Banque du Liban et d'Outre-Mer, the Eastern Commercial Bank, the Bank Misr-Syria Liban, and the Banque libanaise pour le commerce; see Beirut embassy to U.S. Department of State, "Mr. Johnson and the Development Bank," enclosure no. 2 in dispatch 250, November 12, 1953; FN 883a.14/11–1253; 1950–54 Central Decimal File; RG 59; NAB.

37. Raymond Hare, the U.S. Treasury attaché in Beirut, speculated—based on input from EPDB officials and private citizens—that pressure on Chamoun against a separate IBRD-sponsored industrial development bank was coming from several corners. The BSL and its allies like the BNFCI feared the bank would diminish their control over the economy, the British embassy resisted attempts to introduce the IBRD into the Near East as a "wedge for 'American Capital,'" and the communists opposed it for "obvious reasons"; see Beirut embassy to U.S. Department of State, dispatch 342, January 4, 1954; FN 883a.14/1–454; 1950–54 Central Decimal Files; RG 59; NAB. Chamoun asked Klat to come up with a plan that would modify the IBRD proposal so that the bank could dole out agricultural credit; see Beirut embassy to U.S. Department of State, dispatch 250, November 12, 1953; FN 883a.14/11–1253; 1950–54 Central Decimal File; RG 59; NAB.

38. Klat told U.S. embassy officials that Chamoun's scheme was likely to be approved by parliament and would easily obtain private loans ; see Beirut embassy to U.S. Department of State, dispatch 250, November 12, 1953; FN 883a.14/11–1253; 1950–54 Central Decimal File; RG 59; NAB.

39. For date of legal approval as well as Meyer's comments and his detailed report on BCAIF, see Beirut embassy to U.S. Department of State, dispatch 301, November 15, 1954; FN 883A.14/11–1554; 1950–54 Central Decimal File; RG

59; NAB. For date of financial constitution of the bank, see Beirut embassy to U.S. Department of State, dispatch 569, March 30, 1955; FN 883A.14/3–3055; 1955–59 Central Decimal File; RG 59; NAB.

40. Beirut embassy to U.S. Department of State, dispatch 301, November 15, 1954; FN 883A.14/11–1554; 1950–54 Central Decimal File; RG 59; NAB.

41. Saade was also a U.S. embassy informant; see Beirut embassy to U.S. Department of State, dispatch 569, March 30, 1955; FN 883a.14/3–3055; 1955–59 Central Decimal File; RG 59; NAB.

42. At the time of founding BCAIF, the amount of unpaid SCAIL agricultural loans to favored politicians that were guaranteed by the government stood at LL11M. To avoid further abuse of BCAIF loans by those indebted to SCAIL benefiting from government guarantees, a special BCAIF provision stipulated that "no loan shall be extended by the BCAIF to anyone indebted to the government or to the SCAIL with the government's guarantee and who has not paid up the amounts due and their interest on time"; see Beirut embassy to U.S. Department of State, dispatch 301, November 15, 1954; FN 883a.14/11–1554; 1950–54 Central Decimal File; RG 59; NAB. For more on the state-backed operations of SCAIL, see Gates, *Merchant Republic of Lebanon*, 34, 44, 117, 132–33.

43. Local financial circles predicted a slackening in SCAIL business once BCAIF went into operation; see Beirut embassy to U.S. Department of State, dispatch 301, November 15, 1954; FN 883a.14/11–1554; 1950–54 Central Decimal File; RG 59; NAB.

44. BCAIF statutes stipulated that the board of directors be composed of twelve members, eight of whom were to be elected by the stockholders while the remainder four were appointed by the government. Members elected by stockholders at the bank's constitutive meeting held on January 28,1955, included the chairman, Edmond Cachecho (Banque Misr-Syrie-Liban), Boutros Khoury (powerful industrialist and merchant), Munir Abu-Fadel (Intra Bank), Elia Abi-Jaoude (Banque libanaise pour le commerce) and René Letayf (BSL). The later appointment of the third-generation institutionalist Talha Yaffi as BCAIF's manager may have served to appease international interests and heed calls for "rational" and merit-based management. Yaffi served as manager in 1959 (date of appointment not mentioned in related U.S. documents). He is described by the U.S. ambassador Robert McClintock as "an honest and well educated young man" who is not seen as a "first-rate economist" but "passes as an expert in the field of finance." For more on Yaffi and members of BCAIF's board (including its chairman, Boutros Khoury) in 1959, see Beirut embassy to U.S. Department of State, dispatch 692, May 26,1959; FN 883a.14/5–2659; 1955–59 Central Decimal File; RG 59; NAB.

45. On the Eddé family's history and some of its prominent members, including Raymond and Pierre, see Saqr, *'Ailat Hakamat Lubnan*, 200–212.

46. The IBRD special envoy Harold Johnson met with Pierre Eddé during his negotiations with the Lebanese government over setting up a development bank in 1953 and thought him "intelligent and earnest but not much at home in finance";

see Beirut embassy to U.S. Department of State, "Mr. Johnson's Activities in Lebanon," enclosure no. 3 in dispatch 250, November 12, 1953; FN 883a.14/11–1253; 1950–54 Central Decimal File; RG 59; NAB.

47. Achi and Ayache, *Tarikh al-Masarif fi Lubnan*, 161. For reference to "explosive" nature of growth, see ibid., 166.

48. See ibid., 166–67, for detailed statistics on the growth of the sector over time and the difference in growth based on the classification of banks as either Lebanese or foreign.

49. For more on the impact of the creation of the Zionist state on the transfer of capital and services from Palestine to Lebanon, including the contribution to the banking sector (including Intra Bank and Arab Bank), see Hussein Abu el-Naml, "al-Isham al-Filastini," 139–48, and Abu Fakhr, "al-Filastiniyyun fi Lubnan," 149–56.

50. On the impact of these three factors combined, see Achi and Ayache, *Tarikh al-Masarif fi Lubnan*, 157. On the role of petrodollars into the flooding Lebanese capital market, see Badre, "Nahwa Afaaq Iqtisadiyyah Jadidah," 373. On the expansion of Beirut's regional role as financial entrepôt, see Gates, *Merchant Republic of Lebanon*, 115.

51. On the role of laissez-faire policy and exchange deregulation policies in sustaining this growth in the early stages of the merchant republic, see Badre, "Nahwa Afaaq Iqtisadiyyah Jadidah," 373. On the pivotal role of the banking secrecy law in the process, see Achi and Ayache, *Tarikh al-Masarif fi Lubnan*, 165.

52. The number of total banks reached 82 with 128 branches in 1964; see Banque du Liban, "Annual Report for 1964," 9. On *al-Masarif*'s caption, see Tahqiq, "Dhahirat Izdiyad 'Adad al-Masarif fi Lubnan," *al-Masarif*, February 1964, 4–13, 6.

53. Badre, "Nahwa Afaaq Iqtisadiyyah Jadidah," 373.

54. Eddé made these remarks to the paper *Commerce du Levant* on August 6, 1955; see Achi and Ayache, *Tarikh al-Masarif fi Lubnan*, 163.

55. The joint report submitted to parliament's General Assembly was prepared by the Budget and Finance Committee and Administrative and Judicial Committee; see ibid.

56. Ibid.

57. On the "golden period" of growth and nationality-based statistics cited, see Achi and Ayache, *Tarikh al-Masarif fi Lubnan*, 166–67.

58. Ibid.

59. For full text of the law, see Yafi and Yafi, *Majmuat al-Naqd wa al-Taslif*, 1: 4–5. On the income tax law of 1944 and the changes introduced by the Banking Secrecy Law of 1956, see Maurice Nasr, "al-Sirriyyah al-Masrifiyyah," *al-Masarif*, September 1964, 56–65.

60. On numbered accounts and the exclusive right of the bank manager and his deputy to know names, see Article 3 of the Banking Secrecy Law, Yafi and Yafi, *Majmu'at al-Naqd wa al-Taslif*, 4.

61. Between 1943 and 1964, the number of landed parliamentarians dropped from 46 to 23, while the number of businessmen and white-collar professionals rose from 10 each to 17 and 32 respectively; see chart titled "Distribution of Members of Representative Assembly since Independence" in Harik, *Man Yahkum Lubnan*, 31.

62. On the complex historical relationship between merchant and industrial associations, see Baroudi, "Conflict and Co-operation within Lebanon's Business Community," 71–100.

63. Between January 1931 and March 1932, over fifty commercial bankruptcies were declared. In April of 1930, a delegation of bankers, including Michel Trad and Habib al-Dibs, met with Lebanese President Charles Debbas and urged him to ensure that courts carefully vetted the books of companies before confirming a bankruptcy; see Achi and Ayache, *Tarikh al-Masarif fi Lubnan*, 122–23. The banking sector also suffered from a lack of regulation and good bookkeeping practices, however, and between 1931 and 1935, five banks folded. For a list of and details on the affected banks, see Himadeh, *Monetary and Banking System of Syria*, 136, 179, 188.

64. In addition to founding a bankers' association, Himadeh recommended passing a law to regulate all banks, control of banks by a central bank, merging Lebanese banks into joint-stock banks, and hiring of employees with "proper banking education"; see Himadeh, *Monetary and Banking System of Syria*, 291.

65. See Achi and Ayache, *Tarikh al-Masarif fi Lubnan*, 351n62.

66. Eddé's remarks appeared in the local French daily *L'Orient* on July 11, 1958. Ambassador Robert McClintock told Washington that Eddé's declaration was prompted by the disorganized state of the exchange market, and that Eddé might have been overoptimistic in his assessment of the crisis; see Beirut embassy to U.S. Department of State, dispatch 35, July 11, 1958; FN 883a.131/7–1158; 1955–59 Central Decimal File; RG 59; NAB.

67. Since the Lebanese market was too small to meet the U.S. military's need of local currency, the BSL and Lebanese Ministry of Finance offered to do so from the BSL stabilization fund, but at pre-crisis rates and with no guarantee of set market rates; see Beirut embassy to U.S. Department of State, telegram 964, August 6, 1958, FN 883a.131/8–658; 1955–59 Central Decimal File; RG 59; NAB. The embassy later argued that fears of the U.S. troop presence disrupting the market were unfounded, since military expenditures turned out to be smaller than had been anticipated; see Beirut embassy to U.S. Department of State, dispatch 283, November 6, 1958; FN 883a.131/11–658; 1955–59 Central Decimal File; RG 59; NAB.

68. Banks complained that without statutory protection, creditors were vulnerable to sales, unmortgaged property, and concealment of assets by overextended debtors, and they demanded new protective legislation. A five-member committee was formed to make recommendations in this regard. Karame conferred with bankers on October 20, 1958, and arranged for a follow-up meeting three days later; see Beirut embassy to U.S. Secretary of State, October 20, 1958; FN 883.14/102058; 1955–59 Central Decimal File; RG 59; NAB.

69. These senior bankers formed the constitutive assembly of the association. They included Anis Bibi (National Union Bank, general Manager and chairman of the board of directors), Julius Thomson (Chase Manhattan Bank, general manager of the Beirut branch), and Jean Abou Jaoude (Banque libanaise pour le Commerce—general manager and member of the board of directors). For a list of founders and a brief history of the ABL's establishment, see Association of Banks in Lebanon, "Annual Report 1960," 1, and id., *Golden Jubilee Book, 1959–2009*, 10, 22, 23. On the claim that the ABL was the first such association in the Arab world, see ibid., 7. The ABL was legally sanctioned by ministerial decree 1642 and its founding general assembly met on November 18, 1959; see Association of Banks in Lebanon, "Annual Report 1960," 3.

70. Four out of the seven members on the ABL's executive board had to be of Lebanese nationality. On the rules of membership for foreign banks, see Association of Banks in Lebanon, "Annual Report 1960," 12, 13, articles 4 and 6 of the ABL's founding statutes.

71. The three U.S. member banks were Bank of America, City Bank of New York, and Chase Manhattan Bank. For full list of founding bank members, see ibid., 2. The three nonparticipating French banks were the Banque de Syrie et du Liban (BSL), Banque nationale pour le commerce et l'industrie, and Crédit foncier d'Algérie et de Tunisie (CFAT); see Beirut embassy to U.S. Department of State, dispatch 523, January 27, 1961; FN 883a.14/1–2761; 1960–63 Central Decimal File; RG 59; NAB.

72. This rivalry included competition over the control of the central bank.

73. Association of Banks in Lebanon, "Annual Report 1960," 2, and "Annual Report 1964," 5.

74. "al-Hamra al-Shari al-lathi Asbaha Mintaqat al-Bunuk fi Bayrut," *al-Masarif*, November 1963, 50–51.

75. For photos and reports on beach trips, bowling outings, and banquets, see the "Ahl al-Masarif" corner in *al-Masarif*, August 1963, 74–75. Women's roles were also addressed. In its April 1964 edition, the magazine shed light on "the soft side of banking" by running a feature on the everyday life of six young women bankers; see Hasan al-Jindi, "6 Fatayat Muwadhdhafat al-Bunuk," *al-Masarif*, April 1964, 50–51. On banking schools, see *al-Masarif* Public Relations Committee, "Awwal Ma'had Masrifi fi Lubnan," *al-Masarif*, August 1963, 68–69.

76. The four consultative committees were: professional, social, technical, and research and commercial practice; see Association of Banks in Lebanon, "Annual Report 1962," 5. By 2009, there were eleven of these consultative committees; see Association of Banks in Lebanon, *Golden Jubilee Book, 1959–2009*, 13.

77. Regionally, ABL delegates participated in the proceedings of the Arab Chambers of Commerce held in Beirut from 21 to 26 November 1960, and those of Lebanese expatriates held in September of the same year; see Association of Banks in Lebanon, "Annual Report 1960," 5. Internationally, the ABL established contacts with the Swiss and Belgian banking associations, as well as the Banking

Department at World Chamber of Commerce in Paris. ABL president Pierre Eddé paid visits to the heads of the latter two organizations in November 1960; see ibid., 7–8. On plans to set up a joint Lebano-Senegalese bank following Pierre Eddé's tour of some African countries, see Badri Yunis, "Ifriqya Tariq Jadid Tashuqquhu al-Masarif al-Lubnaniyyah." *al-Masarif*, November 1963, 28–31.

78. For the official narrative, see Association of Banks in Lebanon, *Golden Jubilee Book, 1959–2009,* 22. The notion that organizing had become a necessary step in light of the stage of growth of the Lebanese economy was mentioned in passing in the first report in terms of the need to "positively interact" with a long-felt need for public and private organization of the sector. Furthermore, such an acknowledgement was not part of the Articles of Association; see Association of Banks in Lebanon, "Annual Report 1960," 3. In the second annual report, organization was recognized as a "necessary matter in the current stage of development of the Lebanese economy" while asserting that it abided to "the path of a free liberal economy and the system of banking secrecy," see Association of Banks in Lebanon, "Annual Report 1961," 8.

79. Association of Banks in Lebanon, "Annual Report 1960," 12, ABL founding statutes, Article 2.

80. The ABL was also consulted by the government over the proposed social security scheme and expressed its disapproval of the draft. Calls to exempt member banks with branches in the United Arab Republic from nationalization were voiced by ABL delegates at the Arabic Chamber of Commerce conference held in Beirut in November 1960; see ibid., 5–8. Basim al-Jisr, who was a Chehabist technocrat, wrote that the social security scheme and the Law of Money and Credit faced "strong opposition" by businessmen and bankers; see Jisr, *Fuad Shihab,* 101. On the distribution of circulars and memos and laws to association members, see Association of Banks in Lebanon, "Annual Report 1961," 5.

81. The *al-Masarif* reporter Badri Yunis referred to the press and the banks as the "two titans of the Lebanese Economy"; see Yunis, "Sira' al-Jababirah: Bayna al-Sahafah wa al-Masarif," *al-Masarif,* October 1964, 98.

82. Ten more banks joined the ABL in 1961; see Association of Banks in Lebanon, "Annual Report 1961," 3.

83. The ABL clearly linked the expansion of membership at the time to its position on the Law of Money and Credit; see Association of Banks in Lebanon, "Annual Report 1963," 5.

84. EPDB submitted a draft bill to that effect on March 8, 1956; see Badrud-Din, *Bank of Lebanon,* 62n24.

85. The CMC became a legal entity under decree 154 promulgated on June 12, 1959. On the CMC's official mandate, see ibid., 42.

86. The authors of one such account claim that the CMC had no notable role in the history of Lebanese currency and banking; see Achi and Ayache, *Tarikh al-Masarif fi Lubnan,* 179–81. On the appointment of its members two and half years after its creation, see Badrud-Din, *Bank of Lebanon,* 42.

87. Unless otherwise stated, the account here of the conflict between banking factions over control of the CMC is drawn from the U.S. embassy report, largely based on Shoucair's version of events. Shoucair was appealing to the embassy to support his group, claiming that the Bank of America was "unwittingly being used by Beidas to extend Intra Bank's influence and hence Anglo-French interests"; see Beirut embassy to U.S. Department of State, dispatch 322, December 12, 1961; FN 883a.14/12–126; 1960–63 Central Decimal File; RG 59; NAB.

88. Ibid.

89. On the Gemayel-Karame tussle, see ibid. On date of decree 8211 establishing the CMC and the outlining of its aim as that of establishing a central bank, see Badrud-Din, *Bank of Lebanon*, 42–43.

90. The remaining members were Joseph Prince (government commissioner at the BSL); Mohamad Atallah (EPDB representative); and the AUB alumnus and financial expert Abdul-Amir Badrud-Din. On the composition of CMC, see ibid.

91. Articles 121–191 of the Law of Money and Credit regulate the banking profession. For a summary and analysis of the main provisions, including those cited above, see ibid., 55–57.

92. On the statistics gathered by the General Statistical Bureau via a vaguely worded questionnaire, see Beirut embassy to U.S. Department of State, dispatch 1, July 1, 1954; FN 883.14/7–154; 1950–54 Central Decimal Files; RG 59; NAB.

93. On the attempt to introduce an improved "totally new type of questionnaire" and reversion to the old one, see Beirut embassy to U.S. Department of State, dispatch 694, May 3, 1954; FN 883.14/5–354, and dispatch 107, August 13, 1954; FN 883A.14/8–1354; 1950–54 Central Decimal File; RG 59; NAB.

94. CMC instructions were issued under memo 1/62 on September 15, 1962; see Badrud-Din, *Bank of Lebanon*, 44. According to *al-Masarif*, the instructions of memo 1/62 were part of decree 10523 issued on September 10, 1962; see "Awwal T'alimat min al-Masrif al-Markazi," *al-Masarif*, December 1963, 82–87.

95. For a full list of the instructions, see "Awwal T'alimat min al-Masrif al-Markazi," *al-Masarif*, December 1963, 82–87.

96. Association of Banks in Lebanon, "Annual Report 1963," 6.

97. As quoted in Badrud-Din, *Bank of Lebanon*, 43. I was not able to locate full copy of this first memorandum.

98. An English translation of Pierre Eddé's letter/memorandum is reproduced in full in Asseily, *Central Banking in Lebanon*, 19–22.

99. Ibid.

100. Ibid.

101. At least five such meetings were held between the ABL and the CMC; see Association of Banks in Lebanon, "Annual Report 1963," 6. On Chehab wishing both parties to meet, see Beirut embassy to U.S. Department of State, airgram 1025, April 17, 1963; FN 6 LEB; 1963 Subject Numeric File; RG 59; NAB.

102. Under the 1956 law, violators were subject to a prison sentence of from three months up to a year. Under the Law of Money and Credit, this

was increased to from six months up to two years; see Badrud-Din, *Bank of Lebanon*, 56–57.

103. On the different stages of negotiations regarding classification of banks and ABL refusal to entertain any form of classification, see Association of Banks in Lebanon, "Annual Report 1963," 10–11.

104. Violators were subject to interest rate charges on the shortfall not to exceed 3 percent of the interest rate applied on advances against securities (Article 77); see Badrud-Din, *Bank of Lebanon*, 52–53.

105. On the absence of cash reserve ratio requirements until 1969 and subsequent increases, see ibid., 53. On public debate regarding the reserve ratio requirement and opposition by ABL and Naja, see "5 am 10 am 25? Hadhihi Hiya al-Mas'alah," *al-Masarif*, August 1963, 6–9.

106. Badrud-Din, *Bank of Lebanon*, 43–44.

Chapter 4

1. Nasif, *Jumhuriyat Fuad Shihab*, 431.

2. Chapter epigraph: Dhulfiqar Qubaysi, "Nalat al-Lira al-Lubnaniyyah Istiqlalaha," *al-Masarif*, April 1964, 4–6 (5).

3. The catchphrase "No victor and no vanquished" was coined by Saeb Salam, a wealthy Beirut merchant who was the main leader of the 1958 anti-Chamoun rebellion; see Nasif, *Jumhuriyyat Fuad Shihab*, 264.

4. Chehab did not, however, seek to alter the ratio of Christians to Muslims in parliament.

5. Nasif, *Jumhuriyyat Fuad Shihab*, 372. For a sympathetic articulation of Chehabism as a "new style" of governance, see Naccache, "Un nouveau style," 389–99.

6. I borrow the term from Salem, *Modernization without Revolution.*

7. On the need for gradual and slow reform, see Nasif, *Jumhuriyyat Fuad Shihab*, 379. On the priority of administrative reform, see ibid., 389. On redefining the state-citizen relationship, see ibid., 294, 376. On developing the periphery as a means of integration, see ibid., 376.

8. Shehadi, *Idea of Lebanon*, 12.

9. On the different financial regimes that emerged across the Arab world during the period of independence, see Sayyid Ali, *al-Tatawwur al-Tarikhi*, 228–29.

10. Hudson, *Precarious Republic*, 316, puts the number of decrees issued in a single day (June 3, 1059) at 162. Nasif, *Jumhuriyat Fuad Shihab*, 414, however, speaks of 62 decrees in a single day (June 12, 1959).

11. For a detailed list of agencies and laws issued under Chehab, see Kfuri, *al-Shihabiyyah wa Siyasat al-Mawqif*, 257–307. For a concise list of the major laws, institutions, and projects directly related to social welfare, economic development, and public works, see Jisr, *Fuad Shihab*, 57–60.

12. Johnson, *Class & Client in Beirut*, 138.

13. On Chehab's allies among the traditional ruling elite and emerging populist

forces such as the Phalanges, see Hudson, *Precarious Republic*, 301. On Chehab's wooing of the Dandash clan, see Nasif, *Jumhuriyyat Fuad Shihab*, 167.

14. On these "three arenas", see Johnson, *Class & Client in Beirut*, 140–43.

15. Prominent Chehabist military officers included Emile Bustani, Antun Sad, and Gaby Lahoud; see Nassif, *al-Maktab al-Thani*.

16. In the wake of the botched coup led by the Socialist Syrian National Party (SSNP), over 6,000 people were reportedly arrested. The names of President Chamoun and the former MP Raymond Eddé were mentioned in the subsequent trial, and their passports, along those of a handful of other politicians, were revoked; see Hudson, *Precarious Republic*, 305.

17. On the impact of military life and training on Chehabism, see ibid., 95, 103, 375.

18. Jean Lay, a former officer of the French army, was entrusted by Chehab with supervising the reorganization of Lebanon's administration; see ibid., 241–42, and Sad, *Fuad Butrus*, 58–59. On *Père* Louis-Joseph Lebret's reputation as the *éminence grise* of Chehab's administration, see Hudson, *Precarious Republic*, 303. Chehab retained Lebret, a former marine officer in the French navy, as an advisor after the termination of the IRFED mission that the latter headed; see Nasif, *Jumhuriyyat Fuad Shihab*, 395, 401. Another French consultant who had good access to Chehab was the city planner Michel Ecochard, who was head of the engineering division at the Public Works Ministry; see Hudson, *Precarious Republic*, 321. For more on foreign versus Lebanese expert planners under Chehab, see Verdeil, "Politics, Ideology, and Professional Interests," 290–315.

19. See Sad, *Fuad Butrus*, 49–108.

20. On the "rational planning" that characterized Chehabism, see Hudson, *Precarious Republic*, 315. On state restructuring to establish "rational bureaucratic [order] in the Weberian sense," see Johnson, *Class & Client in Beirut*, 142.

21. On the relatively steady rate of increase in the ordinary budget between 1950 and 1961, see Hudson, *Precarious Republic*, 308, table 25. Chehab suppressed a military coup in 1961, and elections (parliamentary and presidential) were held in 1964.

22. A major exception was government spending on public works, which hovered around 17 percent of total expenditures under Chamoun and Khoury but jumped to 30 percent in 1964 under Chehab (see budgetary expenditures by sector listed in ibid., 310, table 27).

23. According to the contemporary Chehabist technocrat Basim al-Jisr, Chehab used to repeat the Aesopian French maxim "Preserve the hen that lays golden eggs" apropos of the services sector; see Jisr, *Fuad Shihab*, 120. On his belief that the main economic challenge facing Lebanon was the limitation of prosperity to Beirut, see ibid., 119. Chehab's dislike of Beirut and its merchants and politicians was "legendary." Because of his preference for living in Sarba in Mount Lebanon, he was dubbed *l'hérmite de Sarba*; see Shehadi, *Idea of Lebanon*, 11.

24. On the main tenets of humanistic economics and Chehab's conversion to

it under the influence of Lebret, see Ra'd, *Tarikh Lubnan al-Siyasi*, 110. On Chehab's general admiration for France and hope for the return of its "historic role" in Lebanon, see Nasif, *Jumhuriyyat Fuad Shihab*, 346–47.

25. Less than two months earlier, the Economic Planning and Development Board of the Ministry of General Planning, which had been set up under Chamoun, and on which AUB institutionalists served, produced a five-year plan for economic development; see Ra'd, *Tarikh Lubnan al-Siyasi*, 25.

26. The IRFED mission to Lebanon was nominally attached to the Ministry of Planning but reported directly to the president; see Hudson, *Precarious Republic*, 314.

27. On the continued predominance of the commercial sector, see Johnson, *Class & Client in Beirut*, 146. On the concentration of industry in Beirut, see Jisr, *Fuad Shihab*, 106.

28. The Shared Account Law was issued on December 19, 1961; see Achi and Ayache, *Tarikh al-Masarif fi Lubnan*, 165.

29. Achi, *al-Nizam al-Naqdi fi Suriya*, 308–9.

30. Ibid., 300.

31. Law of Money and Credit, Articles 12 to 16 and 120, Yafi and Yafi, *Majmu'at al-Naqd wa al-Taslif*, 1: 7–8, 44.

32. On the positions of the planning board and the ABL regarding the powers of the governor and central council, see Badrud-Din, *Bank of Lebanon*, 48–50.

33. See ibid., 65, fig. 4.1, for a chart illustrating the different bodies and departments constituting the central bank, their functions, and the administrative relationships among them.

34. On the governor's rights and duties, including sitting on the board of directors of the IMF, IBRD, and other official international bodies, see Articles 18 to 27, Yafi and Yafi, *Majmu'at al-Naqd wa al-Taslif*, 1: 9–11. The phrase "the widest powers in the general administration and management" is quoted from the Law of Money and Credit's Article 26; see Badrud-Din, *Bank of Lebanon*, 49.

35. See Yafi and Yafi, *Majmu'at al-Naqd wa al-Taslif*, 1: 17, Article 44. On government supervision of the central bank, see Articles 41 to 46, ibid., 1: 17–18.

36. See Yafi and Yafi, *Majmu'at al-Naqd wa al-Taslif*, 1: 17, Article 43 .

37. On composition and mandate of Advisory Committee, see Law of Money and Credit, Articles 35 to 40, ibid., 1: 15–16.

38. See, e.g., Central Bank of Kuwait, "Law no. 32," /www.cbk.gov.kw/en/images/CBK-Law-32-68-En-10-114233-2.pdf.

39. Central Bank of Iraq, *al-Bank al-Markazi al-Iraqi*, 10–11.

40. Achi, *al-Nizam al-Naqdi fi Surya*, 262.

41. Central Bank of Kuwait, "Law no. 32," Article 15.

42. See Yafi and Yafi, *Majmu'at al-Naqd wa al-taslif*, 1: 23n1, Article 70.

43. Badrud-Din, *Bank of Lebanon*, 51.

44. Article 3 of the BSL's Statutes, in Himadeh, *Monetary and Banking System of Syria*, app. 3, 330.

45. Central Bank of Iraq, *al-Bank al-Markazi al-Iraqi*, 11.

46. Ibid., 158.

47. On capping of loans to the Syrian government, see Achi, *al-Nizam al-Naqdi fi Suriya*, 294. On loan restrictions to unproductive capital, see ibid., 264–65.

48. The Central Bank of Kuwait, "Law no. 32," Article 36.

49. Article 3 of the BSL's Statutes, in Himadeh, *Monetary and Banking System of Syria*, app. 3, 330.

50. In exceptional circumstances, the central bank would still have to explore other options with the government, such as cutting expenditures or imposing new taxes, before approving the loan (Article 91). The government was allowed to draw on advances from the bank, but only up to 10 percent of its average annual budget revenue over the past three years, and such advances could not exceed four months' revenues (Article 88). On operations between the bank and the public sector, including the highly restrictive conditions under which the government was permitted to borrow from the BDL, see Yafi and Yafi, *Majmu'at al-Naqd wa al-Taslif*, 1: 30–34, Law of Money and Credit, Articles 84 to 97.

51. Sfeir, "Central Bank and the Banking Law of Jordan," 353–54.

52. Warnings against dwindling capital resources were expressed by Syria's then central bank governor, Izzat Traboulsi; see Achi, *al-Nizam al-Naqdi fi Suriya*, 292.

53. Ibid., 287.

54. At the time of Achi's writing, import deposits were at 15 percent for regular items and 40 percent for luxury imports. On refraining from consumption rediscount and import deposit, see ibid., 289. On open market operations, see ibid., 288. On accepting four-months' rediscounted paper, see ibid., 264–65.

55. Ibid., 264–65.

56. Ibid., 285.

57. On BDL operations affecting money liquidity and volume of credit, see Yafi and Yafi, *Majmu'at al-Naqd wa al-Taslif*, 1: 25–27, Articles 76 to 79. On gold and foreign currency exchange operations, see ibid., 1: 29–30, Articles 81 to 83. On operations with private banks, see ibid., 1: 34–38, Articles 98 to 109.

58. The transfer of BSL staff reduced the need for training of new recruits at the BDL. It was partly due to pressure by the BSL's labor union, led by Gabriel Khoury, who was also the head of Lebanon's General Federation of Trade Unions; see Badrud-Din, *Bank of Lebanon*, 70.

59. Beirut embassy to U.S. Department of State, airgram 224, September 27, 1963; FN 6 LEB; Subject Numeric File; RG 59; NAB. On his alleged "single-handed" drafting of the law, see ibid., enclosure 1. Chehab enlisted the help of the former Nazi Minister of Economics Hjalmar Schacht in drafting the Law of Money and Credit, according to Nasif, *Jumhuriyyat Fuad Shihab*, 419.

60. Beirut embassy to U.S. Department of State, airgram 224, September 27, 1963; FN 6 LEB; 1963 Subject Numeric File; RG 59; NAB.

61. During CMC deliberations, Karame overruled Oughourlian on several controversial points; see Beirut embassy to U.S. Department of State, airgram

1025, April 17, 1963; FN 6 LEB; 1963 Subject Numeric File; RG 59; NAB. On Karame and Klat being the only attendees at the last meeting with the ABL, see Asseily, *Central Banking in Lebanon*, 22.

62. Karim Khalil, "al-Qissah al-Kamilah li Ta'yinat al-Masrif al-Markazi," *al-Masarif*, October 1963, 16–19.

63. On the ABL allegedly backing Klat for governor, see Beirut embassy to U.S. Department of State, dispatch 322, December 12, 1961; FN 883a.14/12–1261; 1960–63 Central Decimal File; RG 59; NAB.

64. This is based on a vivid profile of Oughourlian by Leslie Tihany, first secretary at the U.S. embassy in Beirut; see Beirut embassy to U.S. Department of State, airgram 224, September 27, 1963; FN 6 LEB; 1963 Subject Numeric File; RG 59; NAB.

65. Ibid.

66. Chehab reassured U.S. officials that should Takla take on the job of governor, he would appoint Hussein Uwayni as foreign minister, which would involve "no change in policy because Oueni and Takla saw eye-to-eye on everything, internal and external"; see Beirut embassy to U.S. Department of State, airgram 206, September 16, 1963; FN 6 LEB; 1963 Subject Numeric File; RG 59; NAB.

67. As provided for in the Law of Money and Credit, the directors general of the Ministries of Finance and National Economy, André Tueni and Ihsan Beydoun, were appointed ex officio to the Central Council. For a detailed press account of the appointment saga and short bios of appointees, see Karim Khalil, "Al-Qissah al-Kamilah li Ta'yinat al-Masrif al-Markazi," *al-Masarif*, October 1963, 16–19.

68. When almost a year later Takla was reappointed as foreign minister in President Charles Helou's cabinet, Oughourlian was formally named acting governor of the central bank.

69. Arbitration contracts had been reached between the two parties on both matters and parliament was expected to vote on them. But the Law on Money and Credit designated the central bank governor as the new arbiter, so the issue became primarily a BDL-BSL matter; see "Lubnan Yabda' 'Ahd al-Istiqlal al-Masrifi," *al-Masarif*, March 1964, 68–77, 73.

70. "Bada Lubnan Yaish Ayyam al-Bank al-Markazi," *al-Masarif*, January 1964, 46–49.

71. On Oughourlian's proposals for internal reorganization of the BDL, see "Bada'a Lubnan Ya'ish Ayyam al-Bank al-Markazi," *al-Masarif*, January 1964, 46–49. The IMF's offer of free training for BDL employees was regarded as an opportunity to become less dependent on foreign experts; see "Lubnan Yabda' 'Ahd al-Istiqlal al-Masrifi," *al-Masarif*, March 1964, 68–77, 72. On the role of the French mission and Takla's efforts to involve French and Belgian experts in setting up the currency-issuing department and training its personnel, see "5 am 10 am 25? Hadhihi Hiya al-Mas'alah," *al-Masarif*, August 1963, 6–9, 8. On Oughourlian's visits to European Central Banks, see Badrud-Din, *Bank of Lebanon*, 44.

72. The Ministry of Public Works issued a special information booklet on the

project. Images of the different stages of construction and information on the construction material and companies involved were included. The blurb introducing the brochure boasted the success of the Construction Projects Execution Council in its timely completion of what "many thought would be an unachievable miracle"; see booklet obtained by this author from Banque du Liban Library: Majlis Tanfiidh al-Masharii' al-Insha'iyyah, "Masrif Lubnan" (Wizarit al-Ashghaal al-'Ammah wa al-Naql, 1964). On total cost of project, see "Bada Lubnan Ya'ish 'Ayyam al-Bank al-Markazi," *al-Masarif*, January 1964, 46–49, 49. Fayiz al-Ahdab is listed as a member of the BSL's board of directors for at least the years 1959, 1960, 1962; see Banque de Syrie et du Liban, "Exercice 1959," "Exercice 1960," and "Exercice 1962."

73. Ibid.

74. In addition to a list of high-tech furbishing features, the booklet on construction produced by the Ministry of Public Works and Transport pointed out that electronically powered parking doors were made in Lebanon, and the tiles of the external lobby were from Lebanese quarries; see Majlis Tanfiidh al-Masharii' al-Insha'iyyah, "Masrif Lubnan."

75. "Bada'a Lubnan Yaish Ayyam al-Bank al-Markazi," *al-Masarif*, January 1964, 46–49.

76. Chapter epigraph: Dhulfiqar Qubaysi, "Nalat al-Lira al-Lubnaniyyah Istiqlalaha," *al-Masarif*, April 4–6, 1964, 5.

77. Qubaysi, "Nalat al-Lira al-Lubnaniyyah Istiqlalaha," 4–6.

78. For details of the inauguration ceremony and excerpts of speeches by Takla and Uwayni, see "Tafaseel al-Ihtifal bi Tadsheen Masrif Lubnan" *al-Masarif*, April 1964, 7–9.

79. On repeated complaint of BDL officials about lack of adequate statistics, see Banque du Liban, "Annual Report for 1964," 1, and "Annual Report for 1965," 3.

80. Banque du Liban, "Annual Report for 1964," 5.

81. Ibid., 15. The BDL's praise of Lebanese talent seemed toned down compared to the BSL's assessment of the secret behind Lebanon's growth. In its 1959 annual report, the BSL declared that it was only possible to understand the Lebanese economy "as a function of the skills and ingenuity of the Lebanese"; see Banque de Syrie et du Liban, "Exercice 1959," 25.

82. Banque du Liban, "Annual Report for 1964," 16.

83. In 1964, advances to public sector amounted to approximately LL60M; those to the private sector stood close to LL100M; see ibid., 19. In 1965, the public sector advances went down to LL54M, while private ones increased to around LL105M; see Banque du Liban, "Annual Report for 1965," 23.

84. Unlike the 1965 report, which addressed the question of proliferation of banks and need for their regulation, the 1964 Annual Report matter-of-factly stated the number of banks and their geographic distribution. Other banking statistics were also simply stated; see Banque du Liban, "Annual Report for 1964" and "Annual Report for 1965."

85. For dates of meetings, see Dhulfiqar Qubaysi, "Azmat Thiqah Azmat Bunuk: al-Qissah al-Kamilah li Azmat Shari' al-Bunuk," *al-Masarif*, March 1964, 4–13.

86. The Real Estate Bank's board of directors included the wealthy Beiruti merchant and notable Ahmed Daouk. Backed by his family, Daouk expressed willingness to provide some guarantees, but refused to offer a blanket pledge. On the details of trilateral meetings between the ABL, the BSL, and the BDL, see Dhulfiqar Qubaysi, "Azmat Thiqah Azmat Bunuk: al-Qissah al-Kamilah li Azmat Shari' al-Bunuk," *al-Masarif*, March 1964, 4–13.

87. Members of the bank's Board of Directors were held accountable for liquidating its debt with Debbas receiving the bulk of the blame. For the full text of the court's ruling, see "al-Bank al-Aqari wa al-Bank al-Tijari," *al-Masarif*, 84–90.

88. For excerpts of statements by Takla and Eddé, see Dhulfiqar Qubaysi, "Azmat Thiqah Azmat Bunuk: al-Qissah al-Kamilah li Azmat Shari' al-Bunuk," *al-Masarif*, March 1964, 4–13, 12. For an excerpt from the ministry's release, see ibid., 10.

89. One *al-Masarif* analysis contrasted reports by the French newspaper *Le Monde* affirming the good financial standing of Lebanon with testimony by the BDL's foreign expert Rudolf Manstersky that Lebanese money markets were facing a liquidity crisis; see "Naqs al-Suyulah al-Naqdiyyah," *al-Masarif*, June 1964, 6–9, 6–7.

90. The parliamentarian petitioners were Ghalib Shahin, Abdel Latif al-Zayn, and Anwar al-Sabbah; see "Hakim al-Bank al-Markazi Ya'tarif," *al-Masarif*, Jul 1964, 6–9.

91. See interview with Anis Bibi in "Masarif Lubnan Samidah fi Wajh al-Azamaat," *al-Masarif*, September 1964, 10–13.

92. See interview with Sami Shoucair in "Majmu'at Shuqayr Qadah lil Izdihar wa al-Istiqrar," *al-Masarif*, July 1964, 10–13.

93. See interview with Jabbour in "Damj al-Bunuk fi Lubnan Amr la Mafarr Minhu," *al-Masarif*, August 1964, 16–19.

94. Saab's proposed law included over fifty articles. For text of the draft law, see "Mashru' Qanun bi Insha' Maslahat Ta'min al-Wada'i'," *al-Masarif*, September 1964, 86–91.

95. The excerpt was reprinted in *al-Masarif*, but the newspaper it first appeared in was not identified; see "al-Safqah al-Masrifiyyah al-Lati Tawat Safhah Qadiimah," *al-Masarif*, August 1964, 8–9, which speaks of different newspapers but does not cite their names.

96. Ibid., 8–9.

97. The names of these newspapers were withheld by *al-Masarif*; see ibid.

98. Takla urged reporters to uphold the standards of accuracy, objectivity, and positivity when discussing the central bank; see "Hakim al-Bank al-Markazi Yaquul li *al-Masarif*," *al-Masarif*, May 1964, 44–45.

99. "Hakim al-Bank al-Markazi Ya'tarif . . . ," *al-Masarif*, July 1964, 6–9.

100. "Wad' Masrif Lubnan 24 Malyun fi al-Aswaq Khilal Nisf Shahr Tishreen al-Awwal," *al-Masarif*, November 1964, 8–9.

101. ABL's statement to the press, "Jam'iyyat Masarif Lubnan Ta'tabir al-Hamla al-Sahafiyyah ala al-Masarif Tahdidan li-Salamat Lubnan al-Iqtisidiyyah," *al-Masarif*, October 1964.

102. On the press and the banks as the "two titans of the Lebanese Economy," see Badri Yunis, "Sira al-Jababirah: Bayna al-Sahafah wa al-Masarif," *al-Masarif*, October 1964, 98.

103. As a gesture to show that all was well between the press, the bankers, and the central bank following the signature of the agreement, the ABL held a function in recognition of the central bank's governor, Philip Takla, and invited the Press Syndicate's head, Afif al-Tibi, as guest of honor; see "Wad' Masrif Lubnan 24 Malyun fi al-Aswaq Khilal Nisf Shahr Tishreen al-Awwal," *al-Masarif*, November 1964, 8–9.

104. On the details of the law and its provisions, see "Asbaha Hakim Masrif Lubnan Waziran lil Kharijiyyah," *al-Masarif*, December 1964, 8–11.

105. Banque du Liban, "Annual Report for 1965," 14.

106. The BDL's "Annual Report for 1965" does not indicate how many out of the twenty-two applications were approved; see ibid., 18.

107. See statistics as listed in ibid., 12.

108. Ibid., 13.

109. Takla's first deputy, Joseph Oughourlian, was named acting governor; see *al-Masarif*, December 1964, 8–9.

Chapter 5

1. Chapter epigraph: Helou, *Hayat fi Dhikrayat*, 239.

2. See Riyad Najib Rayyis, "Khamsat Shuhud Yarwun Qissat Yusif Beidas," *al-Nahar*, December 9, 1967, and U.S. embassy Bern to Department of State, telegram 1558, December 7, 1967; FN 6 LEB; Subject Numeric File; RG 59; NAB. Beidas had first sought refuge in Brazil; see Carvalho, "Fall of the 'Genius from Jerusalem.'"

3. See Joseph Farah, "Marwan Beidas Li ad-Diyar," *al-Diyar*, December 27, 2001, and Asfour, *Bank Intra: Qadiyyah wa 'Ibar*, 37.

4. For the best account, see Asfour, *Bank Intra: Qadiyyah wa 'Ibar*. Other accounts consulted for this study include Salameh, *Haddathani Y.S. Qal*, 111–52, and Alamuddin, *Flying Sheikh*, 135–69. Contemporary but poorly referenced accounts include Qubaysi, *Yusif Beidas,* and Sammak, *Nihayat Imbaraturiyyat Beidas*.

5. For a recent yet not entirely reliable study of the crisis, see Dib, *Imbaraturiyyat Intra wa Hitan al-Mal fi Lubnan*.

6. These peers included Hasib Sabbagh, Said Khoury, Zuhayr Alami, Badr al-Fahum, and Abdul Hameed Shoman; see Abu Fakhr, "Al-Filastiniyyun fi Lubnan," and Shoman, *Indomitable Arab*.

7. Beidas's two other partners were Munir Haddad and Fritz Maroum. On

the makeup and activities of International Traders, see Asfour, *Bank Intra: Qadiyyah wa 'Ibar*, 10–12. On his promotion to bank manager at the Arab Bank, see Salameh, *Haddathani Y.S. Qal*, 114.

8. Intra's founding capital of LL6.4M was increased to LL12M in 1953, LL30M in 1959, and finally LL60M in 1962; see Asfour, *Bank Intra: Qadiyyah wa 'Ibar*, 15. Dhulfiqar Qubaysi claims Intra controlled 60 percent of Lebanon's money market while Hanna Asfour cites a more conservative estimate, larger than 15 percent, of its banking operations; see ibid., 16, and Qubaysi, *Yusif Beidas*, 27. Intra's total declared assets in 1965 amounted to LL925M; those of the BDL were a little over a billion liras; see Intra Bank, "Annual Report 1965"; Banque du Liban, "Annual Report for 1965."

9. Intra owned stocks in companies such as Middle East Airlines, the Société financière & immobilière du Port de Beyrouth, Radio-Orient, Casino du Liban, Phoenicia Hotel, Lebanese Cement Corporation, and Baalbek Studios; see Asfour, *Bank Intra: Qadiyyah wa 'Ibar*, 203. Beidas himself was chairman of or on the board of directors of over a dozen companies and banks. For a list, see Badrud-Din, *Bank of Lebanon*, app. 3.

10. In addition to eleven branches in Lebanon, Intra set up branches or offices abroad in Jordan, Qatar, Britain, France, West Germany, Italy, the United States, Sierra Leone, and Gambia. At the time of its collapse, it had subsidiary banks in Lebanon, Switzerland, and Morocco (under construction) and sister banks in Nigeria, Liberia, Brazil, and Greece; see Intra Bank, "Annual Report 1965."

11. Asfour, *Bank Intra: Qadiyyah wa 'Ibar*, 38. On the withdrawal of LL12M in single day, see U.S. embassy Beirut to Department of State, telegram 3292, October 14, 1966; FN 6 LEB; 1963–1966 Subject Numeric File; RG 59; NAB.

12. Yaffi resigned on December 6, 1966. On role of Intra in resignations, see Majid, *Tarikh al-Hukumat al-Lubnaniyyah*, 160–62.

13. The claim that Beidas made secret loans to Nasser first appeared in the German weekly *Der Spiegel* and was reprinted in pro-Saudi daily *al-Hayat*. *Der Spiegel* put the amount at 320M marks, calculated by *al-Hayat* to be equivalent to LL250M. See "Intra Bank: Geheimer Kredit," *Der Spiegel*, October 24, 1966, 139–40, and "Qard Sirri min Beidas Lil Muttahidah," *al-Hayat*, October 27, 1966.

14. "Riwaya 'an Asbab Azmat Bank Intra," *al-Hayat*, October 16, 1966.

15. U.S. embassy Beirut to Department of State, telegram 3292, October 14, 1966; FN 6 LEB; 1963–66 Subject Numeric File; RG 59; NAB.

16. "Faysal: La Yad Lana fi Azmat Lubnan," *al-Nahar*, November 3, 1966. A slightly different version of Faysal's statement was quoted by *al-Hayat*, according to which, Faysal said, "Such [crises] happen in every country when the balance of economic laws governing bank management is disturbed." Faysal made a veiled threat, however, telling the interviewer, "We wish Lebanon well—unless, as the proverb goes, 'I wish him life, but he wants me dead'; in that case I'd feel otherwise" ("Faysal: Tahammalna min Lubnan Isa'at Kathirah wa Narju An Yahtafith bi Hiyadih wa Asalatih al-Arabiyyah," *al-Hayat*, November 3, 1966, cover page).

17. Meouchi was allegedly told by a Saudi embassy official in Beirut that "on Faisal's orders Saudi withdrawals of U.S.$100M [~LL300M] had been made from Intra and other banks." Abdallah's remarks were allegedly made during an encounter he had with a U.S. Department of State officer, Camille Noufal, who relayed them to the U.S. embassy. In a separate communication, the *Christian Science Monitor* correspondent John Cooley reported his conversation with Meouchi to the U.S. embassy in which Meouchi allegedly made reference to an unnamed Saudi embassy official having spoken of Faisal's orders to withdraw funds. According to Cooley, the patriarch expressed his intention to do everything in his power to bring about the fall of the Yafi government and force President Helou to adopt a policy more favorable to Saudi Arabia and the United States and less so to Nasser's United Arab Republic; see U.S. embassy Beirut to Department of State, telegram 3446, October 20, 1966; FN 6 LEB; Subject Numeric File; RG 59; NAB.

18. U.S. embassy Jeddah to Department of State, airgram A-135, October 24, 1966; FN 6 LEB; Subject Numeric File; RG 59; NAB.

19. Reports circulating in Jeddah, and reported by U.S. embassy, of the size of Saudi withdrawals put the amount at roughly U.S.$22M, the equivalent of over LL60M at the time. U.S. embassy personnel in Jeddah requested that Masud, who was a special envoy to several Saudi kings, be protected as a source, indicating that he was not acting on instructions from Al Saud; see U.S. embassy Jeddah to Department of State, telegram 1460, October 18, 1966; FN 6 LEB; 1963–66 Subject Numeric File; RG 59; NAB. Masud was a special envoy of Saudi kings and one of the founders of the kingdom's diplomacy; see "Al-Saudiyyah: Wafat al-Mufad al-Khass li Mulukiha wa Ahad Muassisi Diblumasiyyatiha," *al-Sharq al-Awsat*, December 31, 2000, http://archive.aawsat.com/details.asp?issueno=8059&article=19608#. WvbpitMvzGI.

20. Department of State to U.S. embassy Jeddah, telegram 69262, October 19, 1966; FN 6 LEB; 1963–66 Subject Numeric File; RG 59; NAB.

21. Ali later contacted the U.S. embassy in Jeddah to reiterate that Saudi withdrawals had been "negligible" and entirely private rather than due to government orders. Kuwaiti withdrawals, he added, were less than the earlier estimates of U.S.$53M he had provided but still stood at LL20M; U.S. embassy Jeddah, telegram 1499, October 20, and airgram A-143, October 31, 1966, to Department of State; FN 6 LEB; Subject Numeric File; RG 59; NAB.

22. "Kuwait: La 'Alaqah lana bi Azmat Intra," *al-Hayat*, October 26, 1966, front-page story.

23. On the role of high interest rates in attracting Kuwaiti capital, see U.S. embassy Beirut to Department of State, telegram 3292, October 14, 1966; FN 6 LEB; 1963–66 Subject Numeric File; RG 59; NAB. Abdallah al-Ghanim told U.S. officials of the visit by Beidas and Parker at a British embassy dinner, at which attendees included Undersecretary Khalid Kharafi of Kuwait's Ministry of Commerce; see Kuwait embassy to U.S. Department of State, telegram 351, October 18, 1966; FN 6 LEB; Subject Numeric File; RG 59; NAB.

24. On the global currency crisis and the gold rush during this period, see Harry G. Johnson, "Sterling Crisis," 3–17.

25. Dib, *Warlords and Merchants*, 112–13.

26. The joint declaration was signed in Kuwait on February 2, 1966; see "Bayan Mushtarak li Tashji' Intiqal Ru'us al-Amwal," *al-Masarif*, February 15, 1966, 6–7.

27. Foreign Arab investors in Iraq, whether individuals or companies, were granted the right to fully repatriate their net profits rather than necessarily invest them in Iraq as previously required; see "Tashilat li Ru'us al-Amwal al-Ajnabi-yyah," *al-Masarif*, April 15, 1966, 13. On plans of the Arab Bank in Jordan, see Mustafa al-Junaydi, "Abdul Majid Shuman Yatahaddath ila *al-Masarif*," *al-Masarif*, June 15, 1966, 10–13.

28. See Joseph Mughayzil, "Hatta Yakun Lubnan Khizanat al-'Arab," *al-Masarif*, May 31, 1966, 34–41.

29. Estimates of the drop in the holdings of banks and low liquidity levels were presented by Yusif Sayigh at a panel convened following the Intra crisis. Participants included ABL president Pierre Eddé; former governor of Syria's central bank and Intra consultant Izzat Traboulsi; and the AUB economists Elias Saba and Mohammad Atallah. See "al-Azmah al-Masrifiyyah 'ala al-Mashrahah," *al-Masarif*, December 15, 1966, 12–17.

30. Beidas's open letter, dated October 27, 1966, was published in major newspapers on October 30; see "Beidas: Azmat Intra Mufta'alah Tahdif ila al-Tasallut ala Sharikaat wa Marafiq Hayawiyyah fi Lubnan," *al-Hayat*, October 30, 1966 and "Yusif Beidas fi Bayan Rasmi," *al-Nahar*, October 30, 1966.

31. Oughourlian allegedly used to address Beidas in French, even though Beidas spoke only Arabic and English; see Salameh, *Haddathani Y.S. Qal*, 71. Alamuddin, who had served as a minister under Helou, initially doubted Beidas's account of his meeting with Helou but later came to believe in the conspiracy. Beidas recounted Oughourlian's reaction in New York in his unpublished memoirs. Beidas was incensed by the remarks of Oughourlian, who after all was an "Armenian"! See Alamuddin, *Flying Sheikh*, 136–37. The memoirs, which Alamuddin apparently had access to, were never published, because Beidas and his children were allegedly threatened with assassination should the memoirs be published; see ibid., 139.

32. For the memoir version of Helou's account of events, see Helou, *Hayat fi Dhikrayat*, 232–34.

33. Helou, according to Porter, was in a "tense and somewhat somber mood" throughout their conversation, which took place on December 24, and stated that he wanted to tell Porter "the true story" of the origins of the Intra crisis and the Lebanese government's stance on it; see Beirut embassy to U.S. Department of State, airgram A-558, December 30, 1966; FN 6 LEB; Subject-Numeric File; RG 59; NAB.

34. Beidas boastfully told Salameh that he was "preparing for a major financial and political deal," after which "Lebanon's political future and governance" would revolve around Intra. It would work as follows, according to Edward Baroudy, Beidas's broker and liaison with Sarkis: the central bank would lend LL100M to

Intra, which itself charged interest of 6 percent or more on large loans, at 3 percent, and the difference compounded over Helou's remaining four years in office would finance Sarkis's presidential campaign; see Salameh, *Haddathani Y.S. Qal,* 121, 140–44.

35. Baroudy shadowed Beidas as a companion and entertainer. He had assured Beidas that the interest charged by BDL on the LL100M loan would hover around 3 percent and told his boss that expenses for the next presidential campaign would not exceed LL10M; see Salameh, *Haddathani Y.S. Qal,* 141–42.

36. Asfour, *Bank Intra: Qadiyyah wa 'Ibar,* 39–41.

37. For a detailed account of the events on Friday, October 14, leading up to and including the emergency marathon meeting held by the council of ministers that afternoon, see ibid., 51–54, and Helou, *Hayat fi Dhikrayat,* 236.

38. On the meetings held by the ABL and the Council of Ministers and the decisions taken by the latter, see Association of Banks in Lebanon, "Annual Report 1966," 11–12. On ABL's threat to strike unless enough cash were provided by central bank, see Beirut embassy to U.S. Department of State, telegram 3307, October 17, 1966; FN 6 LEB; 1963–66 Subject Numeric File; RG 59; NAB. On ABL's "recommendation" that the banks close for a few days, see Helou, *Hayat fi Dhikrayat,* 239. According to Hanna Asfour, Eddé did not object to including Intra among the banks that would benefit from the government guarantees, but Philip Takla, Elias Sarkis, and Joseph Oughourlian opposed it; see Asfour, *Bank Intra: Qadiyyah wa 'Ibar,* 57–58.

39. According to Helou, both Najib Alamuddin and Rafiq Naja were completely in the dark as to the financial status of Intra which increased the president's doubts as to the reliability of the bank's declared balance sheet. On Helou's reasoning to exclude Intra, see Helou, *Hayat fi Dhikrayat,* 236–39.

40. Alamuddin blamed an "unholy alliance" of Lebanese Zionists and international interests for the deliberate destruction of Intra; see Alamuddin, *Flying Sheikh,* 145. Yusif Salameh asked, rhetorically, whether the exclusion of Intra from liquidity guarantees offered by the Lebanese government to other banks was due to the Palestinian identity of Intra; see Salameh, *Haddathani Y.S. Qal,* 133. See also Asfour, *Bank Intra: Qadiyyah wa 'Ibar,* 23, and Qubaysi, *Yusif Beidas.*

41. When Beidas recruited his brother-in-law Yusif Salameh to set up an Intra branch in New York, he enlisted the help of his "friend" David Rockefeller, head of the Chase Manhattan Bank, whose brother Nelson was New York State governor at the time. Intra, Beidas told Salameh, had strong relations with several U.S. banks, specially Chase Manhattan and Bank of America; see Salameh, *Haddathani Y.S. Qal,* 122. On the friendship between Hasib Sabbagh and David Rockefeller, see Deeb and King, *Hasib Sabbagh.*

42. U.S. embassy Beirut to Department of State, telegram 2678, February 7, 1958; FN 883A.131/2–758; 1955–1959 Central Decimal File; NAB.

43. In February 1965, Intra financed the import of American wheat and feed grain via an agency of the U.S. government in the amount of U.S.$21M; see Thomas

Brady, "Intra Bank in Debt to Agency of U.S.; Chairman Replaced," *New York Times*, October 27, 1966. In France, Beidas was officially decorated for his multimillion dollar investments that contributed to strengthening the value of French franc; see Asfour, *Bank Intra: Qadiyyah wa 'Ibar*, 24. The Petro-dinar scheme was recounted by Muhsin Dalul, a close aide of Jumblatt's, who reportedly had read the letters at the time Jumblatt received them; see Dalul, *al-Tariq Ila al-Watan*, 109–12. On claims of breaking into the international gold trade and the building of gold refinery in Beirut, see Shihab al-Din, *Daya' al-'Arab Bayna al-Naft wa al-Dhahab*, 195–202.

44. On the breakdown of stock ownership in Intra, see Alamuddin, *Flying Sheikh*, 141. Beidas placed a Lebanese flag on top of the high-rise building Intra purchased on Fifth Avenue in New York; see Salameh, *Haddathani Y.S. Qal*, 118.

45. On October 14, when Intra's collapse was imminent, Yafi allegedly told Najib Alamuddin that Beidas was a "crook" and that he, i.e., Yafi, had in his possession a "confidential report" showing that Intra was in bad shape and could not be saved. Yafi refused to share the said report with Alamuddin; see Alamuddin, *Flying Sheikh*, 138. During parliamentary debates, Saeb Salam blamed the banking crisis on Intra and its alleged mismanagement. He then distributed his speech as a booklet; see "Khitab al-Rais Saeb Salam al-Lathi Irtajalahu fi al Majlis al-Niyabi bi Sadad Azmat Bank Intra," October 31, 1966, Special Collection, Jafet Library, American University of Beirut. Beidas allegedly turned down a request by Salam to finance a real estate development project of the latter's in the region of Doha; see Salameh, *Haddathani Y.S. Qal*, 152. Beidas also declined to grant considerable loans to Abdallah Yafi; see Carvalho, "Fall of the 'Genius from Jerusalem.'"

46. In the eyes of the Lebanese banking establishment, Beidas displayed the "obnoxious traits of nouveau riche"—he was "abrasive, cocky, and overwhelmingly vain" (Carvalho, "Fall of the 'Genius from Jerusalem'").

47. Pierre Eddé "hates the sight of me . . . he even taught his parrot to cackle 'Down with Bedas [sic]!'" Beidas told a writer for *Life* magazine while in Brazil (ibid.). Beidas had allegedly refused to join the Association of Banks in Lebanon (ABL) in 1959 unless he was guaranteed the position of president. According to Hanna Asfour, who later became Intra's representative at the ABL, it took a lot of convincing for Beidas to change his mind and register the bank with the association in 1962; see Asfour, *Bank Intra: Qadiyyah wa Ibar*, 44–45.

48. Beidas was surprised by Jumblatt's defense of Intra. In one of the letters he later wrote Jumblatt from Switzerland, the exiled banker expressed his regret at having bankrolled his political adversaries and thanked Jumblatt for his backing; see Dalul, *al-Tariq Ila al-Watan*, 110.

49. On plans of a general strike across Lebanon in mid-October 1966, see "al-Ittihad al-'Ummali Yabhath Taqrib Maw'id al-Idrab," *al-Nahar*, September 29, 1966.

50. Prime Minister Yaffi allegedly pressured Intra's lawyers to file for debt settlement no later than Monday October 17 lest the government declare Intra bankrupt; see Asfour, *Bank Intra: Qadiyyah wa 'Ibar*, 59.

51. The U.S. government refused to convert the pesos, declaring them invalid. See U.S. embassy Beirut to Department of State, telegram 7730, February 28, 1967, and Department of State to Beirut embassy, November 18, 1966; FN 6 LEB; RG 59; NAB.

52. Salha tried to impress upon the U.S. embassy that Intra's collapse had grave political as well as economic consequences. In an apparently coordinated campaign, an Intra shareholder, Victor Moussa, who was also broker of an Intra deal financing wheat from the United States, called the embassy "immediately after Salha" and repeated the same story; see U.S. embassy Beirut to Department of State, telegram 3349, October 17, 1966; FN 6 LEB; 1963–66 Subject Numeric File; RG 59; NAB.

53. Alamuddin stipulated that the new owners of MEA guarantee the livelihood of MEA employees and that the controlling share somehow be returned to Lebanon, given that traffic rights would not be obtained in the future should the controlling interest cease to be national; see U.S. embassy Beirut to Department of State, telegram 3388, October 18, 1966; FN 6 LEB; Subject Numeric File; RG 59; NAB. Over a month later, Alamuddin adamantly told the U.S. embassy, and the Lebanese press, that MEA was not for sale; see U.S. embassy Beirut to Department of State, telegram 4875, November 30, 1966; FN 6 LEB; 1963–66 Subject Numeric File; RG 59; NAB, and "Alamuddin: Tayaran al-Sharq al-Awsat Laysa lil Bay," *al-Nahar*, November 29, 1966.

54. Chase claimed that Intra's branch in New York had no credit balance with Chase since other offices of Intra owed Chase "substantially" more money. New York's superintendent of banks, Frank Willie, brought suit in the U.S. Supreme Court against Chase and the other two largest American banks, First National City Bank and Bank of America International, to release Intra funds. Foreign banks with branches in the United States expressed concern over the actions of Chase; see Robert Walker, "3 U.S. Banks Sued in Beirut Crisis," *New York Times*, October 20, 1966.

55. Salha also approached the Qatari government and managed to sign an agreement with its ruler, Ahmad Bin Ali Al Thani, under which the latter agreed to freeze U.S.$2.8M Qatari funds (1.9 percent of Intra deposits) for two years under certain conditions. Salha also secured a deal with the Greek shipping tycoon Stavros Niarchos for a U.S.$10M loan in return for sales of MEA stocks; see Asfour, *Bank Intra: Qadiyyah wa 'Ibar*, 73–74.

56. Under the deal, the Kuwaiti government would get a ten-year suspension of income tax on earnings on its shares. The government of Lebanon would also guarantee up to LL25M in bad debts; see U.S. embassy Kuwait to Department of State, telegram 359, October 20, 1966; FN 6 LEB; Subject Numeric File; RG 59; NAB.

57. The president had sent his own emissary, Elias Sarkis, to Kuwait to test the waters. On Helou's letter of support, see "Risalah min Helou ila Hakim al-Kuwayt," *al-Hayat*, November 25, 1966. On Sarkis's visit, see "'Ada Rasul al-Ra'is Helou min al-Kuwayt Mutafa'ilan," *al-Hayat*, November 20, 1966.

58. Kuwaiti funds deposits with Intra were estimated by U.S. officials at LL140M, LL30M of which were those of the Sabah family and the rest held by private Kuwaiti depositors; see U.S. embassy Kuwait to Department of State, telegram 560, December 2, 1966; FN 6 LEB; 1963–66 Subject Numeric File; RG 59; NAB, and Asfour, *Bank Intra: Qadiyyah wa 'Ibar*, 70–71. al-Hayat reported that the deal stipulated the freezing of Kuwaiti holdings amounting to LL170M; see "50 Malyunan min al-Kuwayt li Ta'wim Intra wa Tajmid Wada'i Kuwaitiyyah qimatuha 170 Malyunan," *al-Hayat*, December 2, 1966.

59. An important meeting in this regard attended by Kuwaiti Prime Minister Jaber al Sabah, Intra chairman Najib Salha, and three Chase Manhattan top executives, including the bank's Vice President Jacobson, was held on November 27, 1966; see U.S. embassy Kuwait to Department of State, telegram 546, November 29, 1966; FN 6 LEB; RG 59; NAB.

60. On details of deal signed between Intra and KFTCI, see U.S. embassy Kuwait to Department of State, telegram 560, December 2, 1966; FN 6 LEB; 1963–66 Subject Numeric File; RG 59; NAB. On the withdrawal of the offer, see U.S. embassy Kuwait to Department of State, telegram 697, January 5, 1967; FN 6 LEB; 1967–69 Subject Numeric File; RG 59; NAB. On reports in Reuters that Intra failed to release collateral stock from BDL to seal the deal with KFTCI, see Department of State to Beirut embassy, telegram 111633, January 3, 1967; FN 6 LEB; 1967–69 Subject Numeric File; RG 59; NAB.

61. Helou told U.S. Senator Edward Kennedy when the latter was visiting Beirut that the Kuwaiti offer was the best one so far; see Department of State to U.S. embassy Beirut, telegram 111633, January 3, 1967; FN 6 LEB; 1967–69 Subject Numeric File; RG 59; NAB. For press coverage of Kennedy's visit to Beirut and his meeting with Helou, see "Edward Kennedy wa Zawjatuhu fi Lubnan," *al-Hayat*, November 27, 1966.

62. The first committee, composed of six accountants and a retired judge, Shawkat al-Munla, was tasked with auditing Intra's books, producing a legally binding balance sheet, and examining its banking practices for any wrongdoing. The second committee was entrusted with evaluating Intra's assets. The six accountants of the auditing committee were Joseph Taso, Ali Awada, George Baroudy, Michel Siryani, Adib Khoury, and Ghazi Shamma. The valuation committee was composed of George Jirdaq, Muhammad Khayr Tabbarah, Jean Tohme, and Saadallah Asad; see Asfour, *Bank Intra: Qadiyyah wa 'Ibar*, 62–64.

63. On the dismissal of Price Waterhouse and the appointment of Cooper Brothers, see Alamuddin, *Flying Sheikh*, 148–49.

64. Creditors and shareholders held a majority vote in this first committee. For the full text of Law Intra, see Yafi and Yafi, *Majmu'at al-Naqd wa al-Taslif*, 1999, 2: 28–35.

65. Middle East Airlines chair Najib Alamuddin attributed the appointment of retired judge Shawkat Munla as head of committee to the latter's friendship with Prime Minister Abdallah Yaffi, a sworn enemy of Beidas; see Alamuddin, *Fly-*

ing Sheikh, 148. Several committee members, including the AUB economist Elias Saba , withdrew. Munla was accused of sabotaging the committee's proceedings when it transpired that a majority of members were leaning towards recommending refloating Intra. Hanna Asfour further claims that in order to become eligible to serve on the committee, Munla became a depositor at Intra through an illegal transfer of debt from an actual depositor. The second committee was formed on February 2, 1967; see Asfour, *Bank Intra: Qadiyyah wa 'Ibar*, 96–100.

66. The second committee, created under decree 44, was composed of the BDL governor as chairman and four other members: the chairman of Lebanon's State Council (highest judicial authority), the director general of the Ministry of Finance, a legal expert, and a financial expert suggested by the Ministry of Finance. See full text of decree in Yafi and Yafi, *Majmu'at al-Naqd wa al-Taslif*, 1999, 2: 80–82.

67. Helou, *Hayat fi Dhikrayat*, 239.

68. The AUB economist Talha Yaffi, Prime Minister Abdallah Yafi's nephew, provided Washington with details of the government of Lebanon's proposal of a joint buyout of Intra to its Kuwaiti counterpart; see U.S. embassy Kuwait to Department of State, telegram 359, October 20, 1967; and on the seemingly regular meetings between Shawkat Munla and the embassy's reporting officer in Beirut, U.S. embassy Beirut to Department of State, airgram A-4, June 19, 1967; FN 6 LEB; RG 59; NAB.

69. On Tamraz as discreet representative of U.S. private interests, see Department of State to Kuwait embassy, telegram 174798, April 13, 1967; and on Tamraz explicitly asking the U.S. embassy in Kuwait to "contrive means for him to present a proposition in private to [Kuwaiti Finance Minister] Ateegi," U.S. embassy Kuwait to Department of State, telegram 1040, April 12, 1967; FN 6 LEB; Subject Numeric File; RG 59; NAB.

70. On the significance given by Jaber al-Sabah to Eugene Black's advice and the latter's multiple roles, see U.S. embassy Kuwait to Department of State, telegram 546, November 29, 1966; FN 6 LEB; RG 59; NAB. The American Manager of KTFCI also discreetly passed on information to the U.S. embassy about his boss, chairman Abdul Aziz al-Bahar. Embassy cable identifies his last name, Paulding, and asks Washington to protect him as a source; see Kuwait to Department of State, telegram 725, January 18, 1967; ibid.

71. Parker passed on sensitive information on Kuwaiti withdrawals to U.S. officials on the day Intra stopped payment; see U.S. embassy Beirut to Department of State, telegram 3292, October 14, 1966; FN 6 LEB; RG 59; NAB.

72. Small creditors would be given cash certificates for value claims redeemed at a future date while large ones would hold equity shares in the investment companies that would be spun off from Intra's major assets. On details of Credit Suisse offer, see U.S. embassy Beirut to Department of State, telegram 836, August 2, 1967; FN 6 LEB; RG 59; NAB.

73. The Helou administration sought a speedy transfer of liability to Credit Suisse before the first management committee's mandate expired on August 8.

Credit Suisse final signature, however, was made conditional on a more extensive audit and on talks with large creditors; see U.S. embassy Beirut to Department of State, telegram 1011, August 8, 1967; FN 6 LEB; RG 59; NAB.

74. According to Parker, the Fides offer ran aground in September after the Lebanese government declined to provide full guarantees of the existence and value of Intra assets. On Franco-U.S. discussions of the Credit Suisse offer and another French one by the financier Jules Piquet, see U.S. embassy Beirut to Department of State, airgram A-250, September 20, 1967; FN 6 LEB; 1967–69 Subject Numeric File; RG 59; NAB; and on why the Credit Suisse deal fell through, according to Paul Parker, telegram 1848, September 7, 1967; ibid.

75. The U.S. embassy in Beirut questioned the "dubious reputation" of Antoine Meguerdiche, the local banker representing Credit Suisse, which was further "sullied" by association with the shady British banker Francis Richard Craddock; see U.S. embassy Beirut to Department of State, airgram A-250, September 20, 1967; FN 6 LEB; 1967–69 Subject Numeric File; RG 59; NAB.

76. Tamraz had been building up such support since the preceding spring. By the first week of September, he managed to gain the approval of the Lebanese government, which pledged its advance acceptance of the deal to help Tamraz bring other creditors on board. Prime Minister Rashid Karame also promised that the central bank's emergency discount facilities provided for other banks would equally apply to the newly constituted institution. Prime Minister Saeb Salam's nephew Hani Salam, an Intra shareholder, facilitated the collaboration between Parker and Tamraz; see U.S. embassy Beirut to Department of State, telegram 1848, September 7, 1967; FN 6 LEB; RG 59, NAB, on this and on Parker's severance of ties with BEA. On Parker's "very helpful" role in reviving the Kidder Peabody offer, see Beirut embassy to Department of State, airgram A-265, enclosure 1, "Memorandum of Conversation, Subject Intra Bank," September 26, 1967, ibid.

77. U.S. embassy Beirut to Department of State, airgram A-327, October 11, 1967; FN 6 LEB; 1967–69 Subject Numeric File; RG 59; NAB.

78. Each of the four major creditors held shares equivalent to the amount Intra owed them and was represented on the new board of directors. Half the deposits valued at LL250,000 or less were also converted into shares. Tamraz found claims by original shareholders to be "appealing on both humane and political grounds." But Lebanon's Prime Minister Rashid Karame, who was also finance minister, had stipulated that "all former shares should be zero"; see U.S. embassy Beirut to Department of State, airgram A-265, enclosure 2, September 26, 1967; FN 6 LEB; Subject Numeric File; RG 59; NAB.

79. Hanna Asfour argued that the nullification of original shares was unconstitutional, given that no actual sale took place. For a detailed legal argument against the Kidder Peabody scheme, see Asfour, *Bank Intra: Qadiyyah wa 'Ibar*, 113–29. Yusif Salameh ridiculed the Kidder Peabody scheme, which in his view would have been laughed at in U.S. financial circles; see Salameh, *Haddathani Y.S. Qal*, 138. For Alamuddin's comment, see Alamuddin, *Flying Sheikh*, 160.

80. These articles appeared in *Le Figaro* and *Le Canard enchaîné*. The Kidder Peabody takeover was also portrayed as an attempt to wrest control of valuable shipyard assets owned by the Chantier naval de La Ciotat, in which Intra had a controlling share. The value of La Ciotat was expected to grow after the termination of construction work on a new slipway that could handle the building of tankers up to 300,000 tons, see U.S. embassy Beirut to Department of State, airgram A-412, November 7, 1967; FN 6 LEB; Subject Numeric File; RG 59; NAB.

81. Tamraz also hoped to realize his "private dream" of eventually getting the holding company listed on the New York Stock Exchange through share swaps; see U.S. embassy Beirut to Department of State, airgram A-265, enclosure 2, September 26, 1967; FN 6 LEB; Subject Numeric File; RG 59; NAB.

82. U.S. embassy Beirut to Department of State, airgram A-327, October 11, 1967; FN 6 LEB; 1967–69 Subject Numeric File; RG 59; NAB.

83. U.S. embassy Beirut to Department of State, telegram 3084, October 13, 1967; FN 6 LEB; 1967–69 Subject Numeric File; RG 59; NAB.

Chapter 6

1. Chapter epigraph: Dhulfiqar Qubaysi, "Ba'da Intra Ila 'Ayn," *al-Masarif*, October 15, 1966, 6–7.

2. Salim Hoss proposed that the insurance cover deposits in all currencies, including U.S. dollars; see Hoss, "Daman al-Wadai al-Masrifiyyah fi Lubnan," *al-Masarif*, February 15, 1967, 10–17.

3. Hoss was brought in as a consultant by his close friend Khalil Salem, who at the time was director general of the Ministry of Finance; see Mardini, *Salim Hoss: Qissat Hayatih*, 55.

4. On Beidas unilaterally confirming the issue of a loan guarantee in the amount of U.S.$3M without consulting with board of directors; see Salameh, *Haddathani Y.S. Qal*, 125–26. According to Hanna Asfour, the only two people at the bank that had an intimate knowledge of its finances were Beidas and the Beirut branch manager Iskandar Ayyoub; see Asfour, *Bank Intra: Qadiyyah wa 'Ibar*, 50.

5. Asfour, *Bank Intra: Qadiyyah wa 'Ibar*, 245–47.

6. Ibid., 30.

7. Beidas brought in financial consultants, including the former governor of Syria's central bank Izzat Traboulsi and the former Lebanese minister of economy Rafiq Naja, to help put the bank's books in order; see ibid., 35–36.

8. Qubaysi, "Ba'da Intra Ila Ayn."

9. The Bank of France finally agreed to send the manager of its discounting department to Beirut, to be followed by a team of technicians. Once it transpired that withdrawals after the banking "holiday" were less than expected and did not precipitate capital flight, the momentum for major intervention waned; see U.S. embassy Paris to Department of State, airgram A-659, October 26, 1966; FN 6 LEB; Subject Numeric Files 1963–66; RG 59; NAB.

10. U.S. Department of State to Beirut embassy, telegram 68394, October 18, 1966; ibid.

11. Helou and Gunter met on November 11, 1966; see U.S. embassy Beirut to Department of State, airgram A-405, November 15, 1966; ibid.

12. U.S. Department of State, "Memorandum of Conversation, Lebanese Banking Crisis," November 15, 1966; ibid.

13. John Gunter added that members of the banking community had engaged in dangerous banking practices, which in his opinion, had also been a major factor in Lebanon's rapid economic growth; see U.S. embassy Beirut to Department of State, airgram A-405, November 15, 1966; ibid. Gunter continued to be consulted about central banking in the following year. In August 1967, he told U.S. embassy officials that the government of Lebanon "must learn proper use of central bank" but acknowledged that the new BDL governor, Elias Sarkis, and director general of the Ministry of Finance, Khalil Salem, were talented and starting to catch on; see U.S. embassy Beirut to Department of State, telegram 1382, August 21, 1967; ibid.

14. According to Porter, Beshara Francis, the temporary director of Intra's court-appointed management committee, shared Eddé's concerns and viewed efforts by his predecessor to save Intra's foreign branches as "illegal"; U.S. embassy Beirut to Department of State, airgram A-682, February 1, 1967; ibid.

15. U.S. Department of State, "Memorandum of Conversation, Lebanese Banking Crisis," November 15, 1966, and Beirut embassy to Department of State, telegram 3782, October 28, 1966; ibid.

16. Takla had also held the justice portfolio in the Yaffi government. He resigned from that post on September 7; see Majid, *Tarikh al-Hukumat al-Lubnaniyyah*, 161.

17. The AUB's Yusif Sayigh convened a highly publicized panel to dissect the Intra crisis, which included Elias Saba ; see "al-Azmah al Masrifiyyah 'ala al-Mashraha," *al-Masarif*, December 15, 1966, 12–17.

18. For a list of the major laws and decrees, see Banque du Liban, "Annual Report for 1967," 17. For full texts see Yafi and Yafi, *Majmu'at al-Naqd wa al-Taslif*, 1999.

19. Achi and Ayache, *Tarikh al-Masarif fi Lubnan*, 215.

20. Yafi and Yafi, *Majmu'at al-Naqd wa al-Taslif*, 2: 28, Article 2 of Intra's law.

21. Members of the first management committee, numbering six to ten, were nominated as follows: one by the minister of finance, one by the BDL's governor, one or more of known financial or banking expertise by the BDL's central council, one or more creditors, and one or more shareholders. The committee chair had to be a creditor or shareholder. Under the amended law, the second management committee was composed of: the BDL's governor (chair), the president of the State Council, Lebanon's highest judicial body, the director general of the Ministry of Finance, and a financial or economic expert nominated by the minister of finance. For full text of original and amended law, see ibid., 2: 28–35.

22. For full text of law 28/67, see ibid., 2: 36–58.

23. According to U.S. embassy officials, Eddé himself experienced delays; see

U.S. embassy Beirut to Department of State, telegram 3484, October 20, 1966; FN 6 LEB; Subject Numeric File; RG 59; NAB.

24. Ironically, some of these rules were more stringent than those imposed by the BDL on domestic banks, which the ABL had vociferously resisted; U.S. embassy Beirut to Department of State, telegram A-694, February 6, 1967; ibid.

25. The ABL entrusted Eddé with negotiating the gentleman's agreement on January 13, 1967. The ABL chair then summoned foreign branch managers for one-on-one meetings and "grilled" them on the issues in question; see U.S. embassy Beirut to Department of State, telegram A-694, February 6, 1967; ibid.

26. Ibid.

27. Some small bankers were even calling for nationalization of their banks, according to ABL's vice-president Anis Bibi; U.S. embassy Beirut to Department of State, airgram A-764, February 23, 1967; ibid.

28. U.S. embassy Beirut to Department of State, airgram A-764, February 23, 1967; ibid.

29. U.S. embassy Beirut to Department of State, airgram A-859, March 20, 1967; ibid.

30. U.S. embassy Beirut to Department of State, telegram 3723, October 27, 1966; ibid.

31. Achi and Ayache, *Tarikh al-Masarif fi Lubnan*, 211.

32. For a comparative analysis of the functions and composition of all three bodies, see Achi and Ayache, *Tarikh al-Masarif fi Lubnan*, 210–12.

33. Yafi and Yafi, *Majmu'at al-Naqd wa al-Taslif*, 1: 60, Article 148 of the Law of Money and Credit.

34. Achi and Ayache, *Tarikh al-Masarif fi Lubnan*, 210–12.

35. Ibid., 218–21.

36. On the ceremony's proceedings as narrated by Hoss, see al-Mardini, *Salim Hoss: Qissat Hayatih*, 55–56.

37. Achi and Ayache, *Tarikh al-Masarif fi Lubnan*, 202–3.

38. For a list of banks that were taken over by the Higher Banking Commission, see Achi and Ayache, *Tarikh al-Masarif fi Lubnan*, 213.

39. On calling this period a "golden age," see ibid., 217.

40. See Sayyid Ali, *al-Tatawwur al-Tarikhi*, 233. Estimates of Arab oil revenues in 1974 ranged between U.S.$60B and U.S.$75B, and 1980 revenues were predicted to be in the U.S.$100–130B range; see Hoss, "Development of Lebanon's Financial Market."

41. For a list of these funds, see ibid., 12.

42. Achi and Ayache, *Tarikh al-Masarif fi Lubnan*, 225.

43. The Algerian, State Bank of India, and World Bank loans were LL55M, LL15M, and LL75M respectively; see Hoss, "Development of Lebanon's Financial Market," 40. On lending to international banks in Lebanese liras, Renault's bonds, and Franjieh's comments; see Ache and Ayache, *Tarikh al-Masarif fi Lubnan*, 227.

44. On monetary authorities opposing the internationalization of the Lebanese pound, see Hoss, "Development of Lebanon's Financial Market,"43.

45. On the list of amendments, see Ache and Ayache, *Tarikh al-Masarif fi Lubnan*, 228.

46. According to the veteran banker George Ache, the declared objectives of the National Bank for the Development of Industry and Tourism were to reduce the growing trade deficit, encourage the founding of industrial and touristic companies that would grow national income, provide a suitable venue for investing surplus capital, and create new jobs to address population growth; see Ache and Ayache, *Tarikh al-Masarif fi Lubnan*, 229.

47. Hoss drew on the standard Chihist narrative to explain the growth in industrialization. He argued that negative factors typically cited for the absence of industry, such as the small size of the domestic market, the paucity of long-term capital, and the mercantile Lebanese spirit, were "outweighed by such positive factors as Lebanon's geographic proximity to Arab markets; the manifest initiative and enterprise of the Lebanese entrepreneur; Lebanon's consistent adherence to liberal currency and trade systems and to a non-cumbersome tax system; [and] the availability of a highly adaptable and relatively cheap labor." See Hoss, "Development of Lebanon's Financial Market," 6, 7.

48. On the paucity of open-market financial instruments, see ibid., 26–32.

49. The total volume of trading on the BSE reached a high of LL81M in 1964, a low of LL8M in 1968, and bounced back to LL52M in 1973; see ibid., 38–39.

50. Ibid., 16.

51. For a list of buyouts, see Ache and Ayache, *Tarikh al-Masarif fi Lubnan*, 223. Licenses were sold at a price ranging from LL6M to LL8M; see Hoss, "Development of Lebanon's Financial Market,"21.

52. Ache and Ayache, *Tarikh al-Masarif fi Lubnan*, 219. The insurance sector was also dominated by international corporations—seventy-two out of the eighty-seven insurance companies in operation at the time in Lebanon were foreign-based; see Hoss, "Development of Lebanon's Financial Market," 37.

53. On Hoss's proposal for a free-banking zone, see Hoss, "Development of Lebanon's Financial Market," 23–26.

54. The committee set up by the ABL to establish an Arab banking union was composed of the following members: Anwar Khalil, Numan Azhari, Hisham Bsat, and George Ache; see Ache and Ayache, *Tarikh al-Masarif fi Lubnan*, 229.

55. These included Bank Audi's Infebank and Union bank; see ibid., 230–31.

56. For a brief political history of the first stage of the war in the mid-1970s, see Khalidi, *Conflict and Violence in Lebanon*.

57. For a personal account of Sarkis's term in office by his close advisor, see Baqraduni, *al-Salam al-Mafqud*.

58. Assafir, *50 'Aman: Masrif Lubnan*, 42.

59. Tamraz was the primary financier of Lebanese president Amin Gemayel's right-wing Kataeb party; see Hourani, "Capitalists in Conflict," 137–60.

60. On the economics of this crisis and the BDL response to it, see Dibeh, "Political Economy of Inflation," 33–52.

61. On December 6, 1988, a rocket-propelled grenade burst into the third floor of the BDL's headquarters. The day before, a car bomb had exploded nearby, killing one and injuring seven; see Ihsan Hijazi, "Bank of Lebanon Now a War Target," *New York Times*, December 7, 1988.

Conclusion

1. Epigraph: al-Safir, *50 'Aman: Masrif Lubnan*, 48. Naim was featured portrayed as "The Banker in the Bunker" on the front cover of the January 1990 issue of *Institutional Investor*; see Achi and Ayache, *Tarikh al-Masarif fi Lubnan*, 298. On the role of the BDL as an "economic government," see Salloum, *al-Siyasat al-Maliyyah wa al-Niqdiyyah*, 376. Ihsan Hijazi, "Bank of Lebanon Now a War Target," *New York Times,* December 7, 1988.

2. On Hariri's neoliberal reconstruction project, see Hannes Baumann, *Citizen Hariri: Lebanon's Neo-Liberal Reconstruction* (Oxford: Oxford University Press, 2017).

3. Traboulsi, "Social Classes and Political Power in Lebanon," 28–30.

4. Muhammad Wehbe, "'Ra'is al-Jumhuriyya Laysa Hakaman': Iqrar al-Muwazana Bidayat Makhraj Min al-Ma'ziq," *al-Akhbar*, November 2, 2016.

5. Assafir, *50 'Aman: Masrif Lubnan*, 43–45.

6. See Muhammad Wehbe, "'Ra'is al-Jumhuriyya Laysa Hakaman': Iqrar al-Muwazana Bidayat Makhraj Min al-Ma'ziq," *al-Akhbar*, November 2, 2016.

7. al-Safir, *50 'Aman: Masrif Lubnan*, 9–12.

8. On one of Lebanon's largest operations of money creation and its transfer from public to private funds; see Mohammad Zbeeb, "Bil-Asma' wa al-Arqaam," *al-Akhbar*, January 13, 2017.

9. On the share of bank holdings to GDP, see al-Safir, *50 'Aman: Masrif Lubnan*, 90, 145. On banks' share of public debt, see ibid., 133.

10. On the history of government borrowing as a means of undermining state sovereignty, see Krasner, *Sovereignty: Organized Hypocrisy*, 127–51. On the concept of "colonization through lending," see Birdal, *Political Economy of Ottoman Public Debt*, 1. Conditionality is "the practice of attaching policy-change requirements to loans" by IFIs; see Sengupta, "Politics of Market Reform in India," 38.

11. On the links between Lebanon's commercial banks and its political class, see Chaaban, "I've Got the Power," 2016.

12. International Monetary Fund, Middle East and Central Asia Dept., "Lebanon : Staff Report for the 2015 Article IV Consultation," 10., 10.

13. International Monetary Fund, "Lebanon: Financial System Stability Assessment,", 4.

14. al-Safir, *50 'Aman: Masrif Lubnan*, 235.

15. Saba's 1943 decree levied import duties on all imports. The strike by traders in its wake brought Beirut's economy to a standstill. Camille Chamoun declared

the decree a deviation from Lebanese economy; see Traboulsi, "Social Classes and Political Power in Lebanon," 43–44.

16. Al-Safir, 50 'Aman: Masrif Lubnan, 79–83.

17. These notes were leaked to Beirut's daily *al-Akhbar*, whose dynamic and erudite economics editor, Mohammad Zbeeb, and his team of reporters, including Hassan Chakrani, persistently questioned BDL policy, in sharp contrast to the doting coverage of other Lebanese media outlets; see Chakrani, "Sunduq al-Naqd al-Dawli: Irtibat al-Dawlah wa al-Masarif Masdar al-Khatar al-Awwal," *al-Akhbar*, July 30, 2015.

18. International Monetary Fund, "Lebanon: Financial System Stability Assessment," Executive Summary.

Bibliography

ARCHIVES

U.S. National Archives, National Archives Building [NAB], Washington, DC

General Records of the Department of State, Record Group (RG) 59
Central decimal files: Lebanon, 1950–54, 1955–59, 1960–63
Subject numeric files: 1963–66, 1967–69

International Monetary Fund Online Archives

Executive board documents (EBD) collection
By country: Lebanon, 1946–54

Banque du Liban, Library Collection, Beirut

Banque du Liban (BDL)annual reports, 1964–69
Intra Bank, executive board annual reports, 1962, 1965
Banque du Syrie et du Liban (BSL) annual reports, 1959–62.

American University of Beirut

Intra Bank special collection

Association of Banks in Lebanon, Library Collection, Beirut

Executive board annual reports, 1960–67

Centre des Archives diplomatiques de Nantes (CAN), Nantes, France

Mandat Syrie-Liban Files

Rockefeller Archive Center, Sleepy Hollow, New York [RAC]

Ford Foundation records, grants, 732A
Rockefeller Foundation collection

Newspapers and Magazines
al-Akhbar
al-Diyar
al-Hayat
al-Masarif
al-Nahar
al-Nida'
al-Safir
al-Sayyad
al-Sharq al-Awsat,
Life
The New York Times
Der Spiegel

Books, Articles, Reports, and Theses

Abisaab, Malek. *Militant Women of a Fragile Nation*. Syracuse, NY: Syracuse University Press, 2009.

Abu el-Naml, Hussein. "al-Isham al-Filastini fi Izdihar al-Iqtisad al-Lubnani." In *Awraq Filastiniyah wa Arabiyah: Takriman li-Rif'at Sidqi al-Nimer fi al-Dhikra al-Ula li-Rahilih*, 139–48. Beirut: al-Dar al-Arabiyah lil-Ulum, Nashirun, 2008.

Abu Fakhr, Saqr. "al-Filastiniyyun fi Lubnan: Dawr Thaqafi Mumayyaz wa Isham Mash-hud fi al-'Umran." In *Awraq Filastiniyah wa Arabiyah: Takriman li-Rif'at Sidqi al-Nimer fi al-Dhikra al-Ula li-Rahilih*, 149–56. Beirut: al-Dar al-Arabiyah lil-Ulum, Nashirun, 2008.

Abu-Rish, Ziad Munif. "Conflict and Institution Building in Lebanon, 1946–1955." PhD diss. University of California, Los Angeles, 2014.

Achi, Georges. *al-Nizam al-Naqdi fi Suriya*. 3rd ed. Matbaat Jamiaat Dimashq, 1959.

Achi, Georges, and Ghassan Ayache. *Tarikh al-Masarif fi Lubnan*. Beirut: Banque Audi SAL, 2001.

Alamuddin, Najib. *The Flying Sheikh*. London: Quartet Books, 1987.

———. *The Flying Sheikh: Autobiography*. London: Quartet Books, 1989.

Amel, Mahdi. *Fi al-Dawlah al-Ta'ifiyyah*. Beirut: Dar al-Farabi, 2003.

———. *Muqaddimat Nazariyyah li Dirasat Athar al-Fikr al-Ishtiraki fi Harakt al-Taharrur al-Watani*. Beirut: Dar al-Farabi, 2013.

Anghie, Antony. *Imperialism, Sovereignty and the Making of International Law*. New York: Cambridge University Press, 2005. www.loc.gov/catdir/toc/cam051/2004049732.html.

Asfour, Edmond Y. *Syria: Development and Monetary Policy*. Cambridge, MA: Center for Middle Eastern Studies of Harvard University, distributed by Harvard University Press, 1959.

Asfour, Hanna. *Bank Intra: Qadiyyah wa 'Ibar*. Beirut, 1969.

Asseily, Antoine Edouard. *Central Banking in Lebanon*. Beirut, 1967.

Association of Banks in Lebanon. *The Golden Jubilee Book, 1959–2009.* Beirut: Association of Banks in Lebanon, 2009.

Autheman, André. *La Banque impériale ottomane.* Paris: Ministère de l'économie et des finances, Comité pour l'histoire économique et financière de la France, 1996.

Ayyash, Ghassan. *Azmat al-Maliyyah al-'Ammah fi Lubnan: Qissat al-Inhiyar al-Naqdi.* Beirut: Dar al-Nahar, 1997.

Azhari, Numan. *Nu'man al-Azhari: Nisf Qarn min al-'Amal al-Masrifi Hadhihi Tajrubati.* Beirut: an-Nahar, 2008.

'Azm, Khalid al-. *Mudhakkirat Khalid al-'Azm,* vol. 2. Beirut: al-Dar al-Muttahidah lil-Nashr, 1973.

Badre, Albert Y. "The Economic Development of Lebanon with Special Emphasis on Finance." PhD diss., University of Iowa, 1950.

———. "Nahwa Afaaq Iqtisadiyyah Jadidah." In *'Ahd al-Nadwah al-Lubnaniyyah,* 369–76. Beirut: Dar al-Nahar, 1997.

Badre, Albert Y., and Simon G. Siksek. *Manpower and Oil in Arab Countries.* Westport, CT: Hyperion Press, 1981.

Badrud-Din, Abdul-Amir. *The Bank of Lebanon: Central Banking in a Financial Centre and Entrepôt.* Dover, NH: F. Pinter, 1984.

Balakian, Peter. *The Burning Tigris: The Armenian Genocide and America's Response.* 1st ed. New York: HarperCollins, 2003.

Banque de Syrie et du Liban. "Exercice 1959." Beirut: Banque de Syrie et du Liban, 1960.

———. "Exercice 1960." Beirut: Banque de Syrie et du Liban, 1961.

———. "Exercice 1962." Beirut: Banque de Syrie et du Liban, 1963.

Banque du Liban. "Annual Report for 1964." Beirut: Banque du Liban, June 25, 1965.

———. "Annual Report for 1965." Beirut: Banque du Liban, May 27, 1966.

———. "Annual Report for 1967." Beirut: Banque du Liban, May 30, 1968.

Baqraduni, Karim. *al-Salam al-Mafqud: 'Ahd Elias Sarkis 1982–1986.* 4th ed. Beirut: 'Abr al-Sharq lil Manshurat, 1984.

Baroudi, Sami E. "Conflict and Co-operation within Lebanon's Business Community: Relations between Merchants' and Industrialists' Associations." *Middle Eastern Studies* 37, no. 4, 2001.

Baumann, Hannes. *Citizen Hariri: Lebanon's Neo-Liberal Reconstruction.* Oxford University Press, 2017.

Beinin, Joel, and Zachary Lockman. *Workers on the Nile: Nationalism, Communism, Islam, and the Egyptian Working Class, 1882–1954.* Princeton, NJ: Princeton University Press, 1987.

Birdal, Murat. *The Political Economy of Ottoman Public Debt: Insolvency and European Financial Control in the Late Nineteenth Century.* Library of Ottoman Studies 18. New York: Tauris Academic Studies, distributed by Palgrave Macmillan, 2010.

Burgin, Angus. *The Great Persuasion: Reinventing Free Markets since the Depression*. Reprint. Cambridge, MA: Harvard University Press, 2015.

Calomiris, Charles W., and Stephen H. Haber. *Fragile by Design: The Political Origins of Banking Crises and Scarce Credit*. Princeton, NJ: Princeton University Press, 2014.

Cassis, Youssef, *Crises and Opportunities: The Shaping of Modern Finance*. Oxford: Oxford University Press, 2011.

Cammett, Melani Claire. *Compassionate Communalism: Welfare and Sectarianism in Lebanon*. Ithaca, NY: Cornell University Press, 2014.

Carvalho, George de. "Fall of the 'Genius from Jerusalem.'" *Life*, January 27, 1967, 87–89.

Central Bank of Iraq. *al-Bank al-Markazi al-'Iraqi, 1947–1972*. Baghdad: Matabi' Thanyan, 1972.

Central Bank of Kuwait. "Law no. 32 of the Year 1968 Concerning Currency, the Central Bank of Kuwait and the Organization of Banking Business." www.cbk.gov.kw/en/images/CBK-Law-32-68-En-10-114233-2.pdf .

Chaaban, Jad. "I've Got the Power: Mapping Connections between Lebanon's Banking Sector and the Ruling Class." Economic Research Forum (Egypt) working paper, 2016

Chaitani, Youssef. *Post-Colonial Syria and Lebanon the Decline of Arab Nationalism and the Triumph of the State*. New York: I.B. Tauris, distributed by Palgrave Macmillan, 2007.

Chevallier, Dominique. *Mujtama Jabal Lubnan fi 'Asr al-Thawrah al-Sinaiyyah al-Awrubiyyah*. Beirut: Dar al-Haqiqah, 1993.

Chiha, Michel. *Propos d'économie libanaise*. Beirut: Éditions du Trident, 1965.

Citino, Nathan. *Envisioning the Arab Future: Modernization in US-Arab Relations, 1945–1967*. Cambridge: Cambridge University Press, 2017.

Clay, Christopher. *Gold for the Sultan: Western Bankers and Ottoman Finance, 1856–1881: A Contribution to Ottoman and to International Financial History*. New York: I.B. Tauris, distributed by St. Martin's Press, 2000.

Corm, Georges. "al-Iqtisad fi Muhadarat al-Nadwah al-Lubnaniyyah." In *'Ahd al-Nadwah al-Lubnaniyyah*, 577–85. Beirut: Dar al-Nahar, 1997.

———. *Lubnan al-Mu'asir: Tarikh wa mujtama'*. Translated by Hasan Qubaysi. Beirut: al-Maktabah al-Sharqiyah, 2004.

Dalul, Muhsin. *al-Tariq Ila al-Watan: Rub' Qarn bi-Rifqat Kamal Junblat*. Beirut: al-Dar al-Arabiyah lil-Ulum Nashirun, 2010.

Davis, Eric. *Challenging Colonialism: Bank Misr and Egyptian Industrialization, 1920–1941*. Princeton, NJ: Princeton University Press, 1983.

Deeb, Mary-Jane, and Mary E. King, eds. *Hasib Sabbagh: From Palestinian Refugee to Citizen of the World*. Lanham, MD: Middle East Institute / University Press of America, 1996.

Dib, Kamal. *Warlords and Merchants: The Lebanese Business and Political Establishment*. Reading, England: Ithaca Press, 2004.

————. *Imbaraturiyyat Intra wa Hitan al-Mal fi Lubnan.* Beirut: Dar al-Nahar li-l-Nashr, 2014.

Dibeh, Ghassan. "The Political Economy of Inflation and Currency Depreciation in Lebanon, 1984–92." *Middle Eastern Studies* 38, no. 1 (January 2002).

El-Khazen, Farid. *The Communal Pact of National Identities: The Making and Politics of the 1943 National Pact.* Oxford, England: Centre for Lebanese Studies, 1991.

Franck, Peter G. "Economic Nationalism in the Middle East." *Middle East Journal* 6, no. 4 (October 1, 1952).

————. "Dismemberment of Empire and Reconstitution of Regional Space: The Emergence of 'National' Industries in Damascus between 1918 and 1946." In *The British and French Mandates in Comparative Perspective*, edited by Nadine Méouchy and Peter Sluglett. Leiden: Brill, 2004.

Flandreau, Marc. "Crises and Punishment: Moral Hazard and the Pre-1914 International Financial Architecture." In *Money Doctors: The Experience of International Financial Advising 1850–2000*, edited by Marc Flandreau. New York: Routledge, 2003.

Frangieh, Nabil, and Zeina Frangieh. *Hamid Frangieh: Lubnan al-Akhar.* Beirut: Dar al-Arz, 1993.

Gaspard, Toufic K. *A Political Economy of Lebanon, 1948–2002: The Limits of Laissez-faire.* Boston: Brill, 2004.

Gates, Carolyn. *The Merchant Republic of Lebanon: Rise of an Open Economy.* New York: Centre for Lebanese Studies in association with I.B. Tauris, distributed by St Martin's Press, 1998.

Gehchan, Roger. *Hussein 'Uwayni: Khamsuna 'Aman min Tarikh Lubnan wa al-Sharq al-Awsat (1920–1970).* Translated by Georges Abi Saleh. Beirut: FMA, 2000.

Gendzier, Irene L. *Notes from the Minefield: United States Intervention in Lebanon and the Middle East, 1945–1958.* New York: Columbia University Press, 2006.

Gran, Peter. *The Rise of the Rich: A New View of Modern World History.* Syracuse, N.Y: Syracuse University Press, 2009.

Haddad, Bassam. *Business Networks in Syria: The Political Economy of Authoritarian Resilience.* Stanford Studies in Middle Eastern and Islamic Societies and Cultures. Stanford, California: Stanford University Press, 2012.

Hakim, Carol. *The Origins of the Lebanese National Idea, 1840–1920.* Berkeley: University of California Press, 2013.

Hakim, George. "Tanzim al-Inma' al-Iqtisadi wa al-Ijtima'i fi Lubnan." In *'Ahd al-Nadwah al-Lubnaniyyah*, 227–33. Beirut: Dar al-Nahar, 1997.

Hall, Peter A. *The Political Power of Economic Ideas: Keynesianism across Nations.* Princeton, NJ: Princeton University Press, 1989.

Hanieh, Adam. *Money Markets and Monarchies: The Gulf Cooperation Council and the Contemporary Political Economy of the Middle East.* Cambridge: Cambridge University Press, 2018.

Hanssen, Jens. *Fin de Siècle Beirut: The Making of an Ottoman Provincial Capital*. New York: Oxford University Press, 2005.

———. "'Malhamé—Malfamé': Levantine Elites and Transimperial Networks on the Eve of the Young Turk Revolution." *International Journal of Middle East Studies* 43, no. 1 (February 1, 2011).

Harik, Iliyya. *Man Yahkum Lubnan*. Beirut: an-Nahar, 1972.

Helou, Charles. *Hayat fi Dhikrayat*. Beirut: Dar al-Nahar, 1995.

Helleiner, Eric "The Southern Side of Embedded Liberalism." In *Money Doctors: The Experience of International Financial Advising 1850–2000*, edited by Marc Flandreau. New York: Routledge, 2003.

Heydemann, Steven, ed. "War, Keynesianism, and Colonialism: Explaining State-Market Relations in the Postwar Middle East." In *War, Institutions, and Social Change in the Middle East*. Berkeley: University of California Press, 2000.

Himadeh, Said. *Economic Organization of Syria*. Beirut: American Press, 1936.

———. *Monetary and Banking System of Syria*. Beirut: American Press, 1935.

———. "Mushkilaatunah al-Iqtisadiyyah wa Kayfa Nu'alijuha." In *'Ahd al-Nadwah al-Lubnaniyyah*, 101–11. Beirut, 1997.

Hoss, Salim. "The Development of Lebanon's Financial Market." Conference paper. Beirut: Société Technopresse moderne, 1974.

———. "The Roles of Central Banking in Lebanon." PhD diss., Indiana University, 1962.

Hourani, Albert. *Syria and Lebanon: A Political Essay*. London: Oxford University Press, 1946.

Hourani, Najib. "Capitalists in Conflict: The Lebanese Civil War Reconsidered." *Middle East Critique* 24, no. 2 (2015).

Hudson, Michael C. *The Precarious Republic: Political Modernization in Lebanon*. Boulder, CO: Westview Press, 1985.

Hudson, Peter. "Imperial Designs: The Royal Bank of Canada in the Caribbean." *Race & Class* 52, no. 1 (July 1, 2010).

International Monetary Fund. "Lebanon: Financial System Stability Assessment." Country Report No. 17/21. January 2017.

———. Middle East and Central Asia Dept. "Lebanon : Staff Report for the 2015 Article IV Consultation." Country Report No. 15/190. July 2015.

Intra Bank. "Annual Report 1965." May 31, 1966.

Izz al-Arab, Abd al-Aziz. *European Control and Egypt's Traditional Elites: A Case Study in Elite Economic Nationalism*. Lewiston, NY: Edwin Mellen Press, 2002.

Jisr, Basim al-. *Fuad Shihab*. Beirut: Muassasat Fuad Shihab, 1998.

Johnson, Harry G. "The Sterling Crisis of 1967 and the Gold Rush of 1968." *Nebraska Journal of Economics and Business* 7, no. 2 (October 1, 1968).

Johnson, Michael. *Class & Client in Beirut: The Sunni Muslim Community and the Lebanese State, 1840–1985*. Atlantic Highlands, NJ: Ithaca Press, 1986.

Jones, Geoffrey. *The History of the British Bank of the Middle East*. Vol. 1. Hong

Kong Bank Group History Series, no. 3. New York: Cambridge University Press, 1986.

Keynes, John Maynard. *A Treatise on Money.* Vol. 1. London: Macmillan, 1930.

Kfuri, Tawfiq. *al-Shihabiyyah wa Siyasat al-Mawqif.* Beirut, 1980.

Khalaf, Samir. *Lebanon's Predicament.* New York: Columbia University Press, 1987.

Khalidi, Walid. *Conflict and Violence in Lebanon: Confrontation in the Middle East.* Cambridge MA: Center for International Affairs; Harvard University, 1979.

Khoury, Bishara. *Haqa'iq Lubnaniyyah.* 4 vols. Vol. 3. Beirut: al-Dar al-Lubnaniyyah lil Nashr al-Jamii, 1983.

Khoury, Philip S. *Syria and the French Mandate: The Politics of Arab Nationalism, 1920–1945.* Princeton, N.J: Princeton University Press, 1987.

———. "The Syrian Independence Movement and the Growth of Economic Nationalism in Damascus." *British Society for Middle Eastern Studies Bulletin* 14, no. 1 (1987).

Kingston, Paul W. T. "The 'Ambassador for the Arabs': The Locke Mission and the Unmaking of U.S. Development Diplomacy in the Near East, 1952–1953." In *The Middle East and the United States: A Historical and Political Reassessment,* 3rd ed., 30–50. Boulder, CO: Westview Press, 2003.

———. *Reproducing Sectarianism: Advocacy Networks and the Politics of Civil Society in Postwar Lebanon.* Albany: State University of New York Press, 2013.

Krasner, Stephen D. *Sovereignty: Organized Hypocrisy.* Princeton, NJ: Princeton University Press, 1999.

Landes, David S. *Bankers and Pashas: International Finance and Economic Imperialism in Egypt.* Cambridge, MA: Harvard University Press, 1980.

Longuenesse, Élizabeth. "Système éducatif et modèle professionnel: La mandate français en perspective. L'example des comptables au Liban." In *The British and French Mandates in Comparative Perspective,* edited by Nadine Méouchy and Peter Sluglett. Leiden: Brill, 2004.

Louis, William Roger, and Roger Owen, eds. *A Revolutionary Year: The Middle East in 1958.* New York: I.B. Tauris; Washington, DC: Woodrow Wilson Center Press, 2002.

Mahmasani, Yahya. "A Central Bank for Lebanon." MA thesis, American University of Beirut, 1961.

Majid, Majid. *Tarikh al-Hukumat al-Lubnaniyyah 1926–1996: al-Talif—al-Thiqah, al-Istiqalah.* Beirut: Muassasat "Kalimat" Computer, 1997.

Majlis Tanfiidh al-Masharii al-Inshaiyyah. "Masrif Lubnan." Wizarit al-Ashghaal al-Ammah wa al-Naql, 1964.

Makdisi, Samir A. *The Lessons of Lebanon: The Economics of War and Development.* New York: I.B. Tauris, 2004. www.loc.gov/catdir/bios/holo55/2004303304.html.

Makdisi, Ussama Samir. *Artillery of Heaven: American Missionaries and the Failed Conversion of the Middle East.* Ithaca, NY: Cornell University Press, 2008.

———. *The Culture of Sectarianism: Community, History, and Violence in Nineteenth-Century Ottoman Lebanon.* Berkeley: University of California Press, 2000.

Mardini, Zuhayr al-. *Salim Hoss: Qissat Hayatih*. Beirut: Mu'assasat al-Inma' al-Sahafi wa al Tiba'i, 1989.

Massad, Joseph Andoni. *Colonial Effects: The Making of National Identity in Jordan*. New York: Columbia University Press, 2001.

Medawar, George. "Monetary Policy in Lebanon." PhD diss., Cornell University, 1963.

Menassa, Gabriel. *Plan de reconstruction de l'économie libanaise et de reforme de l'État*. Beirut: Éditions de la Société libanaise d'Économie politique, 1948. http://link.library.utoronto.ca/eir/EIRdetail.cfm?Resources_ID=724441&T=F.

Meyer, Albert J. "Economic Thought and Its Application and Methodology in the Middle East." *Middle East Economic Papers*, no. 2 (1955).

Mitchell, Timothy. *Colonising Egypt*. Berkeley: University of California Press, 1988.

———. *Rule of Experts: Egypt, Techno-Politics, Modernity*. Berkeley: University of California Press, 2002.

Naccache, Georges. "Un nouveau style: Le Chehabisme." In *'Ahd al-Nadwah al-Lubnaniyyah*, 389–99. Beirut: Dar al-Nahar, 1997.

Nagano, Yoshiko. *State and Finance in the Philippines, 1898–1941: The Mismanagement of an American Colony*. Singapore: NUS Press, 2015.

Nasif, Niqula. *Jumhuriyyat Fuad Shihab*. Al-Tabah 1. Beirut: Dar al-Nahar, 2008.

Nassif, Nicolas. *al-Maktab al-Thani: Hakim fi al-Dhil*. Beirut: Mukhtarat, 2006.

Nasr, Salim, and Claude Dubar. *al-Tabaqat al-Ijtima'iyyah fi Lubnan: Muqarabah Susyulujiyyah Tatbiqiyyah*. Translated by George Abi Saleh. Beirut: Muassasat al-Abhath al-rabiyyah, 1982.

Olsaretti, Alessandro, and Michelle Hartman. "'The First Boat and the First Oar': Inventions of Lebanon in the Writings of Michel Chiha." *Radical History Review* 86, no. 1 (2003).

Oughourlian, Joseph. *Histoire de la monnaie libanaise: Une monnaie, un État*. Toulouse: Éditions Érès, 1982.

Owen, Roger. "The Middle Eastern National Economy: Imagined, Constructed, Protected." In *Configuring Identity in the Modern Arab East*. Beirut: American University of Beirut Press, 2009.

———. *State, Power, and Politics in the Making of the Modern Middle East*. 2nd ed. London; New York: Routledge, 2000.

Pauly, Louis W. *Who Elected the Bankers? Surveillance and Control in the World Economy*. Ithaca, NY: Cornell University Press, 1997.

Plumptre, A. F. W. *Central Banking in the British Dominions*. Toronto: University of Toronto Press, 1940.

Porter, Robert S. "Statistical Services in the Middle East." *Middle East Economic Papers*, no. 2 (1955).

Prashad, Vijay. *The Darker Nations: A People's History of the Third World*. New York: New Press, 2008.

Qubaysi, Zulfiqar. *Yusif Beidas: Filastini Halim bi Majd Lubnan*. Beirut, 1978.

Raʿd, Leila. *Tarikh Lubnan al-Siyasi wa al-Iqtisadi 1958–1975.* Beirut: Maktabat al-Saih, 2005.

Rogan, Eugene. *Frontiers of the State in the Late Ottoman Empire.* Cambridge: Cambridge University Press, 1999.

Rosenberg, *Financial Missionaries to the World: The Politics and Culture of Dollar Diplomacy 1900–1930.* Durham, NC: Duke University Press, 2003.

Rutherford, Malcolm. *The Institutionalist Movement in American Economics, 1918–1947: Science and Social Control.* New York: Cambridge University Press, 2011.

Sad, Antoine. *Fuad Butrus: al-Mudhakkirat.* Beirut: Dar al-Nahar, 2009.

al-Safir. *50 ʿAman: Masrif Lubnan.* Beirut: al-Safir, 2015.

Salameh, Yusif. *Haddathani Y. S. Qal.* 4th ed. Beirut: Dar Nelson, 2001.

Saleh, Mohammed Ali El-. "Une évaluation de la gestion mandataire de l'économie syrienne." In *The British and French Mandates in Comparative Perspective,* edited by Nadine Méouchy and Peter Sluglett. Leiden: Brill, 2004.

Salem, Elie Adib. *Modernization without Revolution: Lebanon's Experience.* Bloomington: Indiana University Press, 1973.

Salibi, Kamal. *The Modern History of Lebanon.* London: Weidenfeld & Nicolson, 1965.

Salloum, Abdel Amir. *al-Siyasat al-Maliyyah wa al-Naqdiyyah wa al-Masrifiyyah fi Lubnan: Azamat wa Hulul.* Beirut: Asdiqa' al-Harf, 1991.

Sammak, Faysal. *Nihayat Imbaraturiyyat Beidas.* Beirut: n.p., 1967.

Saqr, Yusuf Saqr. *ʿAʾilat Hakamat Lubnan.* Al-Tabah 1. Beirut: al-Markaz al-Arabi lil-Malumat, 2008.

Sayigh, Yusif Abdallah. *Entrepreneurs of Lebanon: The Role of the Business Leader in a Developing Economy.* Cambridge, MA: Harvard University Press, 1962.
———. *Yusif Sayigh: An Incomplete Autobiography.* Translated by Majid al-Barghouti. Beirut: Riad El-Rayyes Books, 2009.

Sayyid Ali, Abdul Munim. *al-Tatawwur al-Tarikhi lil Anzimah al-Nadqiyyah fi al-Aqtar al-ʿArabiyyah.* Beirut: Markaz Dirasat al-Wihdah al-Arabiyyah, 1983.

Scutt, G. P. Symes. *The History of the Bank of Bengal: An Epitome of a Hundred Years of Banking in India.* Bank of Bengal Press, 1904.

Seikaly, Sherene. *Men of Capital: Scarcity and Economy in Mandate Palestine.* Stanford: Stanford University Press, 2015.

Sen, S. N. *Central Banking in Undeveloped Money Markets.* Calcutta: Bookland, 1952.

Sengupta, Madhura Shashwati Mitu. "The Politics of Market Reform in India: The Fragile Basis of Paradigm Shift." Ph.D. diss., University of Toronto, 2004.

Sfeir, George N. "The Central Bank and the Banking Law of Jordan." *Middle East Journal* 20, no. 3 (Summer 1966).

Sharara, Waddah. *Fi Usul Lubnan al-Taʿifi . . . Khatt al-Yamin al-Jamahiri.* Beirut: Jadawel, 2011.

Shehadi, Nadim. *The Idea of Lebanon: Economy and State in the Cénacle libanais, 1946–54.* Oxford, England: Centre for Lebanese Studies, 1987.

Shihab al-Din, Rashid. *Daya' al-'Arab Bayna al-Naft wa al-Dhahab.* Beirut: Wikalat al-Inma al-Wataniyyah: Maktab al-Abhath wa al-Dirasat, 1980.

Shoman, Abdulhameed. *The Indomitable Arab: The Life and Times of Abdulhameed Shoman (1890–1974), Founder of the Arab Bank.* London: Third World Centre, 1984.

Schuker, Stephen A. "Money Doctors between the wars: Competition between Central Banks, Private Financial Advisors, and Multilateral agencies." In *Money Doctors: The Experience of International Financial Advising 1850–2000,* edited by Marc Flandreau. New York: Routledge, 2003.

Thompson, Elizabeth. *Colonial Citizens: Republican Rights, Paternal Privilege, and Gender in French Syria and Lebanon.* New York: Columbia University Press, 2000.

———. "The Colonial Welfare State in Syria and Lebanon." In *War, Institutions, and Social Change in the Middle East,* edited by Steven Heydemann. Berkeley: University of California Press, 2000.

Traboulsi, Fawwaz. *A History of Modern Lebanon.* London [Ann Arbor, MI]: Pluto Press, 2007.

———. "Saudi Expansion: The Lebanese Connection, 1924–1952." In *Kingdom without Borders: Saudi Political, Religious and Media Frontiers,* edited by Madawi al-Rasheed. New York: Columbia University Press, 2008.

———. *Silat bi-la Wasl: Mishal Shiha wa al-Idiyulujiya al-Lubnaniyyah.* Beirut: Riyad al-Rayyis lil Kutub wa al-Nashr, 1999.

———. "Social Classes and Political Power in Lebanon." Research Paper. Heinrich Böll Stiftung, 2014.

Verdeil, Eric. "Politics, Ideology, and Professional Interests: Foreign versus Local Planners in Lebanon under President Chehab." In *Urbanism Imported or Exported? Native Aspirations and Foreign Plans,* edited by Joe Nasr and Mercedes Volait, 290–315. London: Wiley-Academy, 2003.

Vitalis, Robert. *When Capitalists Collide: Business Conflict and the End of Empire in Egypt.* Berkeley: University of California Press, 1995.

Williams, Jonathan, Joe Cribb, and Elizabeth Errington. *Money: A History.* London: British Museum Press, 1997.

Yaffi, Talha. "The Monetary and Banking System of Lebanon with Special Reference to Monetary Reform." PhD diss., University of Wisconsin, 1959.

Yafi, Muwaffaq, and Abdel Fattah Yafi, eds. *Majmu'at al-Naqd wa al-Taslif.* 5 vols. Vols. 1 and 2. Beirut: Yaffi Ikhwan wa Shurakahum, 1999.

Zeifer, Hayma. "Les élites techniques locales durant le Mandat français en Syrie (1920–1945)." In *The British and French Mandates in Comparative Perspective,* edited by Nadine Méouchy and Peter Sluglett. Leiden: Brill, 2004.

Index

International Statistics Education Centre
(ISEC), 55–56
Intra Bank: BCAIF and, 79, 81; Gulf
capital withdrawals, 132–35;
importance, 129, 131–32, 144,
217n8; international operations,
131–32, 142–43, 144, 158–
59, 217n10; Kuwaiti deposits,
132–33, 135, 223n58; rise of,
131–32; shareholders, 76, 143, 152,
225nn78–79. *See also* Beidas, Yusif
Intra crisis: audits, 147, 223n62;
bankruptcy proceedings, 145,
147–48; causes, 130, 132–36, 137,
154, 156–57; conspiracy theories,
129–30, 133, 137, 139–40, 142–43,
147, 220n40; effects, 7, 12, 128,
129, 132, 144, 153, 154–55; Helou
administration and, 137–42, 144,
145, 146, 147–49, 158; liquidity
problems, 132, 136, 137, 138, 140–
41, 156; management committees,
148, 149–50, 152, 159, 161–62,
223–24n65, 227n14, 227n21;
reactions, 130, 134–35, 141, 157–
58; resolution, 13, 130, 144–53,
161–62, 224n66, 224–25nn72–75,
225nn78–79
Intra's law (Law 2/67), 148, 159,
161–62
Iraq, 18, 21, 30, 107, 110, 111, 136,
167, 219n27
IRFED, *see* Institut international de
formation et de recherche en vue du
développement harmonisé
ISEC, *see* International Statistics
Education Centre
Israel, 82–83, 131, 166, 167, 172, 176.
See also Palestine

Johnson, Harold, 79–80, 203n46
Jordan, 107, 136, 159
Jumblatt, Kamal, 103, 143, 144,
221n48

Karame, Rashid: central bank debates
and, 91, 92, 94–95, 114–15;

Chehab and, 103; as finance
minister, 87, 91, 92, 114–15,
205n68, 225n78; as prime minister,
87, 92, 159, 225n76
Keesing, F. A. G., 50–52, 90
Keynesian policies, 11, 44–45, 46–47,
59–60, 179
KFTCI, *see* Kuwait Foreign Trading
Contracting and Investment
Khoury, Bishara: background, 8;
clique, 115; laissez-faire policies,
45, 99; Oughourlian and, 116; as
president, 3, 8–9, 35, 43, 81, 82,
189n64, 190n67, 190n71, 200n20;
resignation, 45
Khoury, Boutros, 86, 200nn20–22,
203n44
Khoury, Michel, 76–78
Kidder Peabody, 150, 151–52, 172
Klat, Paul, 54, 65, 79, 91, 92, 115,
194n39, 195–96n52, 202nn37–38
Kuwait: banks, 136; capital from, 76,
132–33, 135, 136, 146; central
bank, 107, 110–12; Intra crisis
and, 146–47, 149, 150, 151–52,
222–23nn56–59, 223n61; money
markets, 170
Kuwait Foreign Trading Contracting
and Investment (KFTCI), 147
Kuwait Investment Advisory Board, 150

Laissez-faire policies: Banking Secrecy
Law and, 84; bank regulation and,
7, 70, 94, 97, 102, 125–26, 155,
159, 169; Chehabism and, 61, 97–
98; competing ideology, 9, 51, 52;
criticism of, 51; effects, 44, 62, 83,
99–100, 136; financial deregulation,
5, 9, 43, 45, 49; monetary policy
and, 64, 121–22; rationalizing,
60–63; sociocultural basis, 74,
200nn12–13; supporters, 5–6, 37,
43–44, 45, 73. *See also* Chihism
Law of Money and Credit (1963):
amendments (1973), 168–69;
banking secrecy and, 114–15;
drafting, 54, 90, 92–98, 107–10,

KABIR TAMBAR, *The Reckonings of Pluralism: Citizenship and the Demands of History in Turkey,* 2014

DIANA ALLAN, *Refugees of the Revolution: Experiences of Palestinian Exile,* 2013

SHIRA ROBINSON, *Citizen Strangers: Palestinians and the Birth of Israel's Liberal Settler State,* 2013

JOEL BEININ AND FRÉDÉRIC VAIREL, EDITORS, *Social Movements, Mobilization, and Contestation in the Middle East and North Africa,* 2013 (SECOND EDITION), 2011

ARIELLA AZOULAY AND ADI OPHIR, *The One-State Condition: Occupation and Democracy in Israel/Palestine,* 2012

STEVEN HEYDEMANN AND REINOUD LEENDERS, EDITORS, *Middle East Authoritarianisms: Governance, Contestation, and Regime Resilience in Syria and Iran,* 2012

JONATHAN MARSHALL, *The Lebanese Connection: Corruption, Civil War, and the International Drug Traffic,* 2012

JOSHUA STACHER, *Adaptable Autocrats: Regime Power in Egypt and Syria,* 2012

BASSAM HADDAD, *Business Networks in Syria: The Political Economy of Authoritarian Resilience,* 2011

NOAH COBURN, *Bazaar Politics: Power and Pottery in an Afghan Market Town,* 2011

LAURA BIER, *Revolutionary Womanhood: Feminisms, Modernity, and the State in Nasser's Egypt,* 2011

SAMER SOLIMAN, *The Autumn of Dictatorship: Fiscal Crisis and Political Change in Egypt under Mubarak,* 2011

ROCHELLE A. DAVIS, *Palestinian Village Histories: Geographies of the Displaced,* 2010

HAGGAI RAM, *Iranophobia: The Logic of an Israeli Obsession,* 2009

JOHN CHALCRAFT, *The Invisible Cage: Syrian Migrant Workers in Lebanon,* 2008

RHODA KANAANEH, *Surrounded: Palestinian Soldiers in the Israeli Military,* 2008

ASEF BAYAT, *Making Islam Democratic: Social Movements and the Post-Islamist Turn,* 2007

ROBERT VITALIS, *America's Kingdom: Mythmaking on the Saudi Oil Frontier,* 2006

JESSICA WINEGAR, *Creative Reckonings: The Politics of Art and Culture in Contemporary Egypt,* 2006

JOEL BEININ AND REBECCA L. STEIN, EDITORS, *The Struggle for Sovereignty: Palestine and Israel, 1993–2005,* 2006

Lightning Source UK Ltd.
Milton Keynes UK
UKHW010046100720
366314UK00004B/599